How to Start a Law Firm

Other titles available from Law Society Publishing:

SRA Standards and Regulations: November 2019 Edition
Solicitors Regulation Authority

Junior Lawyers' Handbook
Eloise Skinner

Career Management for Lawyers: Practical Strategies to Plan Your Next Chapter
Rachel Brushfield

Smarter Legal Marketing
Rachel Brushfield

Driving Success in Your Law Firm
Eddie Ross and Sally Holdway

Clarity for Lawyers, 3rd edition
Mark Adler and Daphne Perry

Exit Strategies Toolkit
Tracey Calvert and Helen Carr

Titles from Law Society Publishing can be ordered from all good bookshops or direct (telephone 0370 850 1422, or visit our online shop at **www.lawsociety.org.uk/bookshop**).

How to Start a Law Firm

A Practical Guide to Offering Legal Services

Darren J. Sylvester and Rachel Roche

The Law Society

ISBN-13: 978-1-78446-153-9

Published in 2020 by the Law Society
113 Chancery Lane, London WC2A 1PL

Typeset by Columns Design XML Ltd, Reading
Printed by Hobbs the Printers Ltd, Totton, Hants

The paper used for the text pages of this book is FSC® certified. FSC (the Forest Stewardship Council®) is an international network to promote responsible management of the world's forests.

FSC
www.fsc.org
MIX
Paper from responsible sources
FSC® C020438

Contents

Foreword

The law firms of the future will not look like the law firms of the past. Those of us who entered the legal profession earlier on in the 21st century – or even at the end of the 20th – have already witnessed a significant shift.

The profession is moving away from traditional paths of career progression. Instead, we are learning to accept greater flexibility and innovation, as well as recognising potential in people much earlier on in their careers. Though this move is no doubt a challenge for many firms, we can't deny that it also offers incredible opportunity.

Starting your own legal business or entering a management role no longer depends on the stage of your career. Today's more flexible path of progression in legal careers allows a greater diversity of individuals to do this and shine.

Of course, this book was written in the face of dramatic and immediate change: the COVID-19 pandemic. Among the many other effects on society, lockdown created a period of relative quiet and solitude in which many people chose to re-evaluate their careers. For some, this re-evaluation was outside of their control due to firm closures, furloughs and redundancies.

However legal professionals have found themselves in this position, I suspect that this period of reflection has made a significant number of solicitors more determined than ever to have their career on their own terms. In many cases, this will no doubt mean starting their own law firm or choosing to go freelance.

Starting your own law business is a brave and rewarding thing to do. It's also hard work and not for everyone. The authors of this book, Darren J. Sylvester and Rachel Roche, have set out to create an accessible and exhaustive resource for legal professionals considering this path.

Whether you have plans to launch a major new firm to shake up the industry or simply hope to use the new freelance solicitor regulations to better manage your work/life balance, this book is an excellent starting point. It will help you navigate the specific structural and regulatory challenges of setting up a legal firm, as well as the more universal concerns of all new businesses: how to find clients, how to keep clients and how to stay ahead of the competition.

Whatever your legal ambitions, remember that together we are heralding in a new future for the profession. Now is the time to build an innovative, diverse and inclusive legal space that will benefit us all.

Christina Blacklaws
Former President of the Law Society (July 2018–July 2019)
October 2020

Preface

The legal landscape is shifting beneath us. The growth of digital technology has enabled the profession to experiment with new and innovative ways of delivering legal services, many of which offer client solutions faster, more conveniently and more affordably.

Just like in other industries, there's also a growing awareness of the importance of flexible working arrangements. With so much information now at our fingertips, along with so many different communication tools, there's absolutely no reason to work a traditional 9 am–5 pm role in a traditional firm ... unless you want to, that is.

It's not just the structure of the way lawyers work that's changing. There have been some significant changes to the way we're legally allowed to practise. Specifically, there have been changes to the Code of Conduct that is part of the Solicitors Regulation Authority's (SRA's) new Standards and Regulations (released November 2019). These are the first major changes to the way solicitors are regulated since 2011. The Bar Standards Board (BSB) have also recently published a new version of the BSB Handbook (released February 2020; the latest version came into effect on 1 September 2020). This introduced new regulations and obligations for barristers.

The full implications of these regulations and obligations are covered later in the book, but one very significant change for solicitors is the introduction of the new category of the freelance solicitor. The SRA defines freelance solicitors as those who practise alone, outside of a law firm with no employees. There are many ways to set up your own law firm, but this new category offers up countless possibilities for those who want to work completely independently.

Of course, as the saying goes, *the more things change, the more things stay the same*. We may have a myriad of new digital tools and opportunities to work with, but many of the pressures and challenges of setting up in practice are the same as they've ever been.

This book has been written to provide the information and guidance necessary to set up and manage a legal practice. It offers real-life advice on all aspects of managing a firm, including caring for clients, managing finances, coordinating marketing efforts, embracing technology and staying relevant in an increasingly crowded legal marketplace. But most of all: this book has been written for you.

It's for you if you're just starting your own law firm and aren't sure where to turn for good, solid advice. It's for you if you're sat at a desk in someone else's office wondering about doing something different. And it's for you if you are training to be a lawyer and are considering how your future career could work for you.

We speak from experience. When we set up our law firms, neither of us had access to this kind of practical advice. The process of starting out can be daunting, complex and time-consuming. Through a process of trial and error, we got there in the end and now both enjoy the satisfaction of running our own successful firms. With this book, we've set out to provide all the guidance and advice we wish we'd had during the early days. Our hope is that you won't need to make quite as many mistakes as we did!

Setting up and running a law firm isn't easy, and it's certainly not for the faint-hearted. But with vision, purpose, hard work and organisation (along with a dash of good luck and a moderate attitude towards risk-taking) it can be incredibly rewarding. We hope this book gives you the inspiration and encouragement you need to take your own big step forward, whatever that might look like.

Darren J. Sylvester
Rachel Roche
October 2020

About the authors

Darren J. Sylvester was admitted to the Honourable Society of Lincoln's Inn in 2002 and was called to the Bar in 2003. He has handled many cases in civil litigation (for both claimants and defendants) and is an advocate of alternative dispute resolution. In 2009 Darren qualified as a solicitor and joined a London firm that specialised in professional negligence disputes. He went on to set up his own practice, DJS Law Solicitors, in 2016. DJS Law Solicitors specialises in civil litigation and professional negligence, though also offers services in consumer law, charity law, travel claims, lasting powers of attorney, wills and probate.

Darren is a member of the Professional Negligence Lawyers Association. He runs a free legal advice surgery in Cheshunt, Hertfordshire, and has frequently featured on radio answering legal questions.

Rachel Roche qualified as a legal executive in 2007, then as a solicitor in 2009. She worked as a solicitor at various firms in the West Midlands, then took a year out in 2012–13 to study French and European Law at the Sorbonne in Paris. Rachel set up her own practice, Roche Legal, in 2014. Roche Legal specialises in private client law, including matters involving the Court of Protection and missing persons law.

Rachel is a full member of the Society of Trust and Estate Practitioners and is also a full accredited member of Solicitors for the Elderly. She regularly gives talks to other lawyers on the subject of setting up and running a legal practice, including but not limited to operations, implementing technology, compliance and accounts. Rachel was named Sole Practitioner of the Year at the 2018 Law Society Excellence Awards.

Acknowledgements

When we set up our respective law firms, we did so without a blueprint to guide us. Though we are both ultimately pleased with the trajectory our start-ups took, there's no doubt things could've been more straightforward! With this book, we have set out to remedy that.

We wrote *How to Start a Law Firm* while running our own firms full-time. This has not been an easy endeavour, but we've been motivated by the idea of creating a valuable guide to help aspiring law firm owners. Our hope is that this book will help you to commit the time, energy and expertise towards pursuing your dream.

Our hard work has not been the only thing that has gone into making this book a reality. We have been lucky enough to be able to call on our networks to ensure the finished product is truly representative of setting up and running a law firm.

To Katie Anderson-Morrison, who worked her magic to help bring this book together. Her patience when deadlines occasionally slipped is to be commended. The book is all the better for her involvement.

To Christina Blacklaws, who kindly agreed to write the foreword to this book. Thank you, Christina, for sharing your insight on the question of starting a law firm.

To 15 of our fellow law firm owners, who generously provided personal case studies. Belinda Lester, Simone Bowman, Jessica Hampson, Bill Ward, Sarah Khan-Bashir, Neil Brown, Peter Wright, Shazia Malik, Cosma Vento, Melissa Fish, Anna Newport, Jodie Hill, Mandeep Kaur Virdee, Paul Bennett and Jane Cassell: we thank you for your contributions. They have undoubtedly enriched this book.

To Tim Halstead and Mark Smith, who both gave their time to read and review parts of this book.

To David Crosby, Laura Armentano and Christa Biervliet at the Law Society, who provided guidance and wise counsel during the writing of this book.

And to our families and friends, who accepted when we were not available due to the writing schedule demanded by this book. We thank you for your understanding, your encouragement and your unfailing support.

Rachel Roche

I would also like to thank those professionals who have mentored me over the course of my career. This includes my former boss, Julia Kirkham, who taught me how to be a private client lawyer, as well as the many and varied people that I have worked with since.

Thank you to Stacey McVeighty, my first accountant and the first person I met as a business owner. Stacey was kind enough to introduce me to those in her network who could help me build mine.

Thank you to the fellow business owners (legal and otherwise) who have given me valuable insight into the many strands of business ownership and helped shape the business person I am today. You have been there when I needed to bounce ideas around and when I needed to share experiences and insight.

To my clients and peers, without whom my firm would not be where it is today, and to the many people I've yet to meet on my business journey: I look forward to sharing experiences in the future and to helping you on your own journeys, be that as a law firm owner, a colleague, or simply as a friend.

Darren J. Sylvester

I would like to thank those who taught me at college, university and law school; all of you have made an impact on me and my career. Ian Yule, my A-Level law teacher, deserves a special mention as it was his positive and engaging style of teaching that made me want to go on to study law. I am still in regular contact with Ian today, and am always pleased to contribute to the *A-Level Law Review*, of which he was the chairman of the editorial board.

Thank you to Maurice Brindley of Brindley Jacob Chartered Accountants, who has shared a wealth of experience with me, both during the early days of establishing my business and ever since. I will be forever grateful for the time Maurice spent reviewing and advising my business plan and cash flow forecasts, for which there was no charge. Such kindness will not be forgotten.

Thank you to Rasheed Ogunlaru, my business coach, who was also immensely helpful during the set up of DJS Law Solicitors. Rasheed is very generous with his wisdom, guidance and advice, and we worked together on many occasions to fine-tune ideas. His own book *Soul Trader – Putting the Heart Back in Your Business* helped me confirm this was the right path for me. Thus far, I certainly have no regrets.

My grateful thanks and appreciation to Dawn Robinson, Fellow of the Learning and Performance Institute, whose unparalleled knowledge and experience in law firm IT systems was and remains invaluable.

I would like to extend a huge thank you to Rachel Roche, my co-author, for taking on this vast project with me. The phrase 'two heads are better than one' has definitely proved to be true in terms of the percolation of ideas.

Thank you to the many clients who have instructed DJS Law Solicitors or who have attended the firm's free monthly advice surgeries. Handling your legal matters has been both rewarding and enriching.

Finally, to those I will see in the future: I look forward to discussing both your legal matters and the topics contained in this book. I have no doubt that this will continue to be enriching, especially in these unique, uncertain and unparalleled times.

I will end with Geoffrey Tattersall QC's legal ABC, which is still with me today:

A (assume nothing)
B (believe nobody)
C (check everything)

Abbreviations

ABS	alternative business structure
AI	artificial intelligence
AML	anti-money laundering
BD	business development
BMIF	Bar Mutual Indemnity Fund
BPC	Bar Practice Course
BSB	Bar Standards Board
CAP	Committee of Advertising Practice
CILEx	Chartered Institute of Legal Executives
CLC	Council for Licensed Conveyancers
CLSB	Costs Lawyer Standards Board
COFA	compliance officer for finance and administration
COLP	compliance officer for legal practice
CPD	continuing professional development
CQS	Conveyancing Quality Scheme
EHRC	Equality and Human Rights Commission
EU	European Union
FCA	Financial Conduct Authority
GDP	gross domestic product
GDPR	General Data Protection Regulation
HMCTS	Her Majesty's Courts and Tribunals Service
HMLR	Her Majesty's Land Registry
HMRC	Her Majesty's Revenue and Customs
ICAEW	Institute of Chartered Accountants in England and Wales
ICO	Information Commissioner's Office
IFA	independent financial adviser
IPO	initial public offering
IPReg	Intellectual Property Regulation Board
KPI	key performance indicator
LAA	Legal Aid Agency
LASPO 2012	Legal Aid, Sentencing and Punishment of Offenders Act 2012
LLP	limited liability partnership

LPA	lasting power of attorney
LPC	Legal Practice Course
NBFC	non-banking financial corporations
NCA	National Crime Agency
NI	national insurance
OECD	Organisation for Economic Co-operation and Development
PA	personal assistant
PEP	politically exposed person
PQE	post-qualified experience
PR	public relations
REL	registered European lawyer
RFL	registered foreign lawyer
RTI	real time information
SAR	suspicious activity report
SDT	Solicitors Disciplinary Tribunal
SEO	search engine optimisation
SIPP	self-invested pension plan
SRA	Solicitors Regulation Authority
USP	unique selling point
VA	virtual assistant
VAT	value added tax
VOIP	voice over internet protocol
WIP	work in progress

Chapter 1

Could you start a law firm?

Have you always dreamed of being the boss one day? You're far from alone. Thirty per cent of UK millennials aspire to start their own business,[1] and it's not hard to see why.

The image of the business owner is one that's been much idealised. The concept of not being constrained by normal working hours is clearly a big draw, as is the thought of being able to make all your own decisions about the type of work and clients you take on. This dream has been made even more attractive by the growth of digital technologies, which has made telecommuting a very workable reality. It's not hard to get swept away by the daydream of continuing to work with clients here in the UK while simultaneously exploring travel dreams further afield.

But is this a realistic vision? And what price might it come at?

Our intention is not to put you off starting your own business. Quite the opposite in fact – we're big advocates for what we do! However, we do think it's important to have a clear view of what you're getting yourself into. Only a fraction of the people who want to start their own business will ever take any real steps towards doing so. The reason for this is that it's not as effortlessly easy as the idealised images make it sound.

We're also mindful of the fact that not everyone starts a business purely for the love of it. Some lawyers are pushed towards this route through factors out of their control. This could be due to redundancy or a stagnant labour market. It could be due to health reasons or family commitments. Or it could be due to a bad experience working in a traditional law firm.

Whether you're starting your law firm from a place of excitement or necessity, we believe the outcome can be the same – after a lot of clever strategising and even more hard work, you could find yourself completely in charge of your own working life.

1.1 The benefits of being an employee

Before we really focus on the ups and downs of business ownership, we want to spend a bit of time on what's likely to be your current situation. It may seem counter-productive to dedicate a section of this book to the

[1] *The Millennial Money Survey* by F&C Investment Trust, 2018.

benefits of being an employee. However, it's important to fully understand your current position before you choose to make the jump to another.

1.1.1 Being an employee in a law firm

There are all kinds of reasons to want to be at the helm of your own firm – and we'll get to those shortly – but there are also some very good arguments in favour of staying employed in someone else's.

If you're currently employed in a law firm, you'll almost certainly enjoy easy access to high speed internet, IT support and administration staff, not to mention a fully stocked stationery cupboard. You'll arrive each morning to a clean and tidy workspace, and it's highly likely someone else will have stocked up the tea and coffee facilities. If you receive a troubling or unpleasant communication from a client, there'll be someone on hand for you to seek advice from. If you need to work late to get to grips with some casework, you'll probably have company. If you're unwell and need to take a few days off, your colleagues will step in and keep things ticking over in your absence.

Are you seeing a trend here? When you're employed in someone else's business, you're never on your own. There will always be other people on hand to make tricky decisions or to ensure that the basic office logistics are covered. There are certain freedoms you'll need to give up in order to be a successful employee, but for the vast majority of people this feels like a fair exchange.

You may have felt this way in the past. You may still feel like it now, to a certain extent. The decision to start your own practice isn't necessarily a black and white issue. There are advantages and disadvantages on both sides of the divide. You may well feel that you have an awful lot to gain from striding out on your own – but do keep in mind that there are some key benefits you'll be leaving behind.

1.1.2 Becoming a partner in a firm

You don't necessarily need to leave the comfort of a big firm to be more in control. The traditional ambition of a junior lawyer is, after all, to progress to partner level. Though it can be a long and frustrating trajectory, once you get there you'd have more power to influence business growth and development. You may decide that this is an ideal balance between being employed and being the employer.

For many people this traditional aim just doesn't go far enough. After all, you may make partner only to realise that the existing partners are not the people you'd have chosen to enter into this adventure with. It's highly likely that the other partners will be at different stages of their career to you, and may well have very different priorities. It would be unlikely for everyone involved to have the same aims for the future of the firm.

E lawsociety@clientmail.eu.com

T +44 (0) 370 850 1422

The Law Society

DELIVERY NOTE

Customer Copy

Barbara Palmer
91 Yorkland Avenue
Welling
DA16 2LG

Our RefTLS/7524 **Despatch Date December 4th 2020**

Description	Ordered	Shipped
How to Start a Law Firm (Author:) ;11/20;PUB0461539	1	1

This is a key reason why many lawyers decide to forego the traditional career trajectory and kick start a new law firm all of their own. You may want to do this completely independently, or you may be considering starting out with a group of like-minded, hand-picked legal colleagues. There are huge benefits to doing this, both in terms of your professional and personal lives.

1.2 The core benefits of starting a business

We talk about starting a 'business' in this book, as well as setting up a 'practice' or 'firm'. This is a conscious choice, though we know some members of the legal profession still regard a law firm as being different to other types of business.

As lawyers we do, of course, have a very important role to play – we exist, effectively, to uphold the rule of law and work for the protection of the public. Despite this, it's important to remember that everyday business principles still very much apply. No matter how good a solicitor is at supporting clients or winning cases, their firm won't last long if they neglect to send out invoices or to develop a marketing plan.

We believe there are five core benefits to starting your own business:

- You'll have the opportunity to make your vision a reality.
- You'll be able to make your work more flexible.
- It can be incredibly fulfilling and rewarding.
- You'll be able to make all the decisions.
- You will develop professionally and personally.

1.2.1 You'll have the opportunity to make your vision a reality

When you start from scratch, you can make your working day look however you want. There's no reason to stick with the same old formula, unless that's what works for you.

Some new business owners aspire to become the biggest firm in their city, others are more than content working independently from an office pod in their garden. You may want to focus on commercial success, or you may be more concerned with making a difference in your community. Whatever your vision is, you'll be able to set the agenda in order to make sure you get there completely on your own terms.

1.2.2 You'll be able to make your work more flexible

The word 'freedom' is often used in connection with running your own business. We think 'flexibility' is a better description. Being the boss will give you the opportunity to attend a school event or a yoga class during the middle of the normal working day . . . but that's not to say you won't need to work at other times to catch up.

This flexibility is ideal for those who want to have the power to set their own schedule. You won't need to be chained to your desk between the hours of 9am and 5pm: you'll be able to establish a routine that suits you, rather than your managers.

Equally, you'll likely be able to say yes to more travel and holiday opportunities – though you should expect to be connected to the hotel Wi-Fi whenever possible, ensuring that everything is running smoothly in your absence.

Again, the word to remember here is 'flexibility' rather than 'freedom'. After all, when you own your own business it's not as easy to completely switch off at clocking out time. You may be walking away from the jurisdiction of your current boss, but you'll be embracing potentially hundreds of new ones in the form of clients.

1.2.3 It can be incredibly fulfilling and rewarding

Instead of spending week after week contributing to the success of someone else's business, you'll be working towards boosting your own. It's hard to explain just how rewarding it is to watch a business you've built grow around you in this way.

This is as rewarding as it is challenging, and many people thrive in this sort of environment.

1.2.4 You'll be able to make all the decisions

Though many forward-thinking law firms do now promote innovation by encouraging their employees to think creatively, this isn't the same as being completely in charge of coming up with and implementing new ideas.

If you like to be in charge of any given situation, you're likely to really enjoy taking the helm of your own law practice. As the owner of a firm, you'll also be the chief decision maker! You're likely to find being in control empowering – though do remember that making all the decisions all day, every day may become overwhelming.

1.2.5 You will develop professionally and personally

Most lawyers who choose to go down the route of starting their own firm are ambitious and conscientious. These lawyers are likely to appreciate the value of personal development.

Setting up your own business is best described as an intense learning experience. Generally speaking, law school and professional training is unlikely to have equipped you with the skills you need to transition seamlessly from employee to manager and owner.

Rather, you'll suddenly be thrown in the deep end with the need to learn quickly to stay afloat. You'll have to swot up on subjects as diverse as marketing, accountancy, customer service, employment law, management techniques and office logistics.

Our advice is to embrace this as the learning and development opportunity it is.

1.3 The disadvantages of starting a business

We get it. You're fired up and ready to go and probably don't want to hear about the downsides. But please, hear us out on this one!

It's far better to be fully apprised of a situation before you find yourself in the centre of it. Knowledge is power, and if you know which stumbling blocks are likely to appear in front of you, you'll be much better prepared to move past them without incident. Some potential disadvantages are:

- It's risky.
- It can be highly stressful.
- You'll have to dedicate a lot of time to it.
- You'll need to do jobs you don't like doing.
- You may feel alone.

We discuss each of these points below, and then consider if these downsides can be mitigated.

1.3.1 It's risky

Starting a business is always going to be a risk. Eleven per cent of businesses fail in the first 12 months, while 60 per cent won't survive five years.[2] You need to be prepared for the fact that the odds may not go your way.

Much of the risk here is financial. This is especially true if you're considering putting a significant chunk of capital into the business at the beginning.

However, there are other risks to consider. A failed law firm could set your career back a year or two. It could also be damaging to your mental health. Finally, and perhaps most importantly, it could pose a risk to your family situation.

There's anecdotal evidence to suggest that divorce rates and family breakdowns are more prevalent for entrepreneurs, perhaps due to the high stress and time-consuming nature of this particular beast.

[2] *Business Demography, UK*; 2018, Office for National Statistics.

1.3.2 It can be highly stressful

How do you deal with stress? Many people thrive on a healthy amount, but too much is undoubtedly damaging for our physical and mental health.

A successful business owner needs to have the resilience to manage a fair amount of stress. You'll need to think carefully about whether you have this kind of resilience.

1.3.3 You'll have to dedicate a lot of time to it

If you're thinking about starting a business because you want to work fewer hours, you're likely to be disappointed, at least at the beginning. Your particular vision may be based around less work, more play – but you're likely to have to put in more work initially in order to bring this vision to life.

If you're starting out on your own, you'll find you need to do types of work you've never had to do before in order to get your fledgling business off the ground. Not only will you need to manage clients and casework, you'll also have to handle the administration, the finances and the process of bringing in new clients.

1.3.4 You'll need to do jobs you don't like doing

Speaking of the early days, many of the extra tasks you find yourself responsible for won't be much fun. How do you feel about ordering office consumables, making cups of tea for clients or sending invoices? What about liaising with suppliers, arranging appointments or even cleaning the office?

Though over time you're likely to be able to delegate many of these tasks, either to future employees, or contractors or virtual assistants, at first you're unlikely to have the funds for this expenditure.

1.3.5 You may feel alone

Loneliness is one of the best kept secrets in business. Feeling this way can be especially uncomfortable when you're doing something you've dreamed of for a long time. You may feel ungrateful or illogical for experiencing this. But it actually makes a lot of sense.

When you're an employee in a business, you have colleagues and managers to talk to and make decisions with. If you're dealing with a tricky client, there'll be someone on hand to offer advice or support. When you're running your own business . . . you won't have this. Even if you have an employee or two, you may not feel it's appropriate for you to discuss big picture business issues with them. Ever heard the saying about it being lonely at the top? You may come to understand this better than you wanted to.

1.3.6 Can these downsides be mitigated?

Though these downsides may sound scary, we don't believe any of them are insurmountable. There are many things you can do within your business to ensure that you keep things as sturdy and healthy as possible, even in the very earliest days.

As we said, the more you know about potential risks and downsides right from the beginning, the better able you are to protect against them.

1.4 Is this the path for you?

Weighing up the benefits and disadvantages of starting a firm is one way to try to decipher whether or not this is the path for you.

Ultimately, only you can decide whether or not this is the right time for you to start a law firm. The decision is likely to be based on a whole range of factors, including:

- your career goals;
- your personal values;
- your bravery / attitude to risk;
- your level of motivation;
- your resilience to stress;
- your personal circumstances;
- your resources;
- your family set up;
- your skills and personal qualities;
- your experience.

Lawyers can choose to start a business at any point in their career, with a lot or a little capital, and a lot or a little support from others.

If you decide that now is the time for you to start to build your business, you'll need to start translating your business dreams into a practical reality.

CASE STUDY 1: RACHEL ROCHE

Rachel Roche is a solicitor and the director of award-winning boutique law firm Roche Legal. Roche Legal work within private client law across the York and Harrogate areas. Rachel is also a co-author of this book.

When did you launch your law firm?

I launched Roche Legal on 17 February 2014.

How much knowledge and experience did you have before you started?

I qualified as a solicitor on the 15 September 2009. Prior to this I was a legal executive and had worked as a fee earner in a law firm since finishing my A-levels. I therefore had plenty of legal experience, but in terms of business experience, I had none.

You often hear stories of entrepreneurs having set up business ventures in their early years, such as a tuck shop at school, but the closest I ever came to anything like that was setting up a stall in the garden to sell some toys when I was about 10 years old. It wasn't possible to see the stall from the road and I chickened out of putting a sign up for passing motorists in case someone did actually stop and want to buy something!

In terms of having the confidence to set up in business, this came in a large part from being accepted on the HM Hubbard Law Scholarship. This allowed me to spend a year at the Sorbonne University in Paris completing a Master's degree in French and European Law. I did this in academic year 2012/13 when I was already qualified. Taking time out made me recalibrate several things, including my views about who can set up in business, and what was and wasn't within my reach.

I have always found there to be many misconceptions about setting up a law firm. For example, I was under the impression that you needed large amounts of capital to even get a firm off the ground, or that the cost of professional indemnity insurance would make it prohibitive anyway. Gaining different perspectives from my fellow students at the Sorbonne, who were from all over the world, gave me the wherewithal to question what I wanted for my career.

When I returned to the UK, I set about looking at what was and wasn't possible, starting with completing the Management Stage 2 that I needed, speaking with the Solicitors Regulation Authority and finding an insurance broker. My insurance broker was key in helping me formulate my first business plan. I was put in touch with her by the tutor on the Management Stage 2 course.

A couple of years before I went to Paris, I had been offered partnership at the firm I was working at, but I turned it down. I have very fond memories of that firm and the people in it, but I remember thinking that if I was going to be a decision-maker in a law firm, I'd want a greater degree of control, especially over things like processes and technology. For example, at that time social media was only just starting to be used for business and I would have wanted to harness that.

My friends tell me that I always wanted to set up in business, but I don't remember this at all – although I did always want to be a solicitor, despite there being no lawyers in my family or known to me growing up. Now that I have my business, I can't imagine earning a living any other way.

What would you say is the most important lesson you learned in the first few years of your firm?

I stressed such a lot in the first couple of years and was, frankly, scared to death I'd make a mistake in terms of running the firm. I was always worried about making sure I did everything by the book, especially in relation to the Solicitors' Accounts Rules. Looking back, I need not have burnt so much energy on these things, but I didn't know that at the time. That's not to say that I believe I should have been laissez-faire in any way (I'm certainly not laissez-faire now) but I think I would have relished the experience a little more had I been more relaxed and had more faith in myself.

I find it difficult to really answer the question as to what the most important lesson is that I've learnt in business during the first few years, as I think the experiences I've been through as a whole have helped shaped me and my firm, rather than one or two particular lessons as such. I think that overall I've become a better and more efficient decision-maker; shifted my perspective in a positive way about how things work in business and in the wider economy; learnt a lot about other people (and myself); and generally continued to evolve as a business owner, manager, entrepreneur and person. I still need to work on a lot though, especially how to communicate my expectations to people and to speak up when I'm disappointed or not happy with something.

Can you tell us how you learned this particular lesson?

Some time ago I had to deal with a poor performing fee earner and I didn't do anything about it for months and months. When I did deal with it – although I found it uncomfortable – ultimately, the outcome was positive. This taught me to not put my head in the sand about things that are causing problems. It's important to deal with issues faster and make decisions faster – after all, if you make a decision that turns out to be undesirable, you can always change it! Personally I like change, so it interests me as to why I sat on this particular problem for so long. I suspect it was to do with having to deal with a person, rather than, say, a process, and not wanting to upset that person or cause an atmosphere.

A little while after I had dealt with this problem, I read the book 'Lynne's Laws of Leadership' by Lynne Burdon, a solicitor and managing partner of over 30 years. This book was recommended to me by Darren J. Sylvester, my co-author. In Lynne's book, she talks about putting the firm first. This was so good to read! As obvious as it might sound, I think I've tried for a long time to put people first, and although I'm not saying that this isn't important as well, at the end of the day, it's the firm that needs to come first when deciding strategy and direction, as if there's no firm there will be no people in it anyway.

As a business owner you have so many hats on it's no wonder most of the time I feel like my head is going to fall off! If I didn't know any better, I would have said that running a small business is easier than running a large enterprise, but now I don't think that's the case. For a start, in a large business there are more people and departments to deal with things like HR, marketing, PR, accounts, administration, etc., whereas as a small business owner there's just as much going on but you tend to do a lot of these things yourself. It's a proper juggling act a lot of the time and I think it takes time to learn how to prioritise – and what to prioritise – as things change and evolve relatively quickly.

What changes did you make as a result of this?

I think the main changes I've made are to be a more efficient decision-maker and to be less swayed by other people's opinions. Only you, as the business owner, have a complete picture of what goes on and so, as much as it is wise to speak to others, including staff members and other business owners, ultimately, you'll know what to do. That said, knowing what to do and actually doing it are two different things! Though I believe I am getting better at implementation, I think this will be an ongoing learning curve for me.

In what way do you think this made you a better law firm owner?

This makes me think of the expression 'you snooze, you lose' and again it goes back to making decisions quickly – once you have most of the information you need to make them, that is. I realise now that my personality type typically requires a lot of information before I decide and then act, but this can be inefficient. I try now to use the 80 per cent rule. I ask myself; do I have 80 per cent of the information I need to make a decision? If yes, then I have enough information to decide. Otherwise, I hang on for ages waiting for more information when this is both impractical and weighs down the decision-making process.

What advice would you give to a new law firm owner about this?

Don't be hasty, but don't hang about either. One of my former bosses used to use the expression 'more haste, less speed' and now I actually get it!

Don't be afraid to forge ahead on projects, decisions and changes in direction. You know what you're doing. Other people will be willing to help and give you their input and that's fine, but remember that a lot of the time these other people have their own agendas.

Chapter 2

Choosing the right structure

There's a lot of administration involved in the early days of setting up a law firm. Just as you would with any other type of start-up business, you'll need to set aside some time to put together a dedicated business plan.

One of the first things you'll need to explore in your business plan is the kind of structure your firm will have. This includes whether you will be regulated and what type of business entity you'll operate under.

2.1 Why is structure important?

You might want to think of the structure of your business as the foundations everything else is built on. Before you can start to consider some of the more creative elements of your new business – such as core values, service offerings and branding – you'll need to ensure that all the legal aspects are present and accounted for.

One of the most important decisions you'll need to make, certainly during the early days and perhaps even over the lifetime of your practice, is whether or not you are going to be regulated. Once upon a time this might've been a very easy decision as regulation would probably have been a given, but today's legal marketplace is a great deal more flexible.

The other key structural decision to consider is what business entity you will operate under. Will you be taking advantage of the new freelance solicitor legislation, or will you consider more traditional models such as a partnership, a limited liability partnership (LLP) or a limited company? Alternatively, you may decide that an alternative business structure (ABS) is the right choice for you.

It's well worth noting here that you will not be bound to stick with these decisions for the lifetime of your firm. You can apply for regulation – or indeed, choose not to continue with it – at any point. You can also change your business categorisation from sole trader or partnership by registering with Companies House whenever it makes sense for your business to do so.

Changing from a limited company or LLP to a sole trader or partnership is also possible, though this will not be as straightforward.

At this stage, we recommend familiarising yourself with all the available options. If it all seems overwhelming, remember this: you only need to make a decision about what works best for your business right now. If you think this may change in the long term, set a date six or 12 months in the future to re-assess.

2.2 Choosing a regulator

For some new firms, this will be a very straightforward part of the structural set-up process. Others will have more thinking to do. Before you can consider who the right regulator is for you, you'll need to determine whether you want – or need – to be regulated at all.

2.2.1 Do you need to be regulated?

Law is a protected industry and, generally speaking, only those who have undergone sufficient training are able to offer a full range of legal services. However, there are exceptions to this. It's perfectly possible for those without formal training in the law to legally offer certain types of legal services.

Who are the regulated lawyers?

If you are a regulated lawyer and want to offer a full range of reserved legal services, you'll need to be affiliated with a regulatory body.

This might be:

- **the Solicitors Regulation Authority (SRA)**, which regulates solicitors, registered European lawyers and registered lawyers from further afield;
- **the Bar Standards Board (BSB)**, which regulates barristers and some other specialised legal service businesses in England and Wales;
- **the Chartered Institute of Legal Executives (CILEx)**, which regulates chartered legal executives and CILEx practitioners;
- **the Council for Licensed Conveyancers (CLS)**, which regulates licensed conveyancers as well as some specialist conveyancing and probate solicitors;
- **the Institute of Chartered Accountants in England and Wales (ICAEW)**, which regulates chartered accountants as well as some specialist probate practitioners and firms;
- **the Intellectual Property Regulation Board (IPReg)**, which regulates trademark attorneys;

- **the Faculty Office**, which regulates notaries (some of whom may also be solicitors) in England and Wales;
- **the Costs Lawyer Standards Board (CLSB)**, which regulates costs lawyers.

This isn't an exhaustive list, and we haven't listed regulatory bodies for Scotland or Northern Ireland. However, many of the over-arching principles discussed in this book will apply to other regulators.

Who are the unregulated lawyers?

You don't need to be a regulated lawyer to set up a law firm. So long as you're not claiming (or implying) to be something you're not, anyone can set up a business that offers legal services to members of the public.

However, you will not be able to offer 'reserved legal activities', which are defined in the Legal Services Act 2007, s.12.

Most unregulated lawyers come under the following categories:

- will writers;
- mediators;
- charity and trade union representatives;
- McKenzie friends;
- paralegals.

Which option is right for you?

Regulated firms are very much the traditional model, but as we've already touched upon, there's no sense in continuing to do things the traditional way if you find it no longer serves you.

There are major benefits to being regulated, but there are also some key benefits to not being regulated.

Is being regulated right for you?

The majority of legal professionals are likely to decide they do want the benefit of regulation, at least somewhere down the line.

However, there are downsides to associating your firm with a regulatory body, namely regulatory costs and certificate fees, as well as the need to comply with the rules of said regulatory body. Despite this, many professionals determine these downsides well worth it in the light of the opportunities they receive in return.

These include:

- the right to offer a full range of legal services;
- the prestige of being associated with a regulatory body;

- the ability for your clients to benefit from insurance offered by your regulatory body;
- being part of the community of your regulatory body, including training, conferences and award opportunities;
- the reassurance regulation offers to clients.

Is being unregulated right for you?

Alternatively, there are some key benefits to being an unregulated legal professional. These include:

- fewer constraints;
- zero regulatory costs;
- no practising certificate fees;
- lower insurance premiums;
- the public may not even know the difference!

However, there are also some key downsides to this option. Though it's certainly simpler in some ways to skip regulation altogether, you would need to be very careful to ensure that you weren't presenting your business as something it was not.

For example, only firms that are regulated can include the word 'solicitor(s)' in their name or describe their work in a way that implies they are a solicitors firm.[1] This could seriously impact how successfully you were able to advertise your fledgling firm. Though it's true that many potential clients wouldn't know – or care about – the difference between a regulated and unregulated firm, others would. Savvy clients may well look for a regulated firm as an assurance that the firm is run by experienced solicitors with sufficient insurance in place.

It's also important to consider the legal services you would be able to offer without regulation and whether this would be sustainable. You might want to start a will-writing firm with no intention of employing anyone but yourself. In this case, you may well decide that regulation is an added complication you could do without. However, if you were hoping to one day own a bigger will-writing firm with a dedicated office and a team of staff, you may want to consider whether or not this would be financially viable if you weren't also able to offer reserved probate activities.

How do you make the decision?

We're afraid there's no one-size-fits-all answer here.

Whether or not you choose to be regulated will depend entirely on the legal services you want to be able to offer and the type of firm you plan to run.

[1] Solicitors Regulation Authority Code of Conduct (5.4).

Once again: you don't need to make a long-term decision on this right at the beginning. You might decide to start small and test the water without regulation, with a plan to add regulation, and thus additional services, further down the line.

2.3 Who is the right regulator for you?

If you decide that regulation is the right choice for you, the next question will be which regulator to go for. This is generally an easier decision to make, as the ideal regulator for you will depend on the type of qualifications you have and the services you offer.

2.3.1 Solicitors Regulation Authority

The SRA is the regulatory body for solicitors in England and Wales. The majority of solicitors who are seeking to offer 'reserved legal activities' will need to be regulated by the SRA.

These 'reserved legal activities' come under the headings of:

- the exercise of a right of audience;
- the conduct of litigation;
- reserved instrument activities;
- probate activities;
- notarial activities;
- the administration of oaths.

Plainly speaking, if you want to be able to offer any legal services that fall under these headings, you'll need to be regulated, and that regulation will most likely be provided by the SRA.

SRA Standards and Regulations 2019

The SRA published new Standards and Regulations documentation in November 2019 (**www.sra.org.uk/solicitors/standards-regulations**), which replaced the previous SRA Handbook. These new standards apply to all individuals who are authorised by the SRA to provide legal services (including solicitors and registered European lawyers) as well as authorised firms, their managers and employees.

We believe the new Standards and Regulations documentation has brought about the biggest change to the legal profession in the last two decades. For the first time, two Codes of Conduct have been published: one for individuals and one for firms. You may also be pleased to know that they are the shortest collection of rules and codes published in a long time. This is thanks to the SRA's drive towards making their rules less prescriptive in order to enable solicitors to use their own professional judgement.

These new less-prescriptive Standards and Regulations give the legal professionals they regulate a greater element of flexibility than ever before. This allows solicitors to think creatively in terms of how they are able to offer and market legal services to the general public, and to compete in a regulatory environment that's supportive of innovation, competition and growth.

This is regarded as some of the most modern and forward-thinking legal regulation in the world.

2.3.2 Bar Standards Board

Just like solicitors, barristers are only able to undertake 'reserved legal activities' if they hold a valid practising certificate from the BSB.

Any barrister who doesn't hold a current practising certificate is known as an unregistered barrister. This might be because they are no longer practising or because they're retired. It may also be because they've chosen to provide legal services without a practising certificate.

If a barrister chooses to work as an unregistered barrister, they will still need to act in accordance with the core duties in the BSB Handbook.

In particular, they will need to:

1. ensure that their clients understand that they are an unregistered barrister;
2. make their clients aware that unregistered barristers are not subject to the same regulatory protective safeguards as practising barristers.

Reserved legal activities for barristers are:

- the exercise of a right of audience;
- the conduct of litigation;
- reserved instrument activities;
- probate activities;
- notarial activities;
- the administration of oaths.

It is a criminal offence for unregistered barristers to carry out any of these activities without a valid practising certificate.

2.3.3 Other regulators

Though the SRA and the BSB are the two biggest regulators for legal professionals in England and Wales, there are other regulators that support specialist legal professionals within this jurisdiction.

Chartered Institute of Legal Executives

Legal executives work in a very similar way to solicitors on an everyday basis, but they have undergone significantly different training. While solicitors tend to specialise after their training, legal executives specialise early in their legal education and therefore learn only their chosen specialism to a high level.

Legal executives are regulated by CILEx. They will need to be regulated in order to carry out reserved legal activities within their chosen legal field. However, like barristers and solicitors, legal executives can choose to provide non-reserved legal activities without regulation.

Council for Licensed Conveyancers

A licensed conveyancer is a specialist legal professional who deals with property transactions. In order to become a licensed conveyancer, an individual would need to complete the CLC's training and certification process.

By definition, a licensed conveyancer is only a licensed conveyancer due to their association with the CLC. Because of this, it would not be possible to work as a licensed conveyancer without CLC regulation.

The CLC is also able to regulate solicitors and legal executives who work within the legal areas of conveyancing and probate services (not including reserved probate activities). A legal professional or firm offering these types of services may choose CLC regulation rather than SRA regulation.

This choice would have various benefits, including a simpler regulation model and lower regulatory fees. However, the CLC offers narrower regulation than the SRA. Not only does the CLC only regulate legal activities within conveyancing and probate services, they also only regulate non-contentious work.

Institute of Chartered Accountants in England and Wales

In order to be able to use the title 'chartered accountant' in England or Wales, a professional would need to have worked with the ICAEW to complete a minimum of three years' in-depth training and pass a series of examinations in auditing, financial management, taxation and business strategy. Chartered accountants also have an ongoing commitment to continuing professional development (CPD).

In order to offer certain financial services including auditing, insolvency and business investment, an accountant needs to be regulated by the ICAEW. Though it's perfectly possible for accountants to offer other accountancy and financial services without ICAEW regulation, they wouldn't be able to call themselves a chartered accountant.

The ICAEW is also able to legally regulate chartered accountants to carry out probate work. In order to benefit from this, regulated chartered accountant firms need to apply to the ICAEW to become an accredited probate firm.

IPReg

The IPReg regulates trademark and patent attorneys.

Trademark and patent attorneys are specialist legal professionals who specialise in trademark and patent law. You do not have to be a qualified solicitor or barrister in order to become an attorney.

The trademark and patent attorney certification process is a post-graduate course that can be completed after any undergraduate degree. A professional would need to undertake at least two years of work experience under a qualified trademark or patent attorney. They would then need to pass two qualifying examinations. Like most other regulated legal professionals, trademark and patent attorneys are also required to complete ongoing professional development training on an annual basis.

In order to work as a trademark or patent attorney, you would need to be registered by the IPReg.

The Faculty Office

The Faculty Office is the regulator for notaries. Notaries are qualified lawyers appointed by the Archbishop of Canterbury for the purpose of authorising and certifying signatures, authenticating documents and preparing documents for use abroad.

In order to become a notary, an individual must have a law qualification. They would then need to complete the Notarial Practice Course before applying to the Faculty Office for admittance to the Roll of Notaries.

Approximately half of all notaries also practise as solicitors. Notaries are specifically authorised to carry out certain reserved activities under the Legal Services Act 2007. They can undertake any kind of legal activities except:

(a) contentious matters;
(b) taking cases to court.

It's important to note that though the Faculty Office is headed by the Archbishop of Canterbury, the role of notary is a secular one and has no further connection with the Church of England.

Costs Lawyer Standards Board

The CLSB regulates costs lawyers. A costs lawyer is a legal professional who is concerned with the regulation of all aspects of solicitor costs. In order to be qualified as a costs lawyer, an individual would need to undergo the Association of Cost Lawyers' training programme and then complete a period of supervision. They would also need to commit to ongoing professional development.

In order to work as a costs lawyer, an individual would need to apply for annual practising certification from the CLSB. Without this regulation, legal professionals would not be able to call themselves costs lawyers. An unregulated costs lawyer is known as a non-qualified costs draftsman.

2.4 Choosing a business entity

Regulation isn't the only structural concern you'll need to consider when setting up a law practice. You will also need to consider the rather more general question of which kind of business entity model will be the best fit.

This is important as it sets out the legal rights and requirements of your company. The business entity you choose will determine factors including:

- how you need to register your business;
- how you pay yourself from the business;
- whether or not you are personally liable for any company debt;
- how you complete your annual accounts;
- whether you are in business alone or in a partnership;
- how complicated the set-up process is;
- whether annual accounts, financial reports and other business information need to be available in the public domain.

Options include:

- sole trader;
- partnership;
- limited company;
- LLP;
- ABS.

2.4.1 Sole trader

The simplest way to start in business is as a sole trader. This is likely to be the ideal option for you if you plan to start a small law firm from home under the new freelance solicitor regulation.

There are few legal requirements in terms of this business entity, and you won't need to register with Companies House or publish your annual accounts. In fact, all you'll need to do is tell HM Revenue and Customs (HMRC) that you're self-employed and complete a self-assessment tax return each year.

The main thing to understand about being a sole trader is that there is no real separation between you and the business. Your finances and the business's finances are one and the same, even if you have – as you most certainly should – two separate bank accounts. The business's total profits will be considered to be your income and will need to be declared in full on your self-assessment tax return.

The great thing about this is that it offers a lot of flexibility. You'll be able to take money from the business as and when you choose, with no requirement to pay yourself a consistent wage.

There is no formal winding-down process for those who choose to stop practising as a sole trader, though legal professionals may want to follow the Law Society's advice on how to close down a practice (**www.lawsociety.org.uk/support-services/advice/practice-notes/closing-down-your-practice**).

What are the downsides of being a sole trader?

There are some limitations in choosing this kind of business entity. The main concern here is the fact that there's no legal boundary between your finances and the business' finances. This means you would be personally liable for any debt the business was to incur.

This wouldn't necessarily be a big concern if your overheads were very low, but it might if you were considering investing in a big-ticket item such as business premises.

The SRA's new regulations for freelance solicitors

Historically speaking, barristers are much more likely to be sole traders than solicitors are. As many as 80 per cent of barristers are self-employed,[2] while solicitors are just catching up.

The growth of interest in this area has led to the SRA releasing new rules on freelance solicitors and their regulation in the 2019 edition of their Standards and Regulations.

Solicitors who are regulated by the SRA can choose to register as freelance solicitors. In order to do this, they would need to be prepared to work within the following model.

A freelance solicitor is a self-employed solicitor who:

- practises on their own;
- does not employ anyone else;
- practises under their own name;
- is engaged directly by the client;
- receives fees directly payable to them.

---

[2] PLC: Regulation to the Legal Profession in the UK.

Important things to note from these new regulations are:

1. Freelance solicitors can only offer reserved legal services if they have held a practising certificate for three years or more. Freelance solicitors without this level of experience can still practise, but only with non-reserved activities.
2. A freelance solicitor who is providing only non-reserved legal activities will not need to have their practise authorised, though they will need to notify the SRA that they are doing so.
3. Freelance solicitors can't employ anyone, unless that freelance solicitor only undertakes non-reserved legal activities.
4. The clients of freelance solicitors will have access to the SRA Compensation Fund, provided the freelance solicitor is eligible. However, this doesn't include cover for civil liability losses.
5. Freelance solicitors will only be required to publish costs information if they are providing reserved legal activities.
6. Freelance solicitors cannot operate a client account or hold client money.
7. If freelance solicitors are offering reserved legal services, they will need to obtain adequate and appropriate professional indemnity insurance. If they are not offering reserved legal services, they will not need to hold professional indemnity insurance. Freelance solicitors are exempt from the SRA minimum terms and conditions of professional indemnity insurance.
8. Freelance solicitors should register with the Information Commissioner's Office (ICO) as data controllers.
9. If a freelance solicitor stops trading, they won't need to make any provision for claims received after they cease practising. This can be very cost-effective as freelance solicitors won't need to pay for run off cover.

As of March 2020, 71 solicitors have registered as freelance solicitors in England and Wales.[3] It's predicted that this number will rise sharply over the coming years.

2.4.2 Partnership

Legally, being in a business partnership is very similar to being a sole trader. The only real difference is that there are two (or more) of you instead of one. This may be the ideal choice if you're coming together with colleagues or friends to start a law practice.

[3] 'Freelancers Mull "Chambers" Model to Boost Reach', *Law Society Gazette*, 23 March 2020.

Within a partnership, each partner must register separately with HMRC as being self-employed. Though all partners share management responsibilities and profit, they would all need to submit a separate self-assessment tax return to HMRC each year.

If you were starting a partnership, you would need to put together a comprehensive partnership agreement. Among other benefits, this would allow you to set out right at the beginning who was entitled to what percentage share of the profits. In some cases, this might be simple: if both partners were working full-time on the business and both had invested the same amount of capital, it might seem natural to split the profits on a 50/50 basis. However, if one partner was significantly more experienced, had invested more capital or was able to offer a bigger time commitment than the other, they may wish to negotiate on this matter.

The downsides of being in a partnership

Again, the main concern with the traditional partnership as a business structure is there is no legal separation between the finances of the individuals and the finances of the company. Just like sole traders, the partners in this case would be responsible for any debt that the business incurred.

How do partnerships work in terms of the SRA's freelance solicitor guidance?

Freelance solicitors are defined as solicitors who work alone, so they would not legally be able to come together to form a partnership in any traditional sense.

However, if you did want to work alongside other freelance solicitors in a kind of partnership, it would be possible to consider an arrangement similar in nature to a barristers' chamber. In this kind of arrangement, barristers work from one location and use shared services, but they remain independent entities that don't share profits or have any liability for debts of their respective businesses.

This could be a revolutionary way for freelance solicitors to come together to share resources and boost their individual capabilities.

2.4.3 Limited company

When you register your business as a limited company, it becomes a legal entity in its own right. This means you will no longer be fully liable for any debt the business was to incur.

Many clients will view a limited company as more prestigious and 'official' than a business run by a sole trader. You will likely find it easier to raise investment in the company too, as shares of the company can be sold. Many businesses also find that it is more tax efficient to be a limited company.

In order to start a limited company, you would have to register with Companies House.

The downsides of a limited company

Running a limited company is less straightforward than being a sole trader. It's also more public. Information about the limited company will be published by Companies House and you would need to submit annual accounts to them, as well as an annual corporation tax return to HMRC.

There's a lot more to think about during the set-up process of a limited company. You would be legally expected to follow a set up process entailing:

1. **Choosing a business name.** This cannot be the same or too similar to an existing company name. It will usually include the word 'limited' or 'ltd' at the end.
2. **Choosing directors.** There must be at least one director for the company. You can also choose to appoint a company secretary, though this isn't compulsory.
3. **Nominating shareholders or guarantors.** There must be at least one shareholder or guarantor, though this can be the same person as the director.
4. **Naming anyone who has significant control over your company.** This usually means anyone who has voting rights or more than a 25 per cent share in the company.
5. **Preparing documentation.** You will need to produce 'memorandum of association' and 'articles of association' documentation.
6. **Preparing to keep records.** You will need to make sure you understand the records you'll be legally required to keep.
7. **Registering your company with Companies House.** There are costs associated with this, though they are as little as £12.[4]

2.4.4 Limited liability partnership

An LLP may be a good choice for a group of lawyers who want to open a firm together without personal financial liability *and* without some of the more constraining elements of a limited company. An LLP also confers a lot of the prestige and reassurance of a limited company.

Internally, they offer a very similar structure to a conventional partnership. Each member of the partnership is considered to be a self-employed individual who is taxed through an annual self-assessment. The LLP will

[4] 'Set up a limited company: step by step', **www.gov.uk/set-up-limited-company**.

also need to be registered for self-assessment with HMRC, and annual accounts will need to be sent to Companies House.

There are no shares in an LLP. This can make things more flexible as it means new members can be brought into the partnership without any restructuring of shares.

Speaking of flexibility, LLPs can make their business decisions in whatever way they want. There are no requirements for LLP partners to hold formal board meetings.

The downsides of an LLP

Just like with a limited company, LLPs will need to submit yearly financial reports to Companies House which will then be publicly available.

You may also discover that an LLP is not as efficient in terms of your personal tax bill as if you were a director of a limited company.

An LLP doesn't have a mechanism for holding profit over from year to year in order to invest back into the company. Instead, all profit will need to be allocated among the partners.

As you may imagine, setting up as an LLP is slightly more involved than setting up as a traditional partnership. You will need to:

1. **Choose a name.** This must end in 'limited liability partnership' or 'LLP' and mustn't be too similar to the name of another registered company.
2. **Provide a registered address.** This will be publicly available.
3. **Choose at least two designated members.** Designated members will have more responsibility for the partnership than ordinary members.
4. **Write an LLP agreement.** This must set out how profits are to be shared out; how decisions will be made; what responsibilities designated members and ordinary members will have; and how members can join or leave the LLP.

2.4.5 Alternative business structure

Until 2012, the SRA did not allow non-lawyers to be involved in the ownership or management of a law firm.

As a result of this, the ABS was launched in 2012 as a vehicle for non-lawyers to have some kind of involvement in a law firm. This could be at management level, such as a partner, director or member; or it could be at ownership level as an investor or shareholder.

This may be an ideal structure for your law firm if you want to go into business with a partner who is not a legal professional. For example, if you plan to start a firm with a finance or marketing professional.

In order to register as an ABS, you will need to apply to your regulatory body.

The downsides of an ABS

You may find that the application process for starting an ABS is more onerous than other options. If the non-lawyer (or non-lawyers) will own more than a 10 per cent share in the organisation, they will need to take a suitability test to show they are capable of fulfilling the role.

As part of the conditions for operating an ABS, you will need to show that you have satisfactory arrangements in place for ensuring regulatory compliance.

2.5 Making your structure official

It might seem like something of a marathon just making these two structural decisions about your law firm. If you've made it this far, congratulations!

Make sure you've ticked all the official boxes and have registered with HMRC/Companies House/your regulatory body as necessary – then you can begin the next stage of your business planning in earnest.

CASE STUDY 2: BELINDA LESTER

Belinda Lester is a solicitor and the founder of boutique virtual law firm Lionshead Law Ltd. Lionshead Law specialises in employment, commercial, immigration and technology law. All their services are offered virtually and are not limited by geography or normal office hours.

When did you launch your law firm?

Lionshead Law was launched on 2nd September 2013.

How much knowledge and experience did you have before you started?

I came to the profession relatively late – qualifying in 1999 two months before my 31st birthday. I had studied psychology at university and had no idea what to do after graduation. I ended up travelling for a couple of years – spending about 18 months in my birthplace South Africa and six months in Hong Kong. I definitely had some life experience, therefore, before embarking on my career in the law. I studied the CPE part-time at Leeds Metropolitan University whilst working as a legal secretary to help fund it. I then did my LPC full-time at the College of Law in York and qualified as a solicitor in a general practice firm in Leeds before moving to London shortly after qualification.

When I joined Sprecher Grier Halberstam with one year PQE (specialising in employment law), the partner I was joining to support almost immediately went off on maternity leave and I was left holding the fort. This was undoubtedly a baptism of fire but taught me that, whilst I may not have had the usual amount of experience for someone effectively heading a department, I certainly had the balls! I left Sprecher Grier Halberstam after my first child was born and I knew immediately that I did not want to return. I decided, therefore, to set myself up as a consultant offering employment law services to smaller firms that wanted to provide employment law advice and representation to clients without having to go to the expense and risk of employing an employment lawyer full-time. I started this when my daughter was seven months old, and it was pretty successful. When she was a year old, a firm I had approached to offer my consultancy services to asked me to join them to set up an employment department. I was very clear that I was not looking for a job as I had a one-year-old daughter and that if I was to join them, it would have to be on my terms. They agreed, so I joined as a full-time solicitor who worked 50 per cent of the time from home, and was made a partner after 12 months. The hours and seniority were great, but the pay wasn't, and so when I was head-hunted by their immediate competitor up the road, I jumped at the chance to move on the same terms but almost double the pay. I joined that firm as a partner and worked 10am to 3pm in the office Monday to Thursday and the rest of the time from home. I worked there for about five years and really loved it. However, I became increasingly frustrated at having to charge by the hour/six-minute unit as this way of working was, in my view, seriously hampering my ability to attract new business. I knew that there was a better way of doing things, and so I decided to start my own business – initially a law consultancy offering employment law advice and representation only.

What would you say is the most important lesson you learned in the first few years of your firm?

Things were really smooth in the first few years, to be honest. The firm wasn't regulated by the SRA (it didn't need to be as I was only doing non-reserved activities) and so there was very little to think about in terms of risk management, etc. However, in January 2018 we did become regulated by the SRA so that we could branch out and offer immigration and commercial law services in addition to employment law.

All our consultants work for themselves and from home, so this is quite tricky from a risk and compliance perspective. Insurers need to know exactly what measures have been put in place re: supervision, data protection and overall risk management. I learned very early on that risk and compliance was neither my strength nor something I had any real interest in. I learned that I love being a solicitor and I love the freedom and independence of having my own firm, but that the nitty gritty of actually ensuring that it runs in a way which is compliant is a nightmare.

Fortunately, my mother is a solicitor who specialises in solicitors' negligence and she worked for many years in-house at Zurich. She is an absolute genius when it comes to risk and compliance, so I decided to take her on as my risk and compliance consultant. That has been a Godsend! It's so important to know what you are good at and to get others to help you with the things you're not.

Can you tell us how you learned this particular lesson?

I didn't really need to learn it. I knew straight away that I was going to need help with this aspect of running the firm.

What changes did you make as a result of this?

I implemented all the risk and compliance policies and strategies I was advised to. The firm has a cloud-based document management system so that it's easy for me to access everyone's files to conduct file reviews. I created a handbook for consultants to set out clearly all the policies and procedures they needed to follow when opening files/closing files, sending letters of engagement, etc. We also have regular online 'water cooler' chats to keep in touch, to discuss work and also to just have a natter.

In what way do you think this made you a better law firm owner?

It has allowed me to concentrate on doing what I do best – advising/representing clients and business development, whilst knowing that the firm is running properly.

What advice would you give to a new law firm owner about this?

Recognise your strengths and weaknesses and make sure that you engage people who have strengths that are different from yours – particularly in the key areas. For example, if you're a brilliant lawyer and manager and are really hot at compliance but not great at BD/networking: make sure you find people who are able to grow the business for you as, no matter how fabulous you are, if you can't sell what you do, you won't succeed.

Chapter 3

The first steps of your start-up

One of the most important things you will do during the early days of starting a law firm is to put together a comprehensive business plan.

Not everyone enjoys writing projects like this, and it might be tempting to rush through it. However, trust us when we say that really putting your all into exploring options within your business plan is an exercise that will pay dividends in the future.

A business plan is a document that includes both very practical and more creative considerations. Before you can start putting pen to paper, there are various things to make sure you've fully considered.

3.1 Adopting the mindset of a business owner

We've touched already on how your mindset will be very different as a business owner than it has been as an employee.

3.1.1 Judgement, responsibility and decision-making

You may well have had some degree of autonomy as an employee in a law firm, such as running your own caseload, interviewing clients and drafting documents. However, as a business owner you'll need to exercise judgement and make things happen without anyone overseeing it. You'll also be fully responsible for the outcome and any follow-up, whether this is favourable or unfavourable.

Invariably, as the owner of the business you'll have to make quick decisions – often on the basis of what others don't see – as well as test new ideas, seize new territory and take calculated risks, all without anyone else to approve the decision.

3.1.2 The reality of income

You'll also need to come to a place of acceptance regarding the certainty of your income. Employees are guaranteed work with a salary payment at the end of each month. This provides a great deal of relative safety that you're unlikely to have as a business owner, certainly in the early days.

In the first months you may not even be able to take drawings from the business at all. Many new business owners have to live on savings or borrow money during this period.

Even as the business grows, your owner's salary will be far from fixed. Instead, it will be determined by factors such as:

- how many new clients have been brought in that month;
- how quickly you've been able to complete and invoice for work;
- how promptly invoices have been paid;
- whether there have been any big business expenses.

3.1.3 How does the mindset of a law firm owner differ from that of a self-employed lawyer?

Which path you decide to take for yourself and your law firm will have a big impact on the mindset you'll need to cultivate. Crucially: it's different to aspire to run a law firm than it is to work as a freelance solicitor or self-employed barrister.

Though the technicalities of the two situations are very similar, there's a key shift in mindset. A self-employed lawyer is likely to be focused on doing their work, getting paid and keeping their customers happy. A law firm owner needs to be able to do all these things while also holding a bigger picture in mind.

The law firm owner will need to be concerned with how they can offer increased value and more revenue. They'll also need to let go of the idea of doing everything themselves and consider instead who they can add to their team (whether that's a full-time team or a pool of contractors).

3.1.4 Will it be worth it?!

Owning and running a law firm is not easy. If you expected it to be, you've probably already been disappointed by the number of complicated regulatory and structural decisions involved in the planning stages!

You'll need to be able to accept a certain level of uncertainty and risk as a new normal in your professional life. In addition to this, you'll also need to be able to develop a mindset of determination to succeed, despite the many obstacles and rejections that will be in your way.

As a business owner, you may find it difficult to 'switch off'. You'll always be thinking about your firm, especially in the modern legal environment. Technological advancements and developments are constantly being tried, tested and experimented with in order to offer efficient legal services faster, more conveniently and at a cheaper cost. Though these technological developments offer fantastic opportunities to business owners, they also mean that it's harder than ever to 'clock off' come the evening.

It's also worth pointing out that you'll be constantly learning new skills as a businessperson. This is particularly likely to be the case early on when you may not have sufficient income to outsource tasks such as administration, book-keeping or marketing. This learning is likely to have to take place outside of traditional office hours, especially if you're lucky enough to be bringing in a reasonable amount of client work.

If you want to run a successful business, you'll need to have genuine passion for it, both inside and outside office hours. Whether or not it will be worth it is a question only you can answer! For some people this might be the culmination of a lifetime's ambition, for others it won't seem worth the blood, sweat and tears.

We recommend putting some significant thinking time into what kind of mindset you feel able to cultivate. This exercise is likely to help you determine which path is right for you – running a law firm, working as a freelance solicitor or other self-employed legal professional, entering into a partnership or remaining as an employee.

3.2 Determining your vision

3.2.1 Areas to consider

When you imagine yourself in five years' time, where do you see yourself?

- Are you at the helm of a growing law practice?
- Are you working in your current field of law?
- Are you based in a flash city-centre office?
- Are you working from your converted garage?
- Are you working with the same type of clients you've always worked with?
- Are you doing pro bono or legal aid work?
- Are you working at a significantly higher billable rate?
- Are you working with clients remotely?
- Are you based in a new location?
- Are you surrounded by a team of employees?
- Are you offering a selection of online services?
- Are you working with trusted partners?
- Are you doing innovative work?
- Are you actively pursuing further growth?
- Are you winning awards?
- Are you specialising in the work you love?

The answers to these questions will help you build up a detailed blueprint for what you are trying to achieve. This is your vision, and it's really important to be able to hold on to this image throughout the business planning stage and beyond.

This vision is fundamentally what will shape your short-, medium- and long-term plans for your business. It will help you to make big and small choices, and it will guide you on how to move forwards.

If you're considering entering into business with other professionals, it will be vitally important that all the partners subscribe to a shared vision. If you plan to do things alone, it will be you alone who is responsible for developing and enforcing the vision.

3.2.2 Is your vision realistic?

Ambition is important and we would always advise prospective business owners to think big. However, it *is* also important to ensure that your vision is realistic and feasible.

In addition to acting as a kind of over-arching guiding light during your first years in business, a vision is also what will clearly shine through in your formal business plan. It's important that this comes over as something that's possible for you to achieve, especially if you're using your business plan to apply to third parties for financial support, such as a bank loan.

We'd also like to think that you weren't setting yourself up for failure. Ideally, your vision should reflect what you believe you can achieve based on your personal goals, skills and qualities. It might not be realistic to envision yourself running a solo law firm from a remote beach somewhere when you know you thrive on face-to-face time with clients and colleagues. Equally, if you're more comfortable in a casual work environment, you might want to rethink your plan of running a traditional law firm in central London.

It makes sense to take some real time to contemplate your vision. After all, your vision is essentially the business idea everything else will hinge on. This isn't a stage you should rush through.

3.3 Understanding regulatory requirements and legislation

If you've decided to be regulated, you'll need to make sure you understand all the requirements of your particular regulatory body and work this into your business plan.

Even if you've decided to forego regulation for now, you'll need to be aware of certain legislation that apply to all law professionals and/or businesses operating in the legal field.

These regulatory and legislative requirements will need to be clearly addressed in your business plan. Some will seem very simple to comply with; others may require a bit more innovation and creative thought.

Either way, it's wise to make sure you're well informed right from the beginning in order to save unpleasant and stressful surprises later on. Areas to consider are:

- insurance;
- data and information handling;
- money laundering;
- the Financial Services and Markets Act (FSMA) 2000;
- the Legal Aid Agency (LAA);
- compliance officer for legal practice (COLP) and compliance officer for finance and administration (COFA).

3.3.1 Insurance

Generally speaking, we can all agree that insurance is a very sensible thing to have in place, both in your professional and your personal lives. However, there's a general belief that insurance is prohibitively expensive for new law firms. Many have actually cited this as the reason they decided against going out on their own.

Though insurance – particularly professional indemnity insurance – is certainly going to be a big expense for your business, it's far from an insurmountable stumbling block. There are ways to make it feel more manageable.

Types of insurance to consider are:

- professional indemnity insurance;
- employers' liability insurance;
- public liability insurance
- cyber insurance.

Professional indemnity insurance

Professional indemnity insurance is in place to cover any civil liability claims that may arise from your work in private legal practice. This commonly includes professional negligence claims.

Both the SRA and the BSB require firms who are regulated by them to have professional indemnity insurance. You'll need to have this in place for your firm *before* you begin to practise, and the costs associated with this should be clearly featured in your business plan and cash flow forecast projections.

Professional indemnity insurance with SRA regulation

The SRA requires solicitors in private practice to take out and maintain compulsory professional indemnity insurance in accordance with their rules.

Since 2000, the only way of doing this is to obtain professional indemnity insurance from a participating insurer. This can be harder for a new firm, which has no performance record for insurance companies to consider. We thoroughly recommend that you get advice from a specialist insurance broker.

The approval process is far less straightforward than it is for other types of insurance. Before they make a decision, insurance companies will consider whether your practice:

- is covering work areas within its competence and skill set;
- is sufficiently skilled and competent;
- has a clear plan for growth;
- is fully aware of the competitive and rapidly changing nature of the legal marketplace;
- will be operated and managed properly;
- has contingency plans in place.

In addition to ensuring that all firms have indemnity insurance in place, the SRA rules also insist on a compulsory level of cover.

Table 3.1

Type of firm	Level of cover required
Recognised bodies and relevant licensed bodies (including alternative business structures, limited companies and limited liability partnerships)	At least £3 million for any one claim
Sole practitioners, partnerships and free-lance solicitors	At least £2 million for any one claim

This level of cover is often referred to as 'primary level cover'. Depending on the size of the practice and its exposure to risk, further cover may be required on top of this. A specialist insurance broker will be able to advise on whether your firm might fall into this category.

The traditional model was for all professional indemnity insurance policies to run from 1 October to 30 September. However, the SRA's Participating Insurers Agreement in 2013 removed this requirement. Insurers now offer both 12- and 18-month policies and can start whenever they are required.

New firms who are seeking professional indemnity insurance should:

1. Find a specialist professional indemnity insurance broker to offer you advice.

2. Finalise your business plan: this will need to explain fully the nature and structure of your new firm and what exactly you're seeking to insure.
3. Include a professional CV for yourself along with anyone else who'll be involved in the firm. This should showcase expertise, experience and specialist training.
4. Provide evidence of the financial viability of the practice. You should include projections of turnover, expenditure (including salaries) and any expected injection of external capital. Be prepared to justify these figures!
5. Make sure you've included the cost of your indemnity insurance policy in your cash flow projections, as well as a contingency plan for the insurance excess that would be payable by your firm in the event of a claim.
6. Demonstrate that you have sound risk management policies in place. This will reassure insurers that you are seeking to lower the risk of future claims. You might want to consider obtaining accreditations such as the Law Society's legal practice quality mark, the Lexcel accreditation, or the Conveyancing Quality Scheme (CQS).
7. Notify the insurance company of any circumstances or existing claims that might give rise to a claim during the period they will be insuring you. If you fail to do this, the insurance company would be able to refuse cover in the event of that claim arising.
8. Start early! You'll need to put in applications for insurance around 10–12 weeks before you intend to start practising. This should allow for any hold-ups in the process.
9. Do your research on the insurance companies you apply to. You'll want to consider the insurance company's experience within the solicitor's professional indemnity insurance market. You'll also want to look into the level of claims handling and risk management support they provide.
10. You'll need to make sure you're familiar with the insurance company's policies on the cost of run-off cover, which is the premium you would need to pay to your insurer to cover claims made against your firm for six years after it had ceased trading. The only exception to this is freelance solicitors, who don't have to have run off cover if they cease trading.

SRA Indemnity Rules Solicitors who are regulated by the SRA have to follow the SRA Indemnity Rules. Rule 18 obliges solicitor firms to provide certain information to anyone who makes a claim against the firm or any person insured under the firm's insurance policy. This information includes:

(a) the name of the company the firm is insured by;
(b) the contact details of the insurance firm (including the address);

(c) the firm's contact details.

It's important to note that firms are *only* obligated to release details about their insurance when there's an actual claim being made. This disclosure isn't necessary in the case of a complaint or a threat of a claim. Equally, the claim would need to be of a nature that would be covered by the insurance policy.

If a firm were to refuse to release details of their insurance policy to a claimant, rule 17 of the SRA Indemnity Rules gives the SRA the power to disclose this information on behalf of the firm when appropriate.

Provision of Services Regulations 2009 The Provision of Services Regulations 2009, SI 2009/2999 (which implement European Directive 2006/123/EC on services in the internal market) also impose requirements on law firms in terms of disclosing insurance information.

Regulation 8(1)(n) requires legal service providers to hold professional indemnity insurance and also requires that information about this insurance is given to clients. These regulations oblige law firms to make the following information available:

(a) the insurer's contact details;
(b) the territorial coverage of the insurance. The SRA minimum terms state that this coverage should be worldwide.

As a legal service provider you have four options for sharing this insurer information:

1. You can provide the information on your own initiative.
2. You can make the information easily available to clients at the place where you provide the service or where the contract for the service is made (e.g. a notice on the wall in your office).
3. You can make the information easily available electronically (e.g. on your website).
4. You can include the information in any document you supply which contains a detailed description of the service (e.g. in your terms of business document).

Professional indemnity insurance with BSB regulation

The BSB requires all members who hold a self-employed practising certificate to be a member of the Bar Mutual Indemnity Fund (BMIF). The BMIF is a mutual insurance fund where members pay a premium contribution each year in return for a basic level of cover. All members must renew their professional indemnity insurance annually on 1 April.

The annual cost of the premium will depend on two factors: which area of law barristers practise in; and the annual income of their chambers. They pay a percentage of their annual income; the exact percentage will be determined by their practice area. A new Ratings Schedule is published by the BMIF each year. In 2019, ratings ranged from 0.15 per cent for Family: Children to 6.50 per cent for Revenue: Non-Crown: Non-Contentious.

The amount contributed will determine the level of cover received. It's possible to purchase higher levels of cover (up to £2.5 million) for an additional premium.

Table 3.2

Basic premium	Amount of cover
£100–£399	£500,000
£400–£599	£1 million
£600–£799	£1.5 million
£800–£999	£2 million
£1,000+	£2.5 million

In order to apply to join the BMIF mutual insurance fund, self-employed barristers must submit an Application for Membership and Insurance form. As all policies must be renewed on 1 April, BMIF renewal forms are sent out annually in February

Employers' liability insurance

If a law practice has employees, like all UK businesses it will be required by law to hold employers' liability insurance. This protects the firm from legal liability for personal injury or illness suffered by any employees during the course of their employment. Liable firms must purchase employer's liability insurance in addition to professional indemnity insurance.

The Employers' Liability (Compulsory Insurance) Act 1969 states that employers must have a minimum of £5 million of cover in place. However, in practice insurers provide a minimum of £10 million as standard. Higher limits are available should you require them.

This type of insurance is relatively cheap to purchase and is often provided as part of a business insurance package.

Public liability insurance

Public liability insurance protects businesses from the legal liability for any injuries sustained by members of the public during a visit to the business' premises. This would protect you if, for example, a client made a claim against you after injuring themselves at your office.

This type of insurance isn't actually a legal requirement for businesses, but it's generally recommended for peace of mind. It's often included as part of business insurance packages and, like employer's liability insurance, is relatively inexpensive.

If your law firm is going to be based in your home, we'd advise speaking to the insurance company who provides your buildings and contents insurance. It may be possible for you to add public liability cover on to your existing policy for a small fee.

Cyber insurance

Cyber insurance would protect your firm from any claims made as a result of a cyber security breach. Though this type of insurance is not compulsory, many firms are now seeking it out.

This might be something that provides you with an added sense of security, though, of course, an insurance policy is not a replacement for stringent cyber security procedures.

3.3.2 Data and information handling

If you choose to run a law firm, collecting, processing and storing data will be an unavoidable part of your role.

Though this is unlikely to be a task you'll look forward to, you'l! need to familiarise yourself with the necessary regulation in order to make sure you're able to comply with it.

Data Protection Act 2018 and General Data Protection Regulation

In recent years there's been a great deal of publicity relating to data protection and General Data Protection Regulation (GDPR) concerns. Though there's certainly plenty for law firm owners to concern themselves with here, it's nothing new – data protection has actually been a key part of the day-to-day operations of a law firm since 1984.

Personal data has been regulated by the Data Protection Act 1998 since March 2000. Neither the 2018 European Union (EU) GDPR rules nor the UK Data Protection Act (DPA) 2018 which implements them represent a radical break from the data regime established in 1998. However, it's very important to ensure that you understand both these pieces of legislation and how they will impact how you can use and process client data.

Legal professionals have always been bound by professional duties of confidentiality concerning their clients' personal affairs. Despite this, there is no general exemption from the GDPR. We suggest you consider legal and professional confidentiality requirements as separate but complementary to the statutory data protection regime.

Most law practices will process a wide range of personal data. This will be in relation to the employees of the practice, clients, contractors and other individuals involved in their clients' affairs. The exact nature and volume of this personal data will vary according to the size of your practice and the exact field of law you're concerned with. The type and amount of personal data your practice has will have implications for your approach to GDPR and DPA compliance.

Firms who deal with private client matters such as family law, employment law, children's law, mental health law, medical negligence, immigration, crime or welfare law are likely to process large quantities of personal data. Importantly, much of this data will be classified as 'special category' data. This means personal data that is particularly sensitive and needs special protection. If your firm falls into this category, it will be very important for you to have a good general working knowledge of the GDPR and DPA.

Firms who work mainly with commercial matters such as mergers and acquisitions, corporate finance, commercial property and business affairs are likely to be processing less personal data. The personal data that they do have is likely to be less sensitive. If your firm falls into this category, you will still need to understand how GDPR and DPA legislation applies to you, but less specialised knowledge is likely to be necessary.

Legal professionals will mainly be 'controllers' of data, not 'processors'.

Data controllers must:

- process personal data lawfully, fairly and in line with data protection principles;
- process data in a way that protects the person it belongs to;
- use the right systems for holding and processing data responsibly;
- be accountable;
- co-operate with the Information Commissioner's Office (ICO).

When using personal data, you must ensure the data is:

- processed fairly, lawfully and transparently;
- processed for a specified purpose;
- processed in a way that's limited to what's necessary;
- accurate and up to date;
- kept for no longer than it's needed.

The 2018 legislation made changes that affect all law firms. These changes are:

1. **The introduction of an accountability principle:** the requirement to maintain documentation and demonstrate compliance.
2. **The introduction of subject access requests:** individuals now have the right to see all the personal data a law firm is holding on them. If a request is made, the law firm must respond within a month and provide all information free of charge.
3. **The introduction of a right of erasure:** we all now have the 'right to be

forgotten'. This means that an individual can legally request all information your firm holds on them is permanently deleted.

Information Commissioner's Office

When the Data Protection (Charges and Information) Regulations 2018, SI 2018/480 came into effect in May 2018, they required every organisation or sole trader who processes personal information to pay an annual data protection fee to the ICO, unless they are exempt.

The exact fee depends on the size and turnover on your firm. There are three tiers of fees which range from £40 to £2,900. However, most organisations will pay either £40 or £60 per year. Failure to pay this will result in a fixed penalty fine.

The ICO also has wide enforcement powers conferred on it by Part 6 of the DPA 2018 (ss.142–159). This empowers it to issue four types of notice:

- information notices;
- assessment notices;
- enforcement notices;
- penalty notices.

All four of these notices should be taken very seriously and complied with as soon as possible.

3.3.3 Money laundering

Money laundering is a process where money that has been obtained through crime is funnelled through a more legitimate source in order to hide where it came from.

Legal professionals have to comply with money laundering legislation in order to ensure their services aren't being used with criminal intent. This is particularly important where the legal professional is managing transactions for clients, such as in conveyancing.

Regulation 18(1) of the Money Laundering, Terrorist Financing and Transfer of Funds (Information on the Payer) Regulations 2017, SI 2017/692 requires every legal practice to identify and assess any risk of money laundering and terrorist financing.

Practices must:

- take appropriate steps to identify, assess and understand any money laundering or terrorist financing risks the business might face;
- apply a risk-based approach to compliance with client due diligence obligations;
- have documented policies, controls and procedures that enable the business to manage, monitor and mitigate effectively the different risks that have been identified.

Before you take money into a client account, you must conduct due diligence checks. We also recommend that you set a limit for the cash payments you'll accept. If a client does try to make a bigger cash deposit, you may need to consider whether you think there's a risk of money laundering and whether you should make a disclosure to the National Crime Agency (NCA).

Ultimately, no matter how thorough your risk assessment or how appropriate your controls, some criminals may still succeed in exploiting your legal practice. No area of legal practice is completely free from this risk, though arguably the practice areas of property law, probate and trusts, companies, and charities could be more susceptible. This is because issues around mortgage fraud, tax evasion or parent or offshore companies could be being used to convert, disguise or dispose of criminal proceeds.

However, if you've made sure you have excellent risk assessment policies, controls and procedures in place, you'll be able to justify your decisions and actions to law enforcement agencies, the courts and your supervisory authority in the unlikely event that it be necessary.

Training

Your practice's best defence against money laundering is your staff. They are the people you will need to rely on to implement policies and use judgement to spot any suspicious behaviour.

Regulation 24 of the Money Laundering, Terrorist Financing and Transfer of Funds (Information on the Payer) Regulations 2017, SI 2017/692 requires that you make sure employees:

(a) are made aware of the law relating to money laundering, terrorist financing and the relevant requirements of data protection;
(b) are provided with regular training in recognising and dealing with transactions which may flag up money laundering or terrorist financing concerns. On this subject, you may also want to provide employees with the training and equipment to help identify forged documents.

If you're in the process of building a training programme, you may want to consider:

- which staff will require training;
- how you'll manage different training requirements for different staff;
- what format you'll provide training in;
- how regularly the training should take place;
- how you'll ensure training remains up to date for new and emerging risk factors.

As a starting point, you may wish to consider whether you will choose to run training in-house or whether you'll use a third party training company. Anti-money laundering conferences can be effective, as can providing an anti-money laundering manual as a reference for staff to have on hand. There are also a wide range of online training courses and resources available.

Training will need to take place at regular intervals. This may be every one or two years, depending on the size of your firm, how much involvement your staff have with clients and client accounts and how risky your area of practice is.

It's important to understand that failing to train staff sufficiently could leave your firm vulnerable to sanctions under the Money Laundering, Terrorist Financing and Transfer of Funds (Information on the Payer) Regulations 2017, SI 2017/692. Though insufficient training can be a defence for an individual member of staff who fails to report a suspicion of money laundering, it *isn't* a valid defence when there are terrorist funding charge concerns. This also isn't a defence for the firm owner who should have offered sufficient training.

Making a disclosure

If you or your staff believe that a client may be engaging in money laundering or terrorist financing, you have a legal obligation to make a disclosure to the financial intelligence unit within the NCA.

This disclosure should be made as soon as possible after any concerns have arisen, subject to privilege considerations. A suspicious activity report (SAR) can be made online. The NCA provide an encrypted system which will allow you to submit a disclosure online at any time of day.

Tipping off

If you or another member of your firm do have to make an SAR, it will be important to make sure you understand the ongoing legal requirements of this.

The offences of tipping off are defined in the Proceeds of Crime Act 2002, and amended by the Terrorism Act 2000 and Proceeds of Crime Act 2002 (Amendment) Regulations 2007, SI 2007/3398.

You must not disclose to a third party that an SAR has been made if that disclosure could prejudice any investigation which might need to be carried out. Likewise, it's an offence to disclose that an investigation is being contemplated or carried out if the disclosure might prejudice that investigation.

3.3.4 Financial Services and Markets Act 2000

Whether or not your firm will be able to carry out certain financial activities will depend on how – or if – you are regulated.

The FSMA 2000 allows authorised and regulated law practices to engage in regulated financial activities such as arranging insurance policies for clients.

A law practice can be regulated by:

(a) the Financial Conduct Authority (FCA) (known as Authorised Professional Firms);
(b) becoming an appointed representative of another FCA firm;
(c) a dedicated professional body, such as the SRA or BSB, under Part 20 of FSMA, which is known as the 'exempt professional firm' clause.

Some law practices may be able to rely on a statutory exclusion if they only engage in non-regulated financial activities. Certain consumer credit activities, such as debt collecting, are excluded from regulation under FSMA when these activities are undertaken by solicitors or other professionals authorised by the Legal Services Act 2007 in the course of providing advocacy or litigation services.

You'll need to determine whether or not your firm must be authorised by the FCA, or whether you'll be covered by the exempt professional firm clause. It's important to understand that your firm can't have FCA authorisation *and* rely on the exempt professional firm clause.

The SRA Financial Services (Scope) Rules 2001 set out the financial service activities that law firms can engage in under the rules of the exemption. The SRA Financial Services (Code of Business) Rules 2001 explain how firms are allowed to carry out these exempt regulated activities.

3.3.5 Legal Aid Agency

The Legal Aid Agency (LAA) replaced the Legal Services Commission in April 2013. It is responsible for commissioning and administering civil and criminal legal aid and advice in England and Wales.

If you plan for your firm to offer legal aid services, you will need to bid for a contract from the LAA. Their e-tendering portal has a range of legal aid contracts open to tender.

This may or may not be a straightforward process as the provision of legal aid for both civil and criminal matters has been reduced as a result of the Legal Aid, Sentencing and Punishment of Offenders Act (LASPO) 2012.

3.3.6 COLP and COFA

If you are regulated by the SRA, you will be required to appoint both a head of legal practice and a head of financial affairs and administration. The SRA refers to these roles as a compliance officer for legal practice (COLP) and a compliance officer for finance and administration (COFA).

In practice, these roles are often fulfilled by the same person, especially in start-up law firms.

3.4 Creating your business plan

Once you achieve your desired mindset, determine your vision and understand the various regulatory requirements and legislation that will affect that way your business is able to run, these can all be worked into a formal business plan.

3.4.1 Why is a business plan important?

Your business plan is key when it comes to setting out your vision on paper and bringing your dream to life. The planning you do in this document will focus your thinking on your firm's core ideology, its values, its size, its staff, its premises and many other things.

It's likely to take time to feel clear on all these elements, and therefore writing a business plan is likely to involve many drafts and re-drafts. This is completely normal and a very valuable part of the process: a good business plan cannot – and should not – be rushed.

Not only will your business plan act as a blueprint for you as you begin to put together and run your firm, it will also play a very key role in whether you're even able to get to that point.

If you're seeking third party investment, your business plan will form a key part of your application. Banks or other funding organisations will want to see a detailed business plan as proof that the business has been well thought out and is a good business proposition.

Your business plan will also be important when you come to apply for indemnity insurance cover. Again, insurance companies will look to your business plan for reassurance about the quality of the prospective business and its likelihood of success.

3.4.2 What should a good business plan contain?

The more detailed your business plan is, the better you'll understand how the business should be run, and the easier it will be to proverbially hit the ground running.

Your business plan should be thorough, positive, future-orientated and specific. It should be concerned with the growth of the business, not just the first weeks and months.

It should include information on:

- the structure and legal entity of the business;
- the key personnel who will be involved;

- how (or if) the business will be regulated;
- how the business will comply with legal requirements;
- the vision and aims of the business;
- the legal services the business will provide;
- the type of client the business plans to work with;
- market trends, and how you plan to make these work for your business;
- how you plan to market and advertise your services;
- who your competitors are, and why clients would choose you rather than them;
- how you will manage ongoing staff training obligations;
- where your business will be based;
- the operations systems you will be putting in place;
- how you will use IT systems;
- cash-flow forecasts;
- profit and loss accounts;
- balance sheets;
- a SWOT analysis (your business's greatest strengths, weaknesses, opportunities and threats).

3.4.3 Who can help you with your business plan?

We understand just how daunting putting together a business plan can be, especially if you've never done something like this before. Luckily, there are other professionals who can help you with this.

If you're working with a specialist insurance broker, they will be able to offer advice on putting your business plan together in the light of including it in your application for professional indemnity insurance.

It can also be advisable to work with an accountant to put together financial projections. This will be especially important if you are using your business plan to apply for investment. However, even if you're not seeking third party investment, working with an accountant at the business planning stage can be very helpful. An accountant will be able to offer valuable advice on how to manage your business finances correctly right from the start of your business. They may be able to suggest areas for savings, and they'll also be able to correctly advise you on your responsibilities to HM Revenue and Customs (HMRC) as a business owner or sole trader.

Finally, other business owners can be a fantastic resource during the business planning stage. If you're able to develop a mentor-style relationship with someone who's already running a legal practice, this is likely to reap huge benefits for you. Someone experienced in your field of law who's already gone through many of the issues you're likely to experience will be able to give you extensive advice on what to expect and how to plan for it. You may be able to find a former colleague or employer who is willing to be generous with their experience, or you may be able to access a mentoring scheme.

Whoever you have to help you with your business plan, we recommend you continue adjusting and re-drafting it until you feel confident about moving forward with your business.

CASE STUDY 3: SIMONE BOWMAN

Simone Bowman is a barrister and attorney at law. Her law firm, Bow Law Chambers Ltd, is a growing team of direct access barristers within the legal areas of housing, family, employment, general civil litigation, wills and probate, and actions against public authorities. The firm works across England, Wales, Europe and the Caribbean.

When did you launch your law firm?

I launched the Chambers in September 2016, whilst at law school in Jamaica studying for my conversion law course.

How much knowledge and experience did you have before you started?

Virtually none. Although I have vast experience of case management (initially gained in private practice as a paralegal, trainee solicitor and associate solicitor), I had limited knowledge of setting up and running a practice, especially transferring to the Bar and becoming a barrister sole practitioner. There was limited material available specifically for sole practitioners. I ventured into running my own practice pretty much instinctively.

What would you say is the most important lesson you learned in the first few years of your firm?

After the first two years of running my Chambers, I realised the significance of my business plan. I had not reviewed it within this initial period. Instead, I basically ran away with the euphoria of 'having' a practice rather than devoting sufficient time for 'business development' which included my business strategy as well as efficient case management and recruiting support staff.

This was detrimental for the business and I had to develop a business mindset fast. I had ignited my passion to start the vehicle – the practice – but without fuelling the engine –the business.

For a structured model to work, I think it is vital to invest quality time into your business strategy which can encompass finance, marketing, operations management, peer reviews, working with stakeholders or equality, and diversity and training needs. My business plan therefore determined the chronological action plan to become a successful law firm owner.

Can you tell us how you learned this particular lesson?

Having reviewed my business plan after two years, I realised that I had not set up the robust case management system I had initially considered when preparing my plan.

In order to ease the pressure of costs, I had initially started using a basic Microsoft Office One Drive to store case files and template documents. However, this did not fully comply with GDPR practices. The system I used was cumbersome and I was unable to digitally perform client conflict checks or properly track time recording.

The business was not running efficiently. I realised that I had to invest in a simple cost effective management system that could track time recording as well as managing the diary and case files.

There was also the problem that staff were unsuited for their roles. I did not yet have the requisite skills to seek the qualities for key roles within Chambers.

What changes did you make as a result of this?

I made four key changes as a result of the administrative weaknesses and other aspects that posed threats to the business:

1. I decided to review and update my business plan and general strategy every six months. This allows me to observe what aspects of the practice are running well and what requires improvement.
2. I invested in a simple case management system called CLIO. It works very well for the small practitioner and even linked my existing case files from the Microsoft One Drive. Our remote counsel and consultants in England and throughout the Caribbean are benefiting from the advantages of this system.
3. I immediately enlisted the brilliant services of a local apprenticeship scheme and hired an experienced human resources consultant on an ad hoc basis to assist with recruitment drives. This allowed me to focus more on the needs and objectives of the practice.
4. I decided to downsize my Chambers office rental from a four-person office to a one-person office, merely because our lawyers had no need to be physically in Chambers. We began the trend of remote working from our Chancery Lane offices and still maintain our Croydon office base.

Once I had ironed out these troubling issues, I was now on course to seek out new opportunities as per my business plan and utilise my strengths. I expanded the practice beyond England and the Atlantic Ocean to the warmer islands surrounded by the Caribbean Sea. With my dual-practising qualifications, I can remotely advise, assist and represent both English and Welsh, and Caribbean clients in my specialist areas of cross jurisdictional family, probate and Inheritance Act matters, as well as constitutional law matters. This would not have been possible if I hadn't taken the time to review and focus on my strengths, weaknesses, opportunities and threats.

In what way do you think this made you a better law firm owner?

My experiences have ultimately developed my leadership skills, recognising that I had to delegate or outsource aspects of the practice in order to provide a better client care experience and to be able to adapt to change.

This has led to running a more efficient multi-territorial practice that is continuing to grow.

What advice would you give to a new law firm owner about this?

1. Don't be afraid to embrace your weaknesses – you trained as a lawyer, not as an accountant or IT specialist. Use resources – including this book – to guide you through.
2. Regularly remind yourself of what's in your business plan and update it when necessary. How does the plan define your law practice? Are you staying true to this?
3. Invest in a case management system that works for the type of practice you wish to establish and ensure it is GDPR-compliant.
4. Acknowledge and seek help with ad hoc services, be it IT, HR or training.

Chapter 4

Funding your law firm

One of the biggest challenges of making the decision to go it alone with your own law firm is the question of money. Not only can it be very difficult to walk away from a monthly salary, this leap also generally requires you to be able to put up a not-insignificant sum of money to cover start-up business expenses, not to mention your own living costs.

4.1 How much does it cost to start a law firm?

It is important to note that there is huge variety in the amount it can cost to start your own firm. You would need to have access to a very hefty sum to start out with a city-centre office with a brass plaque on the door. Premises, design, legal secretaries and paralegals all cost money, as would the hefty insurance policy you'd need to cover all of this.

However, this isn't necessarily the best way forward for fledgling law firms. It's perfectly possible to start any business – especially a service-based business such as a law firm – on a proverbial shoestring.

Careful budgeting and an innovative use of freely available technology can help small businesses to get off the ground with little to no third-party financial input. This is especially true if you plan to start your business as a sole trader or partnership and won't have any staffing considerations.

In these cases, we believe the most significant financial considerations are to make sure you can cover the absolute basics:

- Will you be able to cover your mortgage/rent during the first few months, even with very little coming in?
- Will you be able to cover basic living costs such as food and utilities?
- Will you be able to work from home and thus avoid any costs for premises?
- Will you be able to cover the cost of indemnity insurance?
- Will you be able to cover any regulatory costs?

- Will you be able to work using your existing tech, e.g. laptop, printer, smartphone?

If you've been practising for a number of years already, it's likely you'll have many of the resources you'll need to get started. You'll likely have any relevant training or licensing under your belt, along with contacts, legal texts and general know-how. None of this will be beholden to any level of investment, and you may well decide you can therefore manage without.

Of course, this decision is very much based on your vision for your business and what you have set out in your business plan. It's also very dependent on the area of law you'll be working in and the type of client you plan to attract.

A lawyer who'll be working mainly with private clients may be perfectly placed to work from home in the early days and travel to meet clients or, if necessary, invite clients to sign documents at their kitchen table. This may be less appropriate if you plan to work with corporate clients or within certain areas of litigation.

It's also important to consider how you'll be contracting with your clients and how that will affect cash flow.

Many privately paid jobs will produce fairly regular cash flow. For example, if you're drafting wills or power of attorney documents for clients, it's reasonable to expect to be paid fairly quickly once the final documents have been signed and registered.

However, if you're entering the litigation field, there are likely to be different expectations. Your clients may expect to contract with you on a no-win, no-fee basis, and you therefore won't be able to expect any income from a case until it has reached a conclusion. Not only would this mean you wouldn't receive any income from a case during the months you were working on it, you would also have to cover any and all expenses relating to it out of your own pocket.

In these cases, you'd need to very carefully consider how long you'd be able to work without payment, and whether an initial injection of capital would be necessary to get things off the ground.

4.2 How can you keep costs down?

Though every new business is different, there are some key ways you can endeavour to keep costs down. These might help to simplify things in the early days and make it easier for you to focus on gradually building the foundations for a successful business, without any unnecessary expenses.

It can be very tempting to invest money in exciting tools and marketing resources, but there's a good chance you'll regret these expenses later on. Bespoke websites, top-of-the-range business cards and complicated case management software may make you feel more like a 'proper' business . . . but you can get off to a successful (and more streamlined) start without any of these things.

Instead, your calculations for initial costs should be more focused on indemnity insurance, a decent computer and a few basic processes and procedures. You can factor in bigger costs such as branding, web design, marketing and PR later on when funds allow.

In the early days, your best marketing resource is your family and friends. Tell everyone what you're doing – or what you're planning to do – and ask them to help spread the word about your services. You can also ask your current professional network for support. It may also be possible to ask other legal professionals, particularly those who specialise in different areas of the law, to consider referring clients to you.

During the early days, we'd also recommend:

- getting your priorities in order;
- remembering the little things;
- starting to bring in money as soon as you can;
- learning that it's okay to bring less to market;
- being ready to barter;
- making sure you get paid;
- removing emotion from financial decisions.

4.2.1 Getting your priorities in order

There's an almost endless list of things you could spend money on during the early days of launching your business. Many of these will *seem* vital, but the reality is likely to be different.

We suggest sitting down to make a list of absolutely every potential expense you're considering, from licensing fees and insurance to rent, computer equipment, graphic design and office supplies. The list is likely to become unsettlingly large, but don't lose heart yet.

The next stage is to go back down the list and cross off anything that isn't completely necessary from day one. For example, legally speaking you will need to pay insurance costs and licensing fees (assuming the services you're providing need to be regulated), but you're unlikely to need extensive case management software or professionally designed brochures right away.

For the items you really do need, consider the most inexpensive way to get them. For example, you need a place to work, but could you work from home or from a shared co-working space rather than renting an office? You'll need a computer to work from, but could you use an existing laptop or buy one second-hand rather than purchasing something new? You'll need some business cards to hand out to your network, but could you use a pre-designed template rather than commissioning something custom?

Building a business is a really exciting time and we certainly understand the temptation to have everything perfectly in place from day one. However, this mindset is likely to wind up costing you a lot of money that might have been better placed covering your living expenses while you're working on getting things established.

4.2.2 Remembering the little things

There are some significant costs when it comes to setting up a law firm, such as indemnity insurance and regulatory fees. You've probably already given a good bit of thought to how you're going to fund these. However, there are also lots of smaller costs to consider. Internet fees, web hosting costs, office supply bills and finance software subscriptions may seem small in themselves, but they have a nasty habit of adding up fairly quickly.

All these little costs should be treated to the same scrutiny as bigger ones. Ask yourself whether they're really necessary; you might find you don't need them yet, or possibly that you won't need them at all. If costs do really feel necessary, make sure you've done your research and that you're getting the best deal possible.

It's wise to add an additional buffer to any initial finance calculations you make as part of your business plan. This will cover all these unexpected little costs and will make sure your bank balance stays where you expect it to be.

4.2.3 Starting to bring in money as soon as you can

Please don't fall into the trap of believing that everything has to be 'perfect' before you can go to market. The idea that all products and services have to be the very best they can be before you can start selling them is likely to have you toiling away for months and months without a single penny coming in.

The reality is this: when you start a business, you're already on borrowed time. There's only so long you'll be able to keep going on start-up funding or your own savings. If you go for too long without any cash flowing into the business, the whole enterprise will quickly become unsustainable.

Instead, we suggest you embrace the idea that it's completely normal and natural for your product and service offering to change over time. What you offer on day one of your business will – and should – evolve into something different by your first, fifth, tenth or twentieth business anniversary.

In our experience, it's best to create a minimum viable service and start offering it to clients right away. This will provide a revenue stream while you start to develop and build up other areas of business. Obviously, you still need to be able to stand by the quality of the service you're offering; we'd never suggest you put something out there that could negatively impact your long-term aspirations.

Remember: the evolution of products and services is an endless process. It would be impossible to create a 'perfect' option right at the beginning of your business journey. Releasing your product or service earlier in the process does not mean you're settling for less.

4.2.4 Learning that it's okay to bring less to market

Just as each service or product doesn't need to be perfect before you take it to market, it's also true that you don't need to have all your offerings in place before you launch.

You may well have a very clear idea in mind of what your business will look like and which legal services you'll be offering. You may primarily be offering a domestic conveyancing service but are also planning to offer wills and lasting powers of attorney (LPAs). It may seem that in order to start with a bang you'll need to have everything ready to go from day one.

However, we think this is the wrong approach. The need to have all your services ready and raring to go at the same time is likely to delay your launch. The time between leaving a salaried role and actually starting to bring in paying business is crucial – you'll want this period to be as short as possible.

Instead, we suggest you think about what the very core service or services of your new firm will be. Generally speaking, these will be the services you're most experienced in providing and so will be the easiest for you to start offering to the general public.

The benefit of starting a law firm over starting a product-based business is all to do with cash flow. Service-based businesses like law firms don't have significant costs other than insurance – it's likely that the only thing you'll have to invest into each piece of client work is your time. This means you may be able to start generating profit from some of the very first jobs you do.

We recommend you take advantage of this and focus on launching one or two core services initially. Once you've started to bring in clients, and the subsequent income, there'll be plenty of time to develop additional service offerings.

4.2.5 Being ready to barter

How do you feel about getting out and opening up lines of communication with other business owners? Bartering and trading services with other likeminded small businesses is a great way to keep your costs in check.

You may well be able to offer some legal services to other business owners in return for their services. A graphic designer might be interested in creating some designs in return for help with their contracts. An accountant might be open to supporting you with your financial forecasts if you're able to make sure their will is up to date.

Not only will this enable you to access valuable support and services in the early days, it will almost certainly build you some great contacts. These contacts may become paying customers in the future. And even if they don't, they may well pass on referrals who will.

4.2.6 Making sure you get paid

If you've previously always been employed in a law firm, it's likely you have absolutely no experience of chasing up invoices. This will generally have been someone else's job entirely – legal professionals often finish up each job, pass the details onto the finance department and then move on to the next client.

Unfortunately, if you take this approach in your own business it's likely no one will ever pay you! It may be the case that you plan to employ someone in the future to handle these things for you, but in the early days you're almost certainly going to need to do it yourself.

Generally speaking, managing invoices and chasing payments isn't hard. Rather, you'll simply need to make sure you have a system in place. The main thing to be aware of here is the importance of clear communication. Make sure your invoices note the payment terms, i.e. when you would like the payment to be made by (many firms opt for 14 days, but the exact length of time you choose is up to you). If an invoice has not been paid by the deadline, it's perfectly acceptable to send a polite reminder.

Many law firms now choose to take payments on account. This means collecting all or part of the fee for a piece of work before you get started. This removes the risk of your firm being out of pocket for weeks (or months!) after completing a piece of work – or, indeed, of you not being paid for it at all.

Of course, in order to manage invoices and reminders (whether you're taking payment on account or after the work has been completed), you'll need to have an organised system. This doesn't necessarily need to involve complex or expensive case management software. Your accountant may well recommend relatively inexpensive bookkeeping software options, many of which will send out payment reminders automatically. If you really want to keep things simple, a spreadsheet and/or a ring-binder will do the job just as well.

4.2.7 Removing emotion from financial decisions

Many of us have a complicated personal relationship with money and how it's spent. Whatever you do with your personal funds, you're likely to have to adopt a very different mindset when it comes to your business funds.

In order to effectively manage the finances of your business, you're going to need to come to a place where you can remove the emotion from financial decisions. The amount of money coming into your business shouldn't change how much thought is put into each outgoing. Rather, for each potential purchase, ask yourself two questions:

1. Will it make me money?
2. Will it save me money?

If the answer to one or both of these is yes, then feel free to go ahead. If it's no, or if you're not sure, it might be time to go back to the drawing board.

Any purchase, whether it's a new hire, a copy machine, accounting software or an investment in marketing services, should be serving these two broad aims. Continuing to give all these decisions the same careful consideration as you did in the early days of your business will help you to build up – and retain – good financial standing.

It's important to recognise that this careful consideration makes you a sensible business owner. We suggest you develop a thick skin in relation to this and embrace the idea of being a frugal spender. Make sure other businesses and service-providers know that if they want to sell to you, they'll have to make a very strong case for the value of their services. An added benefit of this mindset is that it will keep your fellow business owners from approaching you with their sales pitches unless they're confident that what they have to say is really worth your time.

If you find it difficult to limit your spending only to the essentials, remind yourself that it's for the greater good. The more money you save on non-essentials, the more you'll have to invest in the areas that really matter to you and your vision of the future.

4.3 Is start-up funding available?

Not all new law firm owners will be able to launch their firm on independent savings alone. This might be because their personal savings don't allow it, or it might be because they're launching a bigger firm and therefore need to invest in premises right away.

If you believe that investing more into your business at the beginning is the best way to stay true to your vision, there are multiple ways you might look at raising some finance. Some possibilities are:

- bootstrapping your business;
- crowdfunding;
- angel investment;
- venture capital;
- funds from business incubators and accelerators;
- entering contests and competitions;
- taking out a bank loan;

- loans from micro-finance providers or non-banking financial corporations (NBFCs);
- government programmes that offer start-up capital.

4.3.1 Bootstrapping your business

'Bootstrapping' your business refers to the practice of using your own saved funds *plus* funds you've borrowed from family or friends. This option might work well for you if you need just a little extra cash to be able to hit the ground running.

Not everyone will have this as an option, of course, but if you do it can be a flexible and inexpensive way to give your finances a boost early on.

Pros

- Funds can be easily accessed.
- There are little to no bureaucratic obstacles.
- Attractive interest rates (usually!).
- Flexible repayment terms (again, usually).

Cons

- This is generally only an option for small-scale enterprises.
- Not everyone will be able or willing to ask family or friends for cash.
- It can put pressure on your personal relationships.

4.3.2 Crowdfunding

Crowdfunding is a very modern way to inject funds into your start-up. New business owners can use crowdfunding platforms in order to pitch their business idea and invite advance purchases and/or investment. Though this method is more commonly associated with product-based businesses, it can also work well for service-based businesses.

In order to attempt to crowdfund for your law firm, you would need to write an attractive pitch and publish it on a crowdfunding platform. Your pitch would generally include details about your business model and the potential for growth. This would be read by a community of investors as well as members of the general public who may be willing to support your cause.

If those readers liked your pitch and wanted to support you, they could choose to do so by publicly pledging support and donating funds. Often these funds will be put forward on the understanding that you will provide services in return once the business is up and running.

Pros

- Crowdfunding is essentially a way of creating public interest in your business. It can be an effective method for marketing your business and raising funds at the same time.
- It's a much simpler method than placing your business in the hands of a traditional investor.
- It has the potential to attract the attention of venture-capital investors.

Cons

- There is a lot of competition in the crowdfunding marketplace. It can be difficult to make your business plan stand out.
- Some people will feel uncomfortable with the public nature of crowdfunding platforms.
- You'll likely have to put a lot of effort into publicising your crowdfunding profile in order to get attention.

4.3.3 Angel investment

Angel investors are individuals with large amounts of capital that they are willing to invest in innovative business ideas.

They often work together in groups to scrutinise business proposals in order to select ideal projects to invest in. Think Dragon's Den, but without the cameras or the reality TV scripting.

Pros

- You would receive valuable mentorship alongside capital.
- Angel investors may be more willing to take a risk on a business idea than many other funding options.

Cons

- This type of funding can be very competitive. You may find the application process gruelling.
- Angel investors usually offer smaller sums of investment capital than venture capitalists.

4.3.4 Venture capital

Venture capital funds are managed by professionals with a keen eye for seeking out companies with great prospects. They operate by investing in a solid business rather than an equity.

Once the business they are partnered with is ready to launch an initial public offering (IPO) or receive acquisition offers, the venture capital fund will move on to other investment opportunities.

Pros

- You would receive mentorship alongside the funding opportunity.
- Venture capitalists would be closely involved with the success of your business in order to protect their investment.

Cons

- Though the venture capital fund would be a great support to your business, this support generally only lasts until they have recovered their initial capital. This would likely happen within three to five years, which may seem a slim timeframe.
- You may feel you had less control of your business than you wanted, as you would need to give up a reasonable amount of control in return for the capital.
- You may find it too difficult to get this type of funding as many venture capital funds only work with bigger, more established companies.

4.3.5 Funds from business incubators and accelerators

Brand new businesses can apply to access funds provided by business incubators and accelerators. These sorts of programmes can be found in almost all major cities and are often run by organisations such as universities, non-profit organisations, commercial organisations and venture capital firms.

How each incubator or accelerator programme is funded will vary depending on what kind of organisation is behind it. Some will be heavily reliant on public funders such as local enterprise partnerships, Innovate UK, central government, Big Lottery Fund and the European Regional Development Fund. Others will be funded by the return on investment on the businesses they've previously supported, e.g. by taking a stake in each business.

Though incubators and accelerators fulfil a similar purpose, incubators seek to nurture new businesses while accelerators seek to fast-track them.

Pros

- You would receive mentorship and support in addition to funding.
- A business accelerator/incubator programme would introduce you to other start-up business owners.
- Some programmes include the use of office space.
- There's likely to be more of a training element involved than with other funding options.

Cons

- Acceptance to a programme can be very competitive.
- You may find the programme too prescriptive.
- You may feel that the programme isn't quite long enough to support the growth of your start-up.

4.3.6 Entering contests and competitions

Some investment groups run contests or competitions with business funding as a prize. These competitions require new entrepreneurs to pitch their business ideas against others who are hoping to win funding.

You would be required to present a detailed and comprehensive business plan in order to win confidence from investors.

Pros

- Entering this type of competition often results in media coverage, so you may receive much-needed publicity for your business, even if you don't ultimately receive any funding.
- If you were to win funding, it's often on very good terms.

Cons

- You will be up against a lot of other equally enthusiastic start-ups.
- Some people find losing out on prizes demoralising.

4.3.7 Taking out a bank loan

This might've been one of the first options you considered when thinking about business funding. Though there are many more innovative or 'modern' methods, for many a good old-fashioned bank loan is a great option.

Banks and building societies offer loans to businesses and individuals, though you'd need to approach them with a very solid business plan. This plan would need to include the 'modus operandi' of the business, along with a profit forecast and the estimated time of maturity.

There are two main types of bank loans: working capital loans and funding loans. Working capital loans are short term loans (usually up to 12 months) that are designed to cover everyday business expenses. Funding loans are usually taken out over a longer term (one year or longer) and are used for investments in a business.

Pros

- You may be able to access a large amount of capital.
- There may be less competition than with other funding options.
- You will retain the freedom to be fully in charge of your new business.

Cons

- Funding terms can be variable.
- You won't usually have access to expertise or mentorship alongside funding.
- There is a high risk of loss, as you will need to provide collateral in order for the loan to be granted.

4.3.8 Loans from micro-finance providers or non-banking financial corporations

Micro-finance institutions were set up in order to give access to capital to small-scale entrepreneurs who would find it difficult to access conventional banking capital or loans. This includes people who have poor credit ratings, for whom micro-finance institutions might be one of the very few options.

NBFCs can offer a similar solution for some. NBFCs give out loans that are offered without imposing the legality of conventional banks.

Pros

- This may be a good alternative source of funding if you haven't found success with more traditional methods.
- There are no intermediaries; you'll be able to be in direct contact with financial providers.
- The application process is likely to be less rigorous than other options.
- You will usually be given a decision quickly.
- Micro-finance institutions typically offer lower interest rates.

Cons

- Micro finance institutions and NBFCs are unregulated and operate outside of general banking rules.
- Smaller financial institutions can be less stable and therefore more vulnerable to poor economic conditions.
- The cost of lending may be higher with NBFCs.
- You may find you're not able to borrow as much as you planned.

4.3.9 Government programmes that offer start-up capital

Some government programmes and initiatives offer start-up capital or grants. Some will be available only to certain members of the population, such as entrepreneurs of a certain age, background or ethnicity.

If you're eligible for any of these programmes, you'd be required to submit an exhaustive business plan. This would be scrutinised by the programme committee, who would then choose whether to grant funding.

Pros

- Most government programmes are not-for-profit, which would mean you are likely to be given funding on attractive terms.
- There may be a mentorship element to the funding programme.

Cons

- You may not be eligible for any of these programmes.
- The application and approval process may be long and arduous.

4.4 Do you really need a start-up loan?

4.4.1 Considerations

Ultimately, this is another question that only you can answer. Whether or not you need to take out a start-up loan will depend purely on your business plan and what your vision for your business is.

It goes almost without saying that every law firm is different, as is each legal professional who plans to start one. Your vision and aims will be different to other people. You will have a different expectation of growth. And, importantly, you will have your own individual appetite for risk.

One of the key factors that's likely to play into whether or not you need a start-up loan is staffing. If you plan to take on employees right at the beginning, you'll need to think very carefully about how you're going to pay them.

It may be that your intended staff are already established fee earners that will come with a following. In these cases, you may be confident that they will pay for themselves from the outset. You may want to formalise this by taking on fee earners under the 'consultant' model. In this kind of arrangement, fee earners are remunerated based on the amount of fees they have generated – and that have been paid. In this employment model, you would never pay a fee earner more per month than they've brought in.

You may be planning to take on less-established legal staff, or even other support staff such as a compliance manager or administration manager. In these cases, you wouldn't be able to expect your staff to contribute an income right away – if at all. Instead, it's likely you would need some start-up funding to ensure you had a way to pay staff during the first few months while you were all working to establish regular incomings for the firm.

Many new firm owners (us included!) get caught up in the belief that there's some kind of formula about how much start-up capital is needed in order to ensure success. Perhaps there was some truth to this in the past, but the market is more fluid and flexible than it's ever been and there certainly aren't any 'rules' on this anymore.

It's actually far less expensive to run a law firm now than it was in the past. The way clients want their legal services to be provided is changing, and few now search for adverts in the traditional press or expect to visit a big grand office. The minimal costs of web and email hosting, along with search engine advertising, make marketing a much more affordable endeavour. Travel costs are also much reduced for today's legal professionals, as so many meetings can now be conducted over the phone or using a video messaging platform.

Though in many ways a legal firm is a classic service business, it's not quite as simple as setting up with your laptop and a bit of free time. You'll need to ensure that you have factored in the regulatory and compliance costs, which may seem overwhelmingly large in the time before you've even sent out your first invoice. However, this doesn't necessarily mean you'll need to take out a start-up loan to cover it. In many cases it will be possible to pay these big costs in instalments.

It's also important to note that different types of legal professions are set up with very different payment models. Litigators get paid in a very different way for their work than non-litigators. Once again, if the primary work of your firm will be litigating, you'll need to think very differently in terms of ensuring cash flow in the early days than you will if you are involved in client work with a more straightforward invoicing practice.

4.4.2 Our experience

When Rachel started Roche Legal, it was with a couple of thousand pounds in the bank, a tiny laptop, a Word document that became her business plan and a 12-month contract for indemnity insurance. At the time, the cost of her insurance as a sole trader was less than £3,000 per year. Payments for this were spread over the year, and Rachel was confident that she would be able to write enough wills and LPAs to be able to cover the payments.

Rachel's approach in the early days was very much to keep things simple and as inexpensive as possible. This was made possible as she was married at the time and was able to rely on her spouse to keep paying the rent and overheads, even when she was earning relatively little. She worked from home for the first year, then moved the firm to its own office once it was bringing in enough money to make it a sustainable move.

Darren's experience with starting DJS Law was fairly similar. He was also able to get his firm off the ground without the need for outside start-up funding. This was made possible thanks to some personal savings and the fact that Darren chose to work from a home office, as he still does today.

The cost of the first year of indemnity insurance for DJS Law was £5,000, including insurance premium tax. Darren worked to cover this initial overhead by keeping other costs low and aiming to bring in as many clients as possible. To do this, he:

- charged for many services on a fixed-fee basis;
- offered out-of-hour appointments;
- did home visits for clients in the local area;
- gave free talks and seminars;
- volunteered regularly on a local radio station to answer legal questions.

These techniques allowed Darren to quickly get the word out about his firm and start generating income as soon as possible.

4.4.3 Are there legal requirements for start-up funding?

If you do decide that start-up funding is a necessary element of starting your business, you'll need to make sure you're managing this in a way that's in line with existing legal regulation.

Most regulators will have something to say on the matter of funding and investment in a firm, though generally speaking this will simply involve being transparent about the source of any funds and ensuring that you act in a way that doesn't risk bringing the profession into disrepute.

There are some precedents where legal professionals have been fined by their regulatory bodies for failing to act with integrity in this manner. In 2019 the Solicitors Disciplinary Tribunal (SDT) fined a solicitor £25,000 plus costs for making false claims about the source of business funds when he applied to the SRA for authorisation in 2016 (**www.legalfutures.co.uk/latest-news/solicitor-misled-sra-about-dubious-1m-funder-of-his-firm**).

It's also important to note that if you're starting a law firm with the structure of an alternative business structure (ABS) you may well need authorisation for this from the SRA. They published a guidance page on this in 2014, which was reviewed in late 2019 (**www.sra.org.uk/solicitors/guidance/interest-abs-require-sra-approval/**).

However you decide to fund your start-up law firm, we suggest you carefully check the rules of your regulatory body and insurance providers before you proceed.

CASE STUDY 4: DARREN J. SYLVESTER

Darren Sylvester is a solicitor, non-practising barrister and the founder of DJS Law Solicitors. DJS Law Solicitors specialises in professional negligence claims. Darren is also a co-author of this book.

When did you launch your law firm?

I launched DJS Law on 7 April 2016.

How much knowledge and experience did you have before you started?

Before my practice was authorised by the SRA, I had 6.5 years' post-qualification (PQE) as a solicitor. Prior to that I was six years Call (Lincoln's Inn), so in total I had 12.5 years of experience. I'd worked in various legal environments and in the Ministry of Justice in London, so had acquired knowledge in many areas of legal practice but had never actually run or set up a legal practice myself.

What would you say is the most important lesson you learned in the first few years of your firm?

Firstly, to keep things to a minimum until you have to grow. Early on I made the mistake of paying for expensive practice management software with LEAP when I did not actually need it.

Secondly, marketing, networking and business development are very important and time must be set aside for them. You must make time to work 'on' your business, as well as 'in' your business. Initially I was very focussed on client matters, with marketing, networking and business development being secondary. I have now managed to redress the balance.

Can you tell us how you learned this particular lesson?

While I had budgeted for practice management software, it was an expense that the firm needn't have had at that time. I believe that I may have been persuaded to purchase the package with LEAP because there was a 'free' website design and hosting deal, which I probably considered was cost-effective, but in fact wasn't. I had a list of things to achieve to get the practice going, so where there was an opportunity of 'killing two birds with one stone' I took it. I was enthusiastic about what the software could do for my firm. However, after a while I could see hard-earned money from client fees going on a resource that was not vital to my practice's survival, so took the decision to bring my contract with LEAP to an end.

As for marketing, networking and business development, I was going through some financials and found that I was spending too much time in the office, at my desk, and not getting out more. I was paying for subscriptions to associations whose events I was not attending on the basis that I always had something to do that seemed ostensibly more important. Looking back, I was uneasy about being away from the office and losing valuable fee earning time but came to realise that it was vitally important that I networked in a variety of settings so that people knew who I was and what my firm could offer.

What changes did you make as a result of this?

I realised that while enthusiasm and passion is good, in business it is usually wise to never make an instant decision. I now prefer to run thoughts and ideas past other people and get their input and views before making the final decision. After all, we all have blind spots. While there is a lot to be said for 'running your law firm your way', this can still be achieved by soliciting and considering the views of others.

I now set time aside monthly for marketing and business development (and even a free legal advice surgery on the last Wednesday every month for the benefit of the local community).

In what way do you think this made you a better law firm owner?

I now regularly meet other solicitors who have set up and run their own practices, as well as general business owners. Sharing knowledge and experiences sharpens your judgement. Furthermore, when taking a step back and assessing the position, you will observe matters in a new light and will want to try and do things differently. It is about being in tune with, and conscious of, the ever-changing nature of legal practice and being able to respond accordingly and expeditiously.

Chapter 5

Do you need premises?

Whatever sort of law firm you're planning to launch, you'll need somewhere to run it from. The set-up that makes the most sense for you will depend on both the type of business you'll be running and your own personal circumstances.

If you're going to be running a virtual firm, you may well only need somewhere with enough space for you and a laptop. If you're opening a full-service firm with a group of colleagues, you may need to invest in office premises from the outset.

You'll need to consider all options carefully to decide what's right for you and your firm. The main options, which we consider below, are:

- working from home
- using a co-working space;
- investing in an office.

5.1 Your dream v. the reality

At the risk of ruining all your fun here, we're going to advise caution. Though we fully encourage you to explore ideas for your long-term premises strategy at this point, it's unlikely that you're going to start your firm from your dream office.

Instead, think about what's really necessary at this stage, and – perhaps more pertinently – what's actually achievable in terms of your budget. For many new firms, the answer will be to start trading from home. This means you won't need to commit to a significant monthly rent expense until you're confident you have the income to cover it.

We believe that it's better to work your way up to your ideal workspace in a gradual and sustainable way. Working from your kitchen table may not have been what had in mind when you left your previous firm, but this is often the sensible way to begin. It would be demoralising to jump straight into signing an office lease and then spend the first year of your new life as a law firm director struggling to meet each rent payment.

At this stage, it's important to explore all options for working spaces and be honest with yourself about what is the correct choice for you and your business *right now.* This will almost certainly change as you move forward. In another six months or a year, when your firm has started to get established, you may well want to reassess.

5.2 Could you work from home?

It is said that around 70 per cent of businesses start from home (**www.gov.uk/government/news/backing-for-home-based-business-boom**), so you'd be in very good company if you decided to take this route. In fact, we both started our law firms from home. Rachel's firm, Roche Legal, was based at home for a year before moving to a more permanent office, while Darren's firm, DJS Law, is still happily home-based.

Some more traditional-leaning legal professionals take the view that legal services should be offered from a 'proper' office. However, many of us, and many of our clients, see that the profession has come a long way from its formal roots. It's becoming more and more common for law firms to work flexibly with their clients, and this has meant that home-based firms have been widely accepted into the fold.

A lot of home-based firms manage client appointments by travelling to visit clients either at their offices/homes, or by renting meeting room space as and when they need it. Alternatively, in many areas of law it's perfectly acceptable to invite clients into your home office. In our experience, clients will have no problem with this so long as their work is carried out professionally and at a cost everyone is happy with.

5.2.1 What are the benefits of working from home?

There are some very clear benefits to working from home:

1. **It's free.** One of the major benefits to start-up firms is that working from home comes with no additional overheads. This can take a lot of pressure off in the early days, as there's no need for your business to be able to cover the costs of rent payments or utilities.
2. **It's easy.** There's no need to invest large amounts of time searching for the ideal office space if you have somewhere at home you can set up in. This might be a spare room, the dining room, or even a corner of your living space to begin with. When you choose to start your business from home, there's nothing to stop you from *just getting started*.
3. **It's comfortable.** There are a lot of new things to learn and adjust to when you're starting a new business. There's a lot to be said for going through this adjustment period in the comfort of your own home!
4. **There's no commute.** This is a real benefit in terms of saving time and

money. When you have no commute to worry about, you can spend more time getting on with the important things. There's also no cost for petrol, parking or public transport.

5. **You'll be eligible for some tax reliefs.** If you run your law firm from home, you'll be entitled to claim an appropriate portion of the expenses incurred for electricity, gas, water, insurance and other household costs on your annual tax return (please see the considerations at 5.2.3).

5.2.2 What are the disadvantages of working from home?

As with any choice you make in your business, there will be downsides to consider. Some people experience disadvantages of working from home, including:

1. **Loneliness.** If you work from home on your own, you may find you spend much longer periods alone than you ever have before. For some this may feel like a luxury, for others it can be a big adjustment.
2. **Difficulty separating work from home life.** Working from home can mean the boundaries between when you're working and when you're not can become blurred. If your workspace is just a few steps from your leisure space, you may find yourself 'just finishing something off' or 'just checking in with something' at times when you'd normally be relaxing away from work. It's important to keep your private and family life separate from your working life, and this can be harder to do when you work from home.
3. **Not having a traditional professional image for your firm.** Maintaining a traditional professional image for your firm may be more important in some areas of the law than others. If this is something that's a concern for you, you may feel that a home office isn't an appropriate choice for your business.
4. **Lack of privacy.** You may not want your clients to know where you live. In these cases, using your home address for business correspondence or inviting clients into your home may not be something you're comfortable with.

5.2.3 Claiming expenses for working from home

When you complete your yearly tax return, you'll be able to claim a portion of your household expenses such as electricity, gas, water and insurance as tax free expenses. This can result in a small discount on your annual tax bill.

The amount you can claim is usually worked out on a proportional basis. For example, if you have eight rooms in your house and use two of them for business purposes, you could therefore claim that a quarter of your household expenses were used for business purposes.

If you sell your home, usually the principal private residence relief for capital gains tax would apply, meaning it was exempt from capital gains tax. However, if you have claimed on your tax return that a proportion of your home has been used for business purposes, HM Revenue and Customs (HMRC) could argue that this exemption should no longer apply and that a proportion of any gain should be subject to capital gains tax.

As with business rates, this should not apply if any rooms you use for business are also used for other purposes (e.g. both domestic and business use), but it could apply if you have a dedicated office that is only used for business. It's therefore wise to make sure that no one room in your home is used entirely for business purposes. In practice, this might mean inviting other members of your family to use your home office for activities such as studying, completing homework or doing personal administrative tasks.

5.3 Using a co-working space

In recent years there's been rapid growth in the availability of co-working spaces. This can be a great option for new firm owners who don't want to be based from home but are not yet at the stage of being able to lease their own office space.

In fact, some business owners enjoy the benefits of co-working space so much that they decide to stay long-term, even once they could comfortably afford an office of their own.

5.3.1 The benefits of co-working

There are some fantastic benefits of co-working for both new and more established law firm owners:

1. **Getting out of the house.** Working from home doesn't suit everyone. Many start-up owners will be keen to get out of the house to a dedicated workspace.
2. **Affordability.** Co-working leases are generally more affordable than taking out a traditional lease.
3. **Community.** One of the fantastic things about co-working spaces is that they're very sociable. You'll be able to mix with other business owners throughout the day, which is a real benefit for those who are worried about the loneliness of running their own business.
4. **Networking opportunities.** When you work in a shared office space with lots of other business owners, there will naturally be lots of opportunities for networking. Many co-working spaces run regular events such as mixers or workshops to encourage members to share knowledge and ideas.
5. **Facilities.** Many co-working spaces offer a range of facilities you'd be

unlikely to find in a home office. These include access to professional printers and copiers, reception staff, meeting rooms and coffee machines.

6. **Flexibility.** Co-working spaces often have the benefit of being easy-in and easy-out in terms of contracts. This is ideal for new businesses who don't want to be too heavily committed to anything.
7. **Easy.** When you buy in to a co-working space, you'll get many of the benefits of having a professional workspace without having to manage any of the practicalities yourself. You won't need to furnish the space or manage the cleaning or maintenance. You generally won't even need to make sure the tea and coffee supplies are topped up!
8. **Image.** Some new law firm owners want to ensure their firm has the right image right from day one. A co-working space can provide you with a good address and access to attractive meeting rooms whenever you need them.

5.3.2 The disadvantages of co-working

There's a lot to love about co-working spaces, but there can also be downsides:

1. **Distractions.** Some business owners love the social and community elements of co-working, others will find it stops them getting their important work done.
2. **Lack of privacy.** Many co-working spaces offer open plan offices. For some people this will create difficulties, particularly if you need to be able to discuss client work confidentially.
3. **No control.** The flip side of not having to manage any of the practicalities of your workspace yourself is that you don't actually have any control over it. You won't have any say on the kind of furnishings, decor or tech that's provided.
4. **Workspace neighbours.** Another thing you won't have any control over is the people you share the workspace with. This may result in you making some really good contacts . . . or it may not.

5.4 Investing in an office

5.4.1 How do you know when it's the right time to invest in an office?

There is no perfect formula to determine the right time for a law firm to invest in an office. This is a judgement call that will involve a lot of careful thought and number-crunching.

The type and size of your firm will have a big impact on this, as will the kind of start-up funding you raised for your business. In some cases, you may choose to invest a significant chunk of start-up funding into leasing an office as you launch. In other cases, the possibility of investing in professional premises won't even be on your radar until a few years into operations.

Ultimately, deciding on the right time to invest in an office is a combination of gut feeling and ensuring that finances will allow for it. This will generally depend on factors such as the type of clients you have, the growth strategy of your firm, the location of your firm and any staffing requirements.

Many new law firm owners start to think about this step once their firm is established enough to merit taking on additional staff members. Unless you're running an entirely virtual firm, it's likely you would want a workspace big enough for you and your new member(s) of staff to work in together. This may not be feasible in either a home office or a co-working space.

We do encourage you to be cautious about the financial side of investing in an office. A regular lease or mortgage payment will represent a huge portion of your outgoings, and you need to be confident you'll be able to meet it each month. Running a business is stressful enough without adding significant financial strain into the equation.

Caution aside, making the decision to invest in an office is momentous and represents a very exciting step forward for your firm.

5.4.2 Will you rent or buy an office?

Most business owners will likely look to lease an office, especially in the first instance. However, some will consider the possibility of buying an office. This will usually involve taking out a commercial mortgage.

We'd recommend speaking to a specialist insurance broker to get a clear idea on how much mortgage providers would be prepared to lend your business, and how monthly mortgage payments would compare to the average cost of a lease for a similar office.

If you do have some capital available to use as a deposit, you may decide that buying an office space is a better long-term investment for your business. You may even be able to buy somewhere that would include extra office space to rent out to another business, which would provide an additional income.

However, this is certainly a less flexible solution that renting. You'd need to be certain that the office space you were buying was something that would work for your business for years to come, which may be a difficult decision to make.

Renting an office may work out to be less financially beneficial in the long term, but it's a much more affordable and accessible option for most small businesses. Rented offices also often come with more options for serviced facilities, which can be a big draw.

Additional considerations for buying an office

If you do consider buying an office, we'd suggest seeking as much advice as possible from your mortgage broker and accountant on this. Specifically, you may find that there are benefits to buying the property in a different name to the company.

For example, buying a property in your own name or under a different limited company and then renting it to your business may have benefits including:

- being more efficient in terms of tax;
- keeping the property safe should your business get into financial difficulty;
- making it possible to put the property in a self-invested pension plan (SIPP) later on, which again would have tax benefits.

5.4.3 Should you choose a serviced office or a conventional leased office?

Deciding between a serviced and a conventionally leased office will be a significant decision. This will be a matter of weighing up rental costs versus the convenience that a serviced office can provide.

A serviced office is a kind of halfway house between a co-working space and a traditional office. Your law firm will have its own dedicated office space within a managed building. The managers of the building will handle all the practicalities of your office, from the furniture and decor to the utilities, Wi-Fi, cleaning and housekeeping.

Serviced offices generally have the benefit of additional facilities. This could include coffee shop style break-out spaces, bike storage, and a dedicated reception team, who may even offer mail and telephone handling services. This type of office can also often come with more flexible contract options than a conventional office.

Of course, there are some downsides to this type of office rental. The primary concern is often cost – you'll usually pay a significantly higher monthly rent in return for the added convenience. Some law firm owners may also be uncomfortable with the lack of control they have over their own workspace: you may not be able to do much in terms of changing the decor of your office space or bringing in your own furniture.

5.4.4 What should you look for in an office?

When it comes to choosing the right office for you and your business, you'll need to take the concept of your brand and professional image very carefully into account. The office you choose will have a big impact on how your business is perceived by clients, potential clients and competitors.

We'd advise making sure you have a really clear understanding of exactly where you want to pitch your firm before you sign on the dotted line for leasing or buying an office. After all: your office will represent a significant part of your business' branding.

A flash city-centre office with a fully serviced reception desk, for example, will provoke a very different reaction than a unit in a half-abandoned industrial estate. It's important to make sure the type of office you choose gels well with the level of service, professionalism and – importantly! – the fees you'll be charging.

You'll need to achieve a balance between the two possible client reactions of:

- thinking your office is too ostentatious, therefore your firm will be stuffy, impersonal and the fees will be too high; or
- thinking your office is too scruffy, therefore your firm is sloppy, poor quality and doesn't care about its image.

Achieving this balance might seem complicated, but it can actually be fairly easily done with some careful thought. When you're looking for an office, you may want to use the following checklist as a guide.

Presentation

The way your office is presented, even the look of the building from outside, will make an impression on your clients long before you start your meeting.

You'll need to ensure that your place of business is:

- clean and well-maintained;
- smartly decorated;
- well lit;
- professional.

Space

This can be a tricky decision to make in the early days. You'll want to find a balance between making sure your business has sufficient space to grow *but* not being out of pocket by paying for space you don't need.

The choices you make on this front will depend on your personal growth strategy, but for the most part you'll need to have:

- a reception area;
- a private meeting room;
- sufficient office space for fee earners;
- kitchen facilities;
- toilets (for both staff and clients).

Location

The location of your office will likely have a big impact on the type of clients you bring in. Car parking facilities and proximity to the railway station can both be attractive to clients, but it's unlikely you'd be able to find an office that offers both without paying a very significant premium for the privilege.

You'll need to consider:

- car parking availability;
- proximity to public transport;
- proximity to railway station;
- proximity to other businesses.

Accessibility

It's important to make sure you've considered how accessible your chosen office space is for people with disabilities. Mobility aids such as wheelchairs, crutches or rollators can be impeded by certain office set-ups.

All law firms should aim to be as accessible as possible. However, this is likely to be particularly crucial if your firm works with a large proportion of elderly clients.

Think about whether the office space you're considering has:

- access for wheelchair users;
- sufficiently wide doorways;
- step-free access (or ensuring that a ramp is available);
- a lift as an alternative to stairs;
- accessible seating in waiting and meeting areas.

Will you be able to make alterations?

It may be tempting to take on an office with alterations in mind, but this isn't always a practical solution.

Small adjustments such as giving the place a deep clean, putting up a fresh coat of paint or changing some of the decor can make a big difference to the look of your office. If you have an eye for this sort of thing, this can be a great way to make your office your own.

However, bigger changes might turn out to be more complicated than you originally bargained for! Moving interior walls, extending the office space or improving (or adding) kitchen or toilet facilities are likely to become long, disruptive and expensive jobs. You may also find that planning permission is required.

Unless you have an established law firm with the income to sustain the cost of alterations, it might be wise to find an office space that will work for you with no major changes necessary.

5.4.5 Who will take care of the office practicalities?

The bigger the office, the bigger the responsibility for managing practicalities. When you work from home, there's generally very little to manage in terms of office practicalities over and above the usual home cleaning and maintenance jobs.

However, once you bring a separate office into the equation, there will be a whole range of new jobs and practicalities to consider.

Assuming you haven't chosen a serviced office, someone will need to:

- clean the kitchen and toilet facilities;
- hoover/clean the floors;
- empty the bins;
- clean the windows;
- keep refreshment facilities stocked up;
- do the washing up;
- organise and administrate utilities.

In the early days, it's quite possible that you will need to be chief cook and bottle washer and do all these tasks yourself. Later on, you'll be able to consider delegating these tasks to other staff members or contractors.

5.4.6 Key points to remember

There's no question that moving your law firm into an office of its own is a huge step forward and we certainly encourage you to celebrate and enjoy this stage.

However, this is also a time for sensible and practical thought! Signing the lease on an office space is a big commitment – likely one of the biggest you've made for your business so far – and it's prudent to make sure you've explored all your options and fully thought through the implications of each one.

CASE STUDY 5: JESSICA HAMPSON

Jessica Hampson is a solicitor and the owner and a director of the firm CEL Solicitors. CEL Solicitors specialise in civil litigation and have set out to disrupt the status quo of large law firms. They are based in Liverpool.

When did you launch your law firm?

I started CEL Solicitors in 2016.

How much knowledge and experience did you have before you started?

Having spent 10 years working as a paralegal, being newly qualified and having only a handful of years of management experience, on paper, I didn't have the 'normal' pre-requisite experience and I definitely didn't fit the mould of what a founder should be/look like. I was 29, female, a millennial from a council estate in Liverpool and first in my family to graduate from university. On top of it all, I became a mother in the second year of opening my firm. And yet, this is what I would attribute to making CEL Solicitors unique and the zeitgeist of modern firms. The law is ever evolving and so are directors.

The fact that I didn't have the perfect work experience beforehand is something I want to champion to anyone else considering setting up their own firm.

For me, it was my negative experiences in other firms – particularly the poor treatment I received as a paralegal – that shaped the intention behind me setting up my own firm. I couldn't find a firm that I wanted to be a part of or that excited me, so I created my own.

The message I want to convey is that sometimes knowing what doesn't work for you is just as important as knowing what does. Be brave enough to think 'I can do this myself'.

What would you say is the most important lesson you learned in the first few years of your firm?

The 'why'. As I've outlined, there may never be a perfect time or formula to open a firm. However, there does need to be a perfect reason and purpose behind why you set up the firm. That 'why' is going to be the driving factor in the ups and downs of your journey.

Can you tell us how you learned this particular lesson?

I didn't take a wage in the first two years of opening the firm: money/power/titles shouldn't be your sole reason to set up a firm, nor is this what will get you up out of bed in the morning.

Personally, I wanted to open a 'people before profits' law firm that celebrated staff and client wellbeing, disrupted the industry and fought for the man on the street against big business. That's what gets me through the tough times. That's my 'why'.

What changes did you make as a result of this?

The entire firm is shaped by our 'why'. This is shown in the company's culture and values which are:

- People before profits
- Celebrating excellence in law
- Gratitude

As a result, we have built our company's foundation on those three values and I refer back to them constantly to shape all the decisions we make in the firm. This includes who to hire and work with, what new areas of law to go into and, lately, how to deal with the Coronavirus pandemic. I used this model to shape our policy so it was unique to our firm and represented the values of our people.

Our biggest change and investment are our purpose-built office with staff and mental health at the forefront. Our office includes:

- An amphitheatre to share ideas, give motivational speeches, provide training and listen to and collaborate with all voices.
- Two bars to socialise and celebrate our achievements, including a beer and prosecco tap.
- A chill out zone with softer lighting to take five after a heavy call or to just get away from the screen.
- A breakout zone with pool table and think swings to get creative and mix with staff outside of your immediate team.

As you can see, I am very culture centric.

In what way do you think this made you a better law firm owner?

When comparing Apple with Microsoft, Steve Jobs explained that it wasn't the technology or industry legends that gave Apple the edge, it was his company's values and vision that was superior.

As such our vision – 'We believe people with passion can change the world through the law' – is what gives us the edge on our competition. Our USP is that we provide the legal excellence equivalent of any magic circle firm, but with the heart and feel of a small family-run firm.

By having a solid identity, it's easier to attract partnerships, the right candidates and clients who can identify with what your company authentically stands for. This allows us to identify and work with other companies that are aligned to our vision and values.

What advice would you give to a new law firm owner about this?

Don't underestimate the 'fluffy' stuff. Culture is very important to the success of your firm, albeit culture is also very fragile and can take years to build and minutes to destroy. I strongly believe that happy staff make for happy clients and, therefore, increased profit.

What law firms forget is that their product is their people who provide legal advice. As well as lawyers, we are all salespeople. Ultimately, we are selling a legal service in a very competitive market. I stand by the notion that your firm is only as good as your lawyers.

With that in mind, it floors me how firms don't prioritise their people above all else. People are your asset, your commodity. I think this is the simplest but most progressive thing that companies can do.

This is summarised best in my favourite quote by Zig Ziglar: 'You don't build a business – you build people – and then people build your business.'

Chapter 6

Branding your business

Establishing a brand is one of the most exciting parts of setting up a law firm. For many fledgling business owners, this will be the first opportunity to have something really tangible that shows what you've been working so hard on.

6.1 What is branding?

Simply put, your brand is the image you create around your business in order to publicise your products or services. It's a fairly big and complicated concept that can grow and shift along with your firm. You may find it helpful to think of your business' brand as the personality of your business.

A successful brand isn't made up of any one factor. Rather, it's the cumulative effect of all of your marketing efforts.

This includes:

- your business name;
- your logo;
- the colours you use in your marketing efforts;
- your communication style;
- the kind of photos and images you use;
- your web copy;
- the type of updates you share on social media;
- the way you treat clients face-to-face;
- your networking style.

6.2 Why is branding important for your law firm?

Ultimately, branding is important for your law firm as it will dictate how your business is perceived by potential customers. In other words, how you present yourself will determine whether or not your firm looks like a 'proper' or trustworthy business.

A successful brand will increase your business value and generate new customers. It will enable you to establish a sustainable business – assuming the rest of your business practices are strong enough to support it, of course!

Branding and a strong marketing message will help to generate new clients. Once your brand has become more established in your local marketplace, it will go on to develop a reputation of its own, where existing and potential customers will hopefully attach a positive and trustworthy impression on your logo and brand. This will create trust within the legal marketplace and help to support your advertising efforts.

It's also important to note that a strong brand isn't *just* beneficial in terms of recruiting new clients. It can also be a great way to ensure the people within the firm (you plus any business partners, future employees or contractors) feel great about the service they're providing. A good brand can be an excellent team-building resource as it will enable everyone to visualise how the firm should operate. It's likely to become a real source of pride to the team as a whole and can really help to bring the business together.

6.3 The first steps of branding

Branding is one of those things you could literally spend any amount on. It would not be unusual for a big business to spend hundreds of thousands of pounds on a rebranding process. There is no lid on what you could spend on this, but – as with all financial business decisions – we urge caution.

If you've set aside a significant sum for branding your business and feel that's the right move for you, that's great. However, not all businesses will make this same decision in the early days.

The good news is that you don't need to spend a small fortune in order to establish a successful brand. Working with a dedicated branding agency can be a very expensive endeavour, but freelance graphic designers are often much more affordable. You may be able to find someone by asking around other business contacts, or by attending local networking groups. Alternatively, you'll be able to easily connect with freelance designers on social media or via a Google search.

However, there are a fair few necessary steps it's wise to consider *before* you engage a designer. A lot of the work that goes into the branding process will need to be done by you. Some considerations are:

- your name;
- your ideal customers;
- your unique selling point (USP);
- keywords, imagery and colour;
- keeping communications on brand.

We've explored these first steps below.

6.3.1 What's in a name?

Some new business owners have a very clear idea of what they want to call their firm right from the beginning, others may need a little longer to settle on a final idea. Many legal businesses choose to include a word such as law, legal, solicitors or barristers. This is a popular choice as it will clearly convey the services you intend to offer.

The traditional choice is for legal firms to be named after the surnames of their partners, but there's no real reason to stick to this convention if it doesn't work for you. However, you will need to remember that there are rules governing the names for unregulated law firms, specifically that you *can't* use the words mentioned above: law, legal, solicitors or barristers.

The name you choose for your business is the first opportunity you have to present your business to the world at large. We both opted for reasonably traditional names for our businesses (Roche Legal and DJS Law), but this might not be the right choice for you. If you are planning on starting a virtual or web-based firm, you may want to hint at this in your name. Equally, if you envision that your firm will meet a particular niche, you may want that to be reflected.

Ideally, your business name should be clear, easily memorable and something that gives clients an idea of what to expect from you as a firm.

6.3.2 Who are your ideal customers?

This is the most important question you can ask when you start to develop your brand. There's no sense at all in creating a brand you love if it won't speak to the type of clients you're hoping to attract. For example, creating a very traditional brand featuring a logo with a quill on it wouldn't be a good fit if you were hoping to attract internet-savvy clients who wanted to meet over video connection rather than in person.

We understand that when you first start out in business, you'll likely snap up whatever business opportunities come your way. This can be a necessity when you're working to build an income and ensure your start up can keep trading from month to month.

However, when opportunities are coming up regularly, you'll begin to have the luxury of working with the type of clients you *want* to work with. One excellent way to start working towards this point is to focus your branding and advertising efforts towards these groups right from the beginning.

In order to do this, you'll need to dig a bit deeper to try and get to know your ideal audience as well as you can. Ask yourself:

- How old are they?
- Which areas do they live in?
- What do they do for a living?
- Do they have children?
- What other businesses or services do they use regularly?
- Are they business owners?
- What do they do for entertainment?
- Are they part of any clubs or societies?
- Are they part of certain online communities?

Keep in mind that your target audience will include three parties: your primary audience; your secondary audience; and your influencers:

1. **Your primary audience:** the clients you ideally want to attract.
2. **Your secondary audience:** the people that might help you reach your primary audience. These are typically the families, contacts and connections of your primary audience.
3. **Your influencers:** professional contacts that may pass work on to you. These could include other legal professionals (typically those working in other areas of the law), financial advisors, accountants and existing clients that are pleased with the service you provide and have recommended you to their own network.

Investing the time to determine who your target audience are and what makes them tick can help you to see how to brand yourself in order to attract the type of clients you want to work with.

It can also give you key ideas on where to focus marketing and advertising efforts. After all, it's not going to be cost-effective or a worthwhile use of time to advertise your business out into the ether without considering where you will best reach your target audience.

6.3.3 Your USP

Finding your USP

It's very difficult to succeed in business without being aware of and exploiting your unique selling point. Unless you plan to start your business in a particularly rural area, it's highly likely that there are already lots of firms in your vicinity offering the same legal services that you plan to offer. Your USP is the thing that will make clients choose you over your competitors.

With a service business such as a law firm, it's likely that the thing that makes your firm stand out from the crowd will be something to do with the level of service you offer your clients. Alternatively, your USP could be fee-based or outcome-based.

Your USP could be related to:

- **How you meet with clients.** Will you be inviting clients into your office / home office / meeting room facility, or will you be going to them? Will you meet with clients in their own home in the evening, or will you visit them at work? Will you conduct meetings via video chat?
- **Where you're located.** Will your firm be located centrally? Will your firm be accessible to all clients? Will you be the only law firm physically based in a small town? Will your firm have ample parking facilities? Will your firm be located next to fantastic transport links? Will your firm have a particularly interesting location for another reason?
- **How you'll manage each case.** Will you offer free initial consultations? Will you clients work directly with a fee earner rather than a case handler? Will most of your work be done virtually in order to cut down on costs to the client? Will you offer a no-win-no-fee guarantee? Will you offer additional services as a free gift? Will you focus on offering a high level of customer service? Will you aim to work more quickly than expected? How easy will it be for clients or potential clients to contact you? Will you aim to respond to communications within a specified timescale? Will you use technology in an innovative way?
- **The type of law you are concerned with.** Will you be working within a niche area of the law? Will you be approaching a common area of the law in a new way? Will you be solving a particular problem for your clients?
- **Your community outreach.** Will you do any charity work alongside your client work? Will you offer pro bono work to non-profit organisations? Will you be working with legal aid? Will you be working to raise awareness of certain issues? Will you apply for accreditations? Will you run free legal clinics? Will you offer free legal resources on your website? Will you run legal seminars?
- **The type of client you plan to work with.** Will you work specifically with a certain group of customers? Will most of your customers fall within the same age bracket?

What if it isn't easy to determine your USP?

We want to make clear that it isn't always easy to determine your USP, especially within a saturated market. Some of you may have decided to start your own law firm in order to solve a particular problem or meet a particular need . . . but others will be taking these steps simply because they want to make a change to the format of their working life. It won't always be immediately apparent what will make your law firm appeal to your clients over your competitors' firms.

One of the best ways to try and determine your USP is to write a list of all the features and benefits of your firm. You could use the headings and questions above to really start to get a sense of the personality of your firm and how it might compare to its competitors.

Alternatively, you could approach this in a slightly different way and seek to explore how your law firm will make your clients feel. This may seem touchy-feely, but it is important to spend at least a little time thinking about the emotional needs of your client.

This is important whatever area of law you are practising within. Whether you're working in corporate law, conveyancing or criminal litigation, you will be working towards achieving a specific outcome.

Once the transaction, the process or the court case is resolved, how will your client want to feel? Will they be reassured? Victorious? Relieved? How will you support them throughout this process? Is there something about this that will be unique or that isn't done very often? Perhaps there's something here that your competitors either can't do or that they choose not to?

These questions and considerations can all help you to determine what your USP is, and, subsequently, what the best way will be to publicise it.

6.3.4 Thinking about keywords, imagery and colour

Have you considered the importance of the keywords, imagery and colour you use within branding materials? Even very subtle differences can have a big impact on how your brand is perceived by your target audience.

A business tag line is an excellent way to reinforce the general message you are trying to get across with your branding. For example, when Rachel was looking at the branding for her law firm, Roche Legal, she worked to drill down into exactly what her target audience wanted from their solicitor. She set out to use her tagline to communicate to clients how she hoped Roche Legal would make them feel. The tag line – 'Roche Legal; Reassuring Experts' – was designed to ensure that clients knew they would be supported throughout the process, but also to assure them that their solicitors knew exactly what they were doing in legal terms.

Imagery and colour have a more subconscious effect on how your business's brand will be perceived by clients. Certain colours are likely to provoke certain emotional reactions from clients due to the long-entrenched associations we all have. For example, red can be associated with love, anger or fire. Green can be linked to nature, freshness or envy. Yellow can be the colour of happiness and sunshine. Blue can be associated with calmness, sadness or water. When you use colour in your marketing efforts, you could be communicating more than you realise.

Photos and images should also be carefully chosen. It's important to make sure that any stock images you use as part of your branding efforts reflect the kind of clients you are hoping to reach. For example, failing to ensure the models in the images you use are diverse could make certain groups feel they're not welcome. Using images of only young people when you're primarily hoping to work with elderly people could have the same effect. The level of formality of your firm should also be reflected in your chosen images, as this will be a key way to communicate what you're offering.

6.3.5 Keeping communications on brand

We want to stress that it's not just advertising materials that need to adhere to the brand you are building for your business. Rather, your business should embody its brand in everything it does. This includes all processes and communications, both in person and virtually.

For example, if your brand is very heavily based on the fact that you care about your clients, you'll need to make sure this is clear in the way you manage cases, the way you train your staff and the way you respond to emails.

6.4 Establishing your brand

Once you've determined the personality and brand attributes of your business, it's wise to keep that message as clear and consistent as possible.

One of the ways you will want to start showcasing that message is via the medium of graphic design. This can be a very exciting step forward as it's likely to be the first really concrete evidence you'll have that your firm is a real entity outside of your head.

There are a few things that most businesses are expected to have in order to show their legitimacy. It adds a lot to your business in terms of perceived professionalism to have things such as a logo, business cards and a website. If your business doesn't have these things, you may find it difficult to compete with more established firms:

- logo;
- printed materials;
- website;
- social media presence
- word of mouth promotion.

6.4.1 Finalising your logo

You don't have to spend a small fortune on logo design, but we would suggest working with a graphic designer. If your budget is very tight, you may want to consider using your network or searching online to find a freelancer who is as new to business as you are. You may even be able to barter services in order to help each other out.

There are sources online where you can have a logo 'designed' for you for very little cost, but the final product may end up being generic or poor quality. This route would also mean that you don't get the benefit of advice and expertise from a dedicated graphic designer.

6.4.2 Investing in printed materials

In the past, law firms would've had a great deal of printed materials to hand. Papers such as compliment slips and letterheads were considered a necessity. Though these are certainly still nice things to have, it's important to consider how regularly you would use these. Depending on the area of law you practise in, you'll likely find that most of the communications you send will be via email. You might find yourself spending a fair sum of money on printed stationery which then just gathers dust on a shelf.

There are still some printed materials you're likely to get a lot of value from. At the top of this list is the business card. Business cards are so simple but so effective as a tool to support your networking or word of mouth marketing efforts. Do remember that you don't need to spend a fortune on business cards for them to be effective. There are a lot of inexpensive online printers that can produce business cards for you very quickly. You may even want to take advantage of their online design tools, which enable you to arrange your business cards the way you want them and upload your own images (such as your logo).

You may also be considering investing in printed leaflets or flyers. This can represent a fair outlay, especially for a new business. We'd encourage you to consider whether these are really necessary in order for you to reach your target clients, or whether there is a more cost-effective option. Do remember that you can invest in more printed materials at any point in your business, you don't have to commit to anything before you're ready to do so.

6.4.3 Launching a website

Maintaining an online presence has become a very important part of running a business. Many clients will want to look you up online before they consider getting in touch. In this way, a website can act as a shop window in the first instance, though in practice it can be used for far more than this.

A potential client may end up on your website via a search engine, or they may be following a link from your business card. Either way, your website will be the best way for them to find out more about your firm, the ethos of the firm, and what you're able to offer them. It will also be a place where they can find out what the process of working with you might look like, how you've helped other clients, and how they can get in touch with you.

A website can also provide an excellent hub for you to share resources and downloadable information related to the area of law you practise in.

This kind of education-based marketing approach can be a really effective way to show potential clients that you have the expertise to assist them.

Building your website

There are all sorts of tools available that allow business owners to set up and maintain their own website with little to no technical knowledge. These tools include things like WordPress, Wix and Squarespace. You may decide that you feel confident enough with these tools to set up something simple yourself, especially when you're just getting started.

However, if you're not comfortable with this kind of tool you may find that this is a false economy! Managing your website yourself can be extremely time-consuming. You could put hours upon hours into building something like this, only to find that the end result isn't even close to what you had in mind.

It's probably wise to be honest about your technological capabilities at this stage and consider whether it will end up being worth it to pay someone else to manage this for you. You may find that it actually works out cheaper to do this, both in terms of the time cost you would have to spend on setting things up and on ongoing troubleshooting, and in terms of your sanity!

If you hire someone to build and maintain your website for you, you'll end up with a better-looking website that's built with your firm in mind. The cost of hiring someone to do this will vary hugely, so we recommend that you do your research and shop around before you commit to anything.

Considering the content of your website

It's not just the function and look of your website that will have an impact, you'll also need to think carefully about the content. The work you've done on your business' brand will help you determine the narrative for your content. A web address (URL) is generally chosen that is in keeping with the business name.

Just as you will have considered using professionals to help design and build your website, we'd recommend that you consider using a copywriter to help you put the copy together. As a legal professional, it's likely that you have plenty of experience in writing documents. Do consider, though, that the right copy for your website will be of a very different style! In order to use your website to effectively market your business to your target audience, you'll need to think about who that target audience are and which type of copy is likely to resonate with them.

In most cases, you'll likely come to the conclusion that your target audience won't respond well to legalese and jargon. In these cases, it can be a huge help to have the professional advice of a copywriter who will be able to help you make sure you're communicating exactly the right message.

You might decide that this expense is not a necessity in the first six months of your business. We can certainly understand this! However, we do think it's something worth considering as your business grows and evolves.

It's also important to consider the images you will use on your website. It's great to have your own photographs to use, but it's likely you won't have the budget for professional marketing shots right from day one. In these cases, you may choose to use stock images. This can be an inexpensive way to access high-quality professional images – though you do need to make sure they are properly licensed for the purpose for which you are using them. Again, you'll want to give careful consideration to the type of images you're using to make sure you're effectively reaching out to your target audience.

Do you need to have a blog?

One of the ways some businesses use their website to promote a more education-based type of marketing is by having a blog. Some law firm owners find this to be a fantastic way to connect with their target audience.

If you can write blog posts yourself and publicise them across social media – this can be a very inexpensive way to build visibility online, though there is a fairly significant time commitment. It's important to keep in mind that blog success does not happen overnight and you'll need to keep posting regular, high-quality posts for quite some time before you build momentum.

This may be something you're excited about doing, or it may just seem like a chore. If it's the latter, you may decide that it's not worth it for you to start a blog and that your time would be better spent elsewhere.

6.4.4 Using social media effectively

Social media can be an incredibly useful way to get the word out about your firm and what you have to offer . . . so long as you're using it effectively.

The marketing 'rule of seven' was developed in the 1930s and states that a potential client needs to come across your business an average of seven times before they'll be ready to commit to a purchase. Engaging your target market on social media is a great way to manage this process. It can help you to fairly easily get your brand, name, imagery and logo out in front of your audience.

When setting out to use social media, we'd advise you to think carefully about which platforms you're going to commit to using. LinkedIn is usually a given for people in the legal profession, but you may want to consider using other more consumer-based platforms as well. Which platforms are right for you will depend on who your target audience are and where they are likely to spend their time online. For example, there would be little sense in investing large amounts of time establishing a presence on Facebook if you're primarily targeting corporate clients.

Many law firms find success on social media by using it as a tool to share educational resources. This can be a great way to draw clients in and showcase your expertise as a firm. This is often a much better approach to take than using social media channels purely as an advertising channel, as this is likely to put clients off.

6.4.5 The power of word of mouth

Technology has given us so many innovative ways to market our businesses. However, this doesn't mean you should forget the power of good old-fashioned word of mouth.

The simple act of telling people about your business is a fantastic way to get the word out about who your firm is and the services it will offer. Personality and trust are so important when it comes to business, and many people will be more likely to use your firm's services if they have come across you by way of a personal recommendation.

We suggest you tell everyone and anyone about your firm. Tell your family and friends, of course, but also tell people you meet at social or professional events. Not only is this kind of marketing very effective, it's also completely free. The great thing about word of mouth marketing is that you never know which conversation might lead to your next opportunity. A business contact of ours once happened to mention her business at a supermarket checkout and the person behind her in the queue ended up becoming her biggest client to date. You really can't underestimate the power of word of mouth!

Of course, when you start utilising the word of mouth method, this can start to snowball quickly. Once you tell family and friends about what you're doing, they will hopefully go on to tell other people. Your brother, sister, friend or cousin might find themselves at a dinner party sat next to someone who's looking for a legal professional just like you.

The technical term for someone who spreads the word on behalf of your business is a brand ambassador. Recruiting those around you to play this role is often how law firms start to get their first clients. Don't be afraid to ask your personal network if they can offer you any contacts or introductions, they'll often be very keen to help.

As your law firm starts to get established, your pool of brand advocates will grow. Not only will your family and friends still be speaking on your behalf, you'll also hopefully receive recommendations and referrals from the clients you've already worked with. We can't underestimate how worthwhile it is to gather testimonials and general positive feedback from your clients. Testimonials can be a brilliant resource to use on your website and in other marketing materials to reinforce your branding message.

Nourishing informal referrals as a marketing method is a great way to build the longevity of your firm.

CASE STUDY 6: BILL WARD

Bill Ward is a co-founder of the law firm Ward Trade Marks Limited. He is an ex-aviation professional who went into business with his chartered trademark attorney partner to establish a firm specialising in trademark law.

When did you launch your law firm?

We started Ward Trade Marks Limited in March 2014.

How much knowledge and experience did you have before you started?

The set up at Ward Trade Marks is not typical in that only one of the co-founders, Rachael Ward, is a legal professional (she is a chartered trademark attorney). I am not a legal professional and my role in the business is not fee earning. I wear many hats in the business but the main ones are sales and marketing. The secondary hats I wear are finance, IT and operations.

Before we started, I had plenty of operational and complex process-based experience from my days in the aviation industry. Further, as an ex-aviation professional, I was used to the onerous regulatory environment that commercial aviation operates in. Back in the beginning, that proved very useful for us in getting our firm's regulatory approval in place.

However, I had precisely zero experience in what I was to learn would be the most important area for continued growth and success: sales or marketing. I had to learn how to do this fast.

What would you say is the most important lesson you learned in the first few years of your firm?

Without a doubt the sales and marketing side of a law firm is just as important as the quality of work and level of service provided to the clients. Clients don't simply arrive by divine intervention – you have to embrace marketing and sales in equal measure and word of mouth is not enough. Not being a legal professional meant that I could embrace this rather than shying away from it. 'Sales' still seems to be an alien concept in legal circles. A dirty word if you like, so much so that the industry uses various euphemisms to avoid the term, such as 'business development'.

You can get good at sales without being 'salesy' – no one likes that. You have to be able to put yourself into your prospect's shoes and imagine how you would like the conversation to go if it was you that was doing the hiring.

If you are not skilled at this already, then embrace it as a challenge and get skilled at it. You probably won't want to do that if you will be one of the principal fee earners but either way a) get some training, or preferably b) hire in someone that is skilled in the disciplines needed as soon as you can afford to.

Can you tell us how you learned this particular lesson?

It quickly became clear that you must orientate what to say (whether in writing or verbally) towards serving your prospective client, emphasising the benefits they will receive from you. Traditionally, firms would highlight things like 'we were founded in 1845' or 'we have 15 partners with decades of experience in x/y/z legal areas'. Prospective clients nowadays don't want to hear that. Within reason, they assume you have enough expertise anyway. In any case, such an approach doesn't explain how they will benefit from hiring you, and that's what you have to get across.

Part of the same lesson means that you must resist the temptation to give away advice in those initial screening calls. It's easier not to do this if you aren't a fee earner, but if you are, the temptation to do a lovely 'tap dance' when a prospect starts asking specific questions about the matter is very high. After all, you want to show your expertise. Whilst you may think that you have not given much away, the prospect will often think that they now have all they need and won't come back.

What changes did you make as a result of this?

Aside from ensuring that your marketing collateral is set up correctly, the biggest change for me was how to handle initial inquiries. It's all about a) listening, b) asking the right questions to fully understand the person's situation, and c) showing empathy with the person and their situation. From there you can offer your tailored solution that helps your client to get what they want, or to get what is achievable if they cannot have what they want. You have to be realistic and never over-promise.

You must parse up your process into simple and repeatable elements and document these so that they become part of your firm's culture. Be ready to continually review all of your processes so that you keep on improving. It goes without saying that you need to set up a KPI dashboard and know your numbers. If you don't, you will waste money on marketing activity that doesn't attract a single client.

In what way do you think this made you a better law firm owner?

Quite simply: we can better serve our clients. The ones we feel we can't serve well we don't take on.

Listening carefully to peoples' needs and understanding where they are coming from means that you make fewer mistakes by taking in work that is not a great fit for your firm. This is something you can easily miss if you fail to ask the right questions, fail to listen or rely on assumptions as to what the client wants. Again: if we find that we're not a good fit for each other, we refer the work out to another firm.

What advice would you give to a new law firm owner about this?

Play to your strengths and accept that you cannot do everything. Figure out where you have skills and knowledge gaps (you have to be humble enough to do this) and get them backfilled or hire in the skills and experience you need as soon as possible.

Don't feel that you have to take on every prospect that comes your way and never allow yourself to be beaten down on price. I can say this from experience: clients that 'nickel and dime' at the beginning will be the most demanding every step of the way.

Chapter 7

Finding clients and establishing networks

Let us set the scene. You've perfected your business plan, you've registered your business or self-employed status with HM Revenue and Customs (HMRC), you've obtained a professional indemnity insurance policy, set up your new desk space and made sure your new business phone line is operational . . . what next?

The next task, of course, is to actually start practising. In order to do this, you'll have to gets some clients through the (possibly metaphorical) door. Unfortunately, this stage isn't always as straightforward as it sounds. Many of the business owners we know would agree that your first clients are the hardest to get.

7.1 Why are the first clients the hardest to get?

There are a number of reasons why you may find that it's harder to get your first clients than any subsequent ones.

Chief among these reasons is that the process of pitching your business and bringing on clients is probably something that's completely new to you. It's unlikely that you were heavily involved in this side of things when you were employed, and as a result it may take you some time to start feeling comfortable with this new responsibility.

Another reason why your first clients are the hardest to get is that your firm is unproven and unknown. You won't yet have a band of happy former clients who are advocating for you within their networks. Indeed, even your own family and friends might want to wait to see how you get on before they bring their business to you!

7.1.1 How do law firms get their first clients?

It's unlikely that your first clients will be completely unknown to you. Most new law firms pick up their first clients from within their existing professional or personal networks.

This may come from offering services on a 'mates rates' basis for family and friends. Not only will this give you some experience and income, it will also assure those family and friends that you're good at what you do and may encourage them to recommend you to other people. You could also ask those that you've done some work for on this basis to write testimonials for you, and perhaps even share their positive reviews on social media.

You may have made connections in your previous employment that will help to bring in your first clients. Depending on the type of employment contract you had (specifically whether there were restrictive covenants with restraint of trade clauses) you may have been fortunate enough to have taken some clients with you when you left. If there were clients you had a particularly good relationship with, they may be keen to seek you out at your new firm in any event.

7.1.2 Do you need to launch an advertising campaign?

Paying for an expensive advertising campaign is far from the only way to bring clients on board. Indeed, it may be wise to hold off on doing something like this until your business is a bit more established.

It might be wise to focus your initial efforts on building word of mouth advertising through face-to-face networking and social media in the first instance. This will help you to get your first clients on board and to start to perfect your customer service and workflow processes.

Once you feel you're ready to welcome in more clients, you might want to consider running a small advertising campaign online or in a local publication. Using this platform to focus on letting potential clients know where you are, what you could do for them and why they should retain you is likely to be the most effective approach.

7.2 Developing an active mindset about selling

Connecting with potential clients is not something that will come naturally to everyone. For some people, the idea of standing up at a networking event and pitching your law firm might well seem excruciating.

This is one of the reasons why it can be easy to fall into the trap of saying to yourself '*if I do good quality work, people will hear about me*', or '*client referrals are the best type of advertising*', or even '*something will turn up, it always does*'. However, what these three assurances all have in common is that they all encourage you to sit back at your desk and wait for work to come knocking.

The reality is that things don't always work out this way, especially if you're relatively new to the marketplace. Being passive about marketing your business and advertising your services could very well lead to not getting enough work to cover your overheads. In reality, if you want to be successful, you'll need to go out and bring the business in yourself.

There are plenty of ways to approach active selling, and it doesn't have to be done in a way that makes you uncomfortable. For example, networking meetings can be an incredibly effective way to make new contacts, but as we've already touched on: they're not for everyone! If you have a fundamental belief in the value and expertise of your firm, you'll be able to find a way to advertise it that makes you feel good about the process.

7.3 Making yourself visible

One of the most important considerations for a new law firm is to make sure you're visible. You need to put yourself in sight and in mind for your clients, as this is the way to ensure you'll be their first thought when they're in need of the legal services you offer.

There are lots of ways to make your firm visible in this way. Some of the more obvious choices are the traditional ones: networking and business events. There are also many ways you can make yourself visible without physically being in the same location, such as via social media or contributing to industry publications.

Though you'll undoubtedly find some of these methods less daunting than others, we think it's important to aim for a mixture. Doing this will help you to reach out to as many potential clients as possible and will help to give your business a really solid foundation.

Of course, it's not enough to just be out in the world, either physically or virtually. You'll also need to make a good impression while you're there! We encourage you to develop a networking persona in line with the branding of your firm. If your firm's unique selling point (USP) is to be clear, crisp and concise, for example, you'll need to make sure you embody this while speaking at events and don't drone on and on about industry-specific information. Equally, if your branding focuses on your warmth and approachability as a law firm, you'll need to be prepared to offer kind words and understanding in your efforts with social media.

The golden rule here is to focus on making a connection with your audience that will resonate with them. Your audience will need to like you, get to know you and subsequently come to trust you before they are ready to commit to working with you. You can nurture this process by showing that you know what your clients need from you and by making it clear how you will meet those needs.

The final phase of selling is known as the convincing phase. This should be managed by emphasising the connection that's been made with effective communication. Once potential clients reach a point where they believe in the benefits you're offering them and have faith that you understand them, they're very likely to want to become clients.

Below we will look at making yourself visible:

- in person;
- online;
- using traditional marketing methods.

7.3.1 In person

Some ways to make yourself visible in person are:

- networking events;
- business fairs and expos;
- talks and seminars;
- business lunches with clients;
- offering free legal advice.

Networking events

There are many different formats of networking events on offer. Which one is right for you will depend on both your own personal preferences and on where you're more likely to connect with your target clients? Do remember, though, that the power of networking is often not in meeting directly with potential clients. Rather, it's about connecting and building professional relationships with other business owners. These business owners will become excellent brand advocates for you, both in their professional networks and their personal ones.

If you're completely new to this kind of networking, you might not be sure how to pitch yourself. Many networking groups encourage an atmosphere of personal connection. You'll be encouraged to show your personality in a way that will enable you to stand out from the crowd and make authentic connections. This can be an excellent way of doing business – but do keep in mind that 'being yourself' does not necessarily mean being your most relaxed self! At a business networking event, as with other in person opportunities, you should be your *true professional self*. This will obviously be different from the true self you would be when at home with family or out with friends.

If you want to attend networking events on an ongoing basis, you'll usually have to join one or two networking organisations. Before you commit to any one group, make sure you've visited as many groups that run in your area as possible. As we've said before, there's a fair amount of variation in the structure and tone of this kind of event, and you'll likely find that some suit you and your business more than others.

Business fairs and expos

Attending business fairs and expos can be a great way to make yourself visible, whether you're there as an exhibitor or just as an attendee. Setting up your own stand with some attention-grabbing on-brand materials can be a great way to get chatting to potential clients and contacts, though this might not be in budget for everyone, at least not in the early days of your business.

If you're attending a business fair or expo, we recommend going armed with more business cards than you think you'll need! Approach the exercise with the focus of making valuable contacts, not to directly sell your services. We'd suggest keeping an eye out for complementary business owners who may share a target audience with you. For example, if you're a conveyancer, estate agents would be naturally valuable contacts. Alternatively, if you offer private client law, you might be interested in making connections with businesses who do a lot of work with new parents or elderly people.

Keep in mind that much of the networking at this sort of events takes place away from the exhibition booths. Don't be afraid to strike up conversations in the entry queue or the cafe.

Talks and seminars

There are two ways that you can make talks and seminars work for you. The first is to attend talks and seminars that are being run by other people. Many business organisations, city councils and universities run regular business events. You'll often find that these are free or inexpensive, and can be a great way to learn new skills, get ideas and meet other business people. Remember to take plenty of business cards with you and make sure you engage with other attendees as much as possible.

A more proactive way to make use of talks and seminars is to host your own. If you have capacity at your premises, or have access to an inexpensive event space, you might want to invite some of the business people you've come across at networking events to a talk on an aspect of the services you offer that's likely to be of interest to them.

Alternatively, you could contact other relevant organisations to offer to deliver a talk for them on a new case, legislative developments or changes in the law. As an example: if you deal in contract law, offering to run a free seminar for a local business networking organisation on the legalities of small business contracts could prove very fruitful.

This method does involve a fair time investment as you'll need to set aside time to prepare the talk (including creating slides and handouts) and deliver it. In return, you'll get the opportunity to showcase your knowledge, answer questions and introduce yourself to potential clients. All the effort involved will be well worth it if your firm is able to take on new paying clients as a result.

Business lunches

Business lunches with clients are one of the most traditional ways of marketing your firm. Once you've taken on a medium-to-big client or two, it can be very beneficial to invest a bit of time and money in developing your professional relationship over lunch. This type of engagement generally allows you to get to know the client better on a personal level and explore any common interests (for example, music, art, sports). This can be a great way to encourage clients to bring more work your way in the future and/or recommend you to others.

If you're trying to keep costs down, or if you aren't confident enough to invite a client for a full-blown lunch, inviting a client to meet for coffee can be a good alternative to this.

Offering free legal advice

In recent years, many legal aid initiatives, law centres and Citizens Advice Bureaux have suffered from lack of funding. This means that free legal advice, guidance and support for low-income individuals has never been more necessary and important.

You may choose to consider offering some form of free legal advice yourself. Though this won't necessarily lead to paying clients, it's a really effective way of increasing your visibility within your community. You never know what opportunities this may lead to in the future. More importantly, you may feel that this is an excellent way to use your skills and expertise to give back or make a difference.

You could, for example:

- contact your local Citizens Advice Bureau to invite them to refer anyone they are unable to assist to you;
- offer to do work on a pro bono basis for local charities;
- volunteer at a free legal surgery;
- produce free advice booklets or resources;
- offer to write advice pieces for a local publication.

This is something we have found to be a valuable exercise within our own law firms. Darren's firm DJS Law run a free legal advice surgery each month, and for three years were featured regularly on a radio station answering legal questions. Rachel's firm Roche Legal produce free eBooks and printed information booklets on areas of their expertise.

Though these initiatives allow both of our firms to provide free legal information to those who may not be able to pay, they have the added benefit of helping to strengthen our brand personalities and increase our visibility.

Getting involved in doing something like this might be particularly relevant for your firm if your business vision or brand is based strongly on the idea of being friendly, approachable or responsible.

7.3.2 Online

Some ways to make yourself visible online are:

- having an effective website;
- working with search engines;
- using social media;
- building an email newsletter;
- investing in content marketing.

Having an effective website

We've touched already on what an important tool your website is for branding and marketing purposes. We've included it again here as it's a key consideration for being visible online.

When you hand someone your business card, connect with them on social media, pop up in someone's search results or are recommended by a third party, visiting your website will be the natural next step. As a result, your website will become the first major point of contact these potential clients will have with your business.

With this in mind, it's important that your website fully embodies your values and your brand, as well as properly showcasing the services you offer.

To make sure your website is working as effectively as possible, you may want to consider:

- Ensuring everything is accurate and up to date. The best way to do this is to review the website on a regular basis and fix any problems as soon as you're aware of them.
- Including your full contact information, including photographs and information about any client-facing employees.
- Ensuring that the design is professional and appropriate for your business.
- Linking to any social media accounts, blogs or other publications your firm is involved with.
- Including verified client testimonials.
- Ensuring that your website is fully accessible and can be used by those using assistive technology.
- Is the design and layout of your website efficiently 'converting' visitors? A website visitor 'converts' when they take some kind of action, e.g. download a resource, sign-up to your newsletter or request a call-back.

Your website might not source leads for you on its own, but it will provide an online hub for you to direct the leads you find elsewhere to. For example, someone you meet either in person at a networking event or on a social platform such as LinkedIn could then refer to your website to find out more about your firm and your services before they make the decision to get in touch with you directly.

Working with search engines

The more likely it is that your website can be found in the results of major search engines, the more likely this will help to raise your profile. It's particularly important to think about how your website performs in results for the type of search term your potential clients will be using. For example, though it is helpful if your firm comes up first when clients search for your name, you'll also want to find a way to be connected with those clients who are searching terms such as 'will writers in Nottingham' or 'find an injury claim solicitor in London'.

There are some relatively straightforward ways to improve your luck with search engines. As a first step, we'd suggest setting up a profile with Google My Business. This allows you to appear in Google's local business listings, which will show up on a map when individuals search for local services in their area. You will be able to regularly review and update this information, and your clients will be able to rate and review your services.

Another easy way to consider using search engines to increase your visibility is search engine advertising. You can pay to make your website appear when individuals search certain key phrases. The cost of this kind of advertising varies greatly, as it depends how popular your chosen keywords are. In order to bring costs down and ensure you're reaching your ideal clients; it might be wise to narrow your search results. So, instead of paying for the search term 'trademark attorney', you might have more success – and a smaller bill – with the term 'York trademark attorney'.

Though it is possible to improve your website's search engine optimisation (SEO) yourself, once you have the budget to do so you'll almost certainly want to consider hiring an SEO specialist. The time it would take you to learn enough about SEO to implement your own successful pay per click campaign would almost certainly be better spent elsewhere in your business! If you're concerned about keeping costs down, a local SEO agency is likely to be an economical option, especially as this will then free up a big chunk of your time to focus on fee earning.

It is, of course, important to have a basic understanding of how these technologies work. You'll need this in order to make an accurate assessment of what to expect if you do decide to outsource this work. However, this is specialist knowledge and you are by no means expected to be an expert on everything.

Using social media: the benefits

Engaging in social media can be a great way to raise the profile and general awareness of your practice (and yourself). Platforms such as Twitter, LinkedIn and Facebook business pages give you the opportunity to shape the message of your firm and shine a spotlight on areas of your practice you want to promote.

The businesses that use social media most effectively are those that use their energies primarily to provide a resource to their target audience, rather than aiming to directly sell. You may well have an online network consisting of more than 400 people, but you need to be careful of how you approach them. Most people use social media to learn new things, get entertained and make connections. They're unlikely to want to engage with a social media feed that's populated with blatant adverts.

If you're unsure what kind of information your firm should be sharing on social media, we recommend following the DICE method. Each time you consider posting something, ask yourself if it is DICE: different, interesting, compelling and engaging.

Focusing on making your social media feed useful and interesting to the exact target group you want to engage is a great way to attract the attention of that group and hopefully convert a portion of them into actual paying clients.

It's also wise to be mindful of how you can build reciprocal relationships on social media. Helping to amplify the messages of other small business can have twofold benefits:

1. It can help to support your brand as a helpful business that's involved in its community.
2. That small business may help to amplify your messages in return.

Of course, you'll need to consider carefully which other small businesses to engage with. There are some obvious downsides to promoting the work being done by your direct competitors! However, there are plenty of ways to connect with like-minded businesses that share a target audience with you but *don't* offer the same services.

Other law firms can be a great starting point; there will be plenty of firms that have a similar ethos to yours but don't offer the same legal services. You can also look outside the legal industry and make connections with other small businesses who your clients may be interested in, and vice versa.

Once you've started to identify these small businesses, retweeting or sharing their articles, photos or success stories – perhaps along with a few complimentary words – can be a great way to start to build on your online relationships. This will also reflect well on you and may even generate attention for you as a firm.

Twitter in particular is a great online space for commenting, sharing content, or for publicising events or special offers (such as firms who are taking part in the Free Wills Week initiative). On the other hand, LinkedIn is an ideal resource for building professional credibility and showcasing expertise. It's a great place to share longer-form writing and opinion pieces, as well as to highlight speaking engagements and professional awards.

Using multiple social media platforms in tandem can help you to harness your online network and really make it work for you. If you do this well, we believe there is unlimited potential that can lead to rapport, respect, relationships and – perhaps most importantly – results.

What about the downsides of social media?

Though being visible on social media has many benefits, there are also some potential downsides to consider. You will need to be aware of the possibility of breaching confidentiality, the risk of defamation and the platform it gives clients to air complaints or grievances. Once again, the more aware you are of these potential downsides, the better prepared you will be should any of these issues arise.

Before you start engaging in social media in earnest, we'd recommend taking a close look at some professional advice on the issue. The Law Society published a practice note on social media in December 2019 which will help to prepare you for this (**www.lawsociety.org.uk/support-services/advice/practice-notes/social-media**).

If your law firm has employees, you will need to think very carefully about how the firm as a whole will use social media. We suggest putting together a clear social media policy and making sure everyone has a copy. This will help to avoid misunderstandings and unwise posts that might otherwise land your firm in hot water.

Building an email newsletter

Though it can be incredibly beneficial to have a significant number of online followers, there's still a great deal of value in delivering a regular email newsletter.

When you register each new client with your firm, we recommend giving them the option of joining your email newsletter. This can be done very simply; just include an opt-in check-box on your standard registration forms.

Once existing clients are on your email newsletter, you'll be able to drop into their inbox on a regular basis with updates from your firm. This can be a way to provide relevant information, good news stories, details of special offers and reminders about the services you offer.

It's worthwhile to recruit existing clients rather than just potential new ones as your newsletter can be a great way to easily keep in touch and encourage return business. It will also keep your firm and the great work you do fresh in their minds and will hopefully remind them to keep recommending you to their own networks.

It can also be beneficial to encourage potential clients to sign up for your newsletter. This can be a good way to build rapport with potential clients and help them move towards making the decision to engage your services.

When planning your newsletter, we'd suggest thinking carefully about how regularly to send it out. There's no exact right or wrong answer here. You'll want to find a balance between:

(a) ensuring that you keep in regular contact to build on like-know-trust energy; and
(b) not sending newsletters out so often that your readers get annoyed.

Whatever frequency you choose, we suggest you aim to be as consistent as possible.

Investing in content marketing

'Content marketing' may be new terminology, but it's far from a new idea. In essence, content marketing is the idea of producing content that is useful to your audience, with the ultimate aim of positioning yourself as the expert they'll come to when they're ready to buy into the services you offer. This can also be called education-based marketing.

More traditional forms of content marketing include newsletters and writing articles for relevant publications. However, there's no reason to restrict yourself to only these forms of content! The growth of the internet and social media has opened up all sorts of other options for business owners seeking to grow their visibility and influence.

Ideas include:

- videos;
- blog posts;
- podcasts;
- online articles;
- infographics;
- PDF guides;
- eBooks.

Investing time and/or money into developing these resources can help you to provide informative, interesting and useful content on a regular basis. Not only will this give you plenty of material to share on social media channels for your audience to consume, there's also the hope that they'll then go on to share your resources with their own networks.

You may also want to consider the benefit of offering certain resources for download on your website. The usual way to do this is to collect email addresses and send the resources that way, which then has the benefit of boosting your email newsletter list. Legally, you'll need to make sure it's clear to site visitors that they're choosing to opt-in to your mailing list by giving you their email address and downloading resources. You may want to include an opt-in check-box for this, or it's also equally legitimate to include a suitably worded disclaimer to this effect.

Investing in content marketing can impress your existing clients, help to secure new clients and open avenues to new opportunities.

There's a good argument for spending time creating this sort of content in the early days of your business when you're not yet busy with client work or fee earning. This would be a good use of time that might otherwise be unproductive and would be very likely to reap dividends in the future.

7.3.3 Using traditional marketing methods

You're lucky enough to be starting a business with all kinds of digital marketing opportunities at your fingertips, but this doesn't mean you should forego traditional marketing methods altogether.

There's certainly still value in many kinds of traditional marketing and we'd advise you not to overlook this entirely. How important these methods are for your business will likely depend on your target audience and how tech-savvy they are. Think carefully about how your ideal clients are likely to seek legal professionals, and therefore how receptive they might be towards traditional offline advertising.

We do advise some caution when it comes to traditional marketing methods. Certain types of advertising that would've been a given for law firms a few decades ago have now disappeared almost completely, such as The Yellow Pages. Local papers were also once an excellent resource for finding local services, but how likely are your audience to check the back of the paper now when they could do a quick online search instead?

It's also important to consider how much more expensive traditional print marketing can be than digital ones. This is especially important to keep in mind in light of two of the main drawbacks of traditional methods:

1. It's far more difficult to ensure the impact of traditional marketing methods, which makes it hard to track return on investment.
2. Traditional marketing methods have far less of a direct impact, which may not be ideal if you're hoping for an early boost for your firm.

Though we do still think traditional marketing methods are an important consideration, we'd suggest allocating a much smaller budget to this than to online marketing.

Offline sources you may want to consider are:

- adverts in local papers;
- billboard signage;
- petrol station advertising;
- printed brochures and flyers;

- sponsoring local events;
- adverts in other business' publications;
- sponsoring local sports teams.

Many law firms invest in printed brochures or flyers. These are fairly cheap to produce in bulk and can be a great resource when you want to have something tangible to hand to clients at business events. These will likely always have a place in a law firm's marketing strategy, as so many clients like to have something, they can take away with them for later reference. Printed materials can be handed to new clients, left on your reception desk or even distributed around local businesses.

What about return on investment?

Though there are certainly many successes to be had with traditional marketing methods, it can also represent a much bigger outgoing with much more uncertainty about the return on investment.

Getting a good return on your investment is obviously important but can be very hard to predict. DJS Law was approached about six months after it had started up by a local GP surgery. The surgery asked DJS Law if it would consider putting an advert in their patient appointment booklets. The statistics on this looked good: the booklets would be seen by the surgery's staff members as well as all patients, their family members and their carers. This equated to a monthly distribution of 1,000–3,000 booklets.

Though this originally looked like a good opportunity, the advert ultimately didn't provide a good return on investment. The lesson here is to really consider how likely it is that another business's audience will be right for your business – and whether that audience might be receptive to your advert in that context. With hindsight, it's perhaps clear that people visit their GP and pick up appointment booklets because they're unwell, not because they're on the lookout for legal services. We suggest that you very carefully consider each marketing opportunity of this kind and ask some searching questions before you decide to proceed.

It's not always easy to predict how much interest a traditional advert will generate. Sometimes the numbers just don't work out as you expected. Another traditional marketing method that DJS Law have explored is billboard signage. The firm invested in a reasonably large billboard in their local area. The sign was at the front of a large 24-hour supermarket, so was subject to a huge amount of footfall.

The DJS Law billboard was in place for two years. Work did flow in from it, and the advert did pay for itself, but considering the position of the advert and its eye-catching format, it didn't generate the clients and revenue it really should've. It's worth asking the question whether a large static advert is the best use of your firm's marketing budget, or whether it might be money better spent on something more up-to-date and dynamic.

7.4 The legalities of marketing

However you choose to advertise your business, there are certain things you will need to keep in mind. As a business, you have both a moral and a legal responsibility in this sense.

All businesses are bound by law to ensure that their marketing methods are accurate, decent, truthful and socially responsible (**www.gov.uk/marketing-advertising-law**). You will also need to follow the Committee of Advertising Practice (CAP) Non-broadcast Code for any print, online or traditional offline marketing (**www.asa.org.uk/codes-and-rulings/advertising-codes/non-broadcast-code.html**), or the CAP Broadcast Code for any television or radio advertising (**www.asa.org.uk/codes-and-rulings/advertising-codes/broadcast-code.html**).

You will need to keep abreast of any marketing regulations or restrictions that have been put in place by your regulatory body.

The Solicitors Regulation Authority covers this in paragraph 8.9 of the Code of Conduct for Solicitors, RELs and RFLs, which says:

> You do not make unsolicited approaches to members of the public, with the exception of current or former clients, in order to advertise legal services provided by you, or your business or employer.

This message is repeated in paragraph 7.1(c) of the SRA Code of Conduct for Firms. This standard means that as a regulated solicitor you are not allowed to make direct or specifically targeted approaches to individual members of the public in person, by phone or by any other means.

The BSB also has some restrictions on advertising. Though traditionally barristers obtain work from solicitors and so would not need to advertise to clients, this changed slightly in 2004 when direct access rules came in.

Thanks to direct access, in some circumstances members of the public can now instruct barristers directly themselves. This means that many barristers are now seeking to market their services to potential clients.

In doing this, barristers will need to ensure that they are not knowingly or recklessly publishing inaccurate or misleading advertising material, as this would be in breach of the BSB Handbook rule rC19. Barristers are specifically advised to be careful about making comparisons between themselves and other legal professionals as these can often be regarded as legally misleading.

7.5 Referral work

If you are doing good quality legal work and you look after your clients, it's likely that they will recommend you to their family and friends. This can be a fantastic source of work, as well as a welcome reassurance that your clients are genuinely happy with your services.

It's important to note that referrals for your firm don't have to be restricted to satisfied clients. Rather, this is something that you as a business owner can reach out to other business owners about.

As a law firm, you will often get enquiries asking if you do types of law that you don't. In these cases, instead of just answering 'no, sorry' and moving on, consider the value in setting up reciprocal arrangements with firms who do offer those services (but don't offer the services you do).

Other legal professionals and related business can be an excellent source for new work. There's a lot to be gained from seeking to cross-promote with other business who have a similar client base. For example, if your local estate agent is running a seminar on stamp duty changes, why not mention it in your email newsletter in return for the estate agent mentioning your conveyancing services in theirs?

Many businesses will already have their own set of contacts in place when you approach them. This doesn't necessarily mean that you will be met with an automatic 'no'. There may well be scope to secure work away from their existing contacts if you can demonstrate that you are innovative, easy to work with, and can deliver work on time and at the right price.

When referrals work well, both the client and the referrers will be happy with the services provided. Don't underestimate the power of the phrase 'is there anyone else you know who might benefit from our services?'

7.5.1 Referral regulation

Before you begin to make referral connections, we'd recommend you familiarise yourself with the regulation on this.

Paragraphs 5.1–5.3 of the SRA Code of Conduct for Solicitors, RELs and RFLs are concerned with referral arrangements. The purpose of these guidelines is to protect the interests of clients and to ensure that their trust and confidence in their law firm is not jeopardised by these kinds of arrangements.

The SRA's principles (**www.sra.org.uk/solicitors/standards-regulations/principles/**) include the following principles for free sharing and referral arrangements:

> You act:
> 1. in a way that upholds the constitutional principle of the rule of law, and the proper administration of justice.
> 2. in a way that upholds public trust and confidence in the solicitors' profession and in legal services provided by authorised persons.
> 3. with independence.
> 4. with honesty.
> 5. with integrity.
> 6. in a way that encourages equality, diversity and inclusion.
> 7. in the best interest of each client.

In 2013, the Legal Aid, Sentencing and Punishment of Offenders Act (LASPO) 2012 introduced a ban on referral fees in personal injury cases. All legal professionals need to comply with LASPO regulation at all times, as well as the guidelines of their regulatory body.

If you are found to be ignoring these, it's likely your regulatory body will take enforcement action against your firm. This could be because you are actively accepting referral fees in restricted cases, or because you have failed to address the issues and risks that are associated with referral arrangements.

If your practice wishes to accept referral work from other firms or businesses, there's absolutely no reason not to do this, so long as you ensure that you are following all relevant regulations.

Solicitors with referral, fee sharing or 'white label' agreements in place will need to:

- keep accurate records of all past and present fee sharing, referral and 'white label' arrangements;
- declare all arrangements as part of their practising certificate renewal process;
- regularly review procedures and policies on this matter.

7.6 Diversification of clients: how many do you really need?

There's no exact formula to determine how many clients your law firm will need. Rather, this will depend on:

- the type of services you're offering;
- your current resources;
- how quickly you want to grow;
- the cost of your overheads;
- how busy you're comfortable being.

When you first start out, it's likely that you'll welcome in almost any client who comes your way. This can be a necessary factor of running a start-up firm – often you can't afford to turn away business. However, as you grow, you'll earn the ability to be pickier about the type of client you take on.

You may find that there are certain types of clients you enjoy working with more than others, types of services you find more professionally fulfilling, certain types of work that feel more stressful than they're worth, or even certain options that are more lucrative!

7.6.1 Are some clients more valuable than others?

It's not just about the number of clients you get in the door – it's also important to consider the lifetime value of each type of client.

Some clients will come to you for one service and then may never have reason to work with you again. With others you'll build a more long-term professional relationship and may work with them on a repeat basis. Over time you'll come to see which types of client and which types of services have the greatest potential for repeat business, and you may find that it makes sense to gravitate more towards that kind of work.

Equally, you may find that some clients who've only given one instruction will go on to highly recommend your firm within their networks. This type of client will still significantly contribute to your firm financially, and therefore should also be considered as having a high lifetime value.

7.6.2 How will you track clients?

It's likely to be well worth your time to put a simple system in place for tracking new enquiries. There are plenty of software packages that will do this for you, but it can be done equally well in a spreadsheet.

We'd recommend tracking:

- how initial enquiries come in;
- who has referred clients (as an aside: we suggest sending thank you notes);
- what type of service they're interested in;
- what your conversion rate is on enquires.

In addition to providing you with some very valuable data, a system like this will also help to ensure that all prospective clients are properly followed up.

You may also want to consider embracing the idea of running a data-driven law firm and tracking more specific details about your clients. It's unlikely that you'll work with a homogenous client base. Most legal professionals will work with a wide range of clients of different ages, genders, backgrounds, occupations and income levels.

Tapping into this data will reveal the diversification of your client base, as well as highlighting the work you enjoy doing and the clients you enjoy doing it for. Exploring this can make you more aware of key market segments where you will be able to play to your strengths.

7.6.3 Should you specialise or offer a one-stop legal shop?

As your firm grows, you'll be able to identify whether it makes more sense for you, your brand and your growing client base to offer an array of services, or whether you'll find more success as a specialist.

There can certainly be benefits of offering integrated and seamless services in terms of increasing the lifetime value of each client. It's not just legal practitioners who are seeing the benefit of this – there has been a growth in accountancy firms creating alternative business structures (ABSs) in order to provide services including will writing, trust and lasting powers of attorney (LPA) services. Likewise, we're aware of conveyancing firms opening or merging with estate agencies in order to act as their own referral source for conveyancing work and related services.

Though this strategy is certainly attractive and effective for many law firms, others see more value in specialising. It can certainly be easier to brand and market a more specialist firm, as it will be much clearer who your ideal clients are. You're also likely to prefer this option if you want to work solely within your own area of expertise and build up a fantastic reputation for what you do.

7.6.4 But really, how many clients should you take on?

Most of us are in business for two key reasons:

(a) to provide a valuable service to clients;
(b) to make a profit.

It may seem like the best thing to do as a new business is to work with as many clients as possible. Though this may seem intuitively correct, this isn't necessarily true. In reality, taking on too many clients too quickly could lead to problems.

If you're over-loaded, you're likely to have issues with effectively servicing work, meeting deadlines and correctly managing client communications. This is especially likely to be the case if you're a sole practitioner, as you'll have to manage compliance, marketing, administration and reception duties – as well as doing the actual fee-earning.

We've touched on this a few times already, but we do really believe in the value of keeping things simple to begin with and building slowly. Doing things in this way will help you to build a more sustainable firm that's likely to stand strong for many years to come. It will also enable you to gradually assess the skills, attributes and personnel your team needs to acquire.

In order to understand how many clients, you will need – or want – to take on, you'll need to look very carefully at your numbers.

You'll be able to determine how many new clients to aim to take on each month by considering:

- your average fee per client;
- the number of client meetings you held in the last month;
- the number of clients who retained you in the last quarter;
- your average engagement rate;
- the cost of client acquisition (monthly marketing cost divided by the number of new clients per month);
- the monthly cost of non-negotiable overheads;
- the budget you'd like to have per month to invest back into your business.

Exploring these numbers and doing some calculations with them will help you to get a general sense of how many clients you should be aiming to take on per month. Keeping track of client data with a simple spreadsheet or an inexpensive online resource will help you to get a true understanding of your data in order to make more informed decisions about how to move your firm forwards.

As a final note here, if it seems like the number of clients you need to take on in order to cover costs seems impossibly large, you may need to look instead at your fees, as they may be unsustainably low.

CASE STUDY 7: SARAH KHAN-BASHIR

Sarah Khan-Bashir is a solicitor and the founder of SKB Law (a trading name of Shire Solicitors). SKB Law is an award-winning firm specialising in family law. The firm is based in West Yorkshire. Sarah was awarded an MBE in 2014 in recognition of her work with Mosaic, a Prince's Trust educational charity.

When did you launch your law firm?

The initial set-up was a partnership in 2007, then I went solo in 2017. I then rebranded the firm to suit my own style and launched with a new trading name in 2019.

How much knowledge and experience did you have before you started?

I qualified in 1998 and worked for the West Yorkshire Police in their civil litigation department. I worked there for seven years before deciding to open up a law firm in partnership with another civil lawyer.

I had zero knowledge of running my own practice as I'd always worked for other people. This meant that I took a leap of faith! However, we did have the advantage that the other partner did have some prior knowledge as they'd previously set up a firm in another city.

What would you say is the most important lesson you learned in the first few years of your firm?

Networking is key. Not just for creating a regular source of work, but also to run your thoughts and ideas past other sole practitioners. As a sole practitioner you can quite easily influence change within your firm, but rather than doing this on the spur of the moment, it's good to run things by other sole practitioners to find out what did and didn't work for them.

Can you tell us how you learned this particular lesson?

We felt we were quite self-sufficient as a partnership and did well, but as changes in the law took place and the 2008 recession hit, we had to adapt our business model.

As partners we were quite different in our approaches and I found this difficult to navigate. I sought advice from others in my position and slowly but surely connections were made through work or events. These networks became a useful source of support and I was able to move the practice in a direction I felt would be more beneficial to our clients. This ultimately led to me becoming a sole practitioner who felt confident to go it alone.

It's quite lonely as a sole practitioner, but when I faced certain challenges, I could find a way through them using my network. Be honest about your concerns and someone will always help. The biggest challenge for me was rebranding as I was concerned about confusing clients and losing the goodwill of the years under the previous name. If I hadn't had others to consult with, I may never have proceeded with the rebrand.

What changes did you make as a result of this?

Because of the help I had received through networking, I found this was a key but often underrated business skill. I wanted to share this with others, especially those thinking of entering the legal profession. As a result, I co-created the SKB Law Academy. We developed employability workshops and worked with many schools and universities. These workshops gave advice on how to brush-up on those all-important business skills which aren't often taught. The importance of networking very early on in your legal journey is a key message in these workshops.

In what way do you think this made you a better law firm owner?

I was able to give back to the community I served. It also helped develop my team, as they were all involved in the delivery of the workshops. It gave them confidence and a 'feel good' factor.

Working within the legal industry can be exhausting. Getting involved with the academy allowed staff to see an aspect of being a lawyer they may not have considered before, while also adding to their skills as lawyers.

Ultimately: if my team were happier, my clients tended to be too.

What advice would you give to a new law firm owner about this?

As well as running a law practice, consider adding a heart to your business. Ask yourself how your firm can help the community you serve by giving something back.

Being a sole practitioner is incredibly hard work and adding some social mobility work can make things so much more worthwhile. The side effect of this is that it won't hurt your profile, either! Work with existing initiatives or, if you yourself can see a gap in certain needs in your locality, create something new.

Chapter 8

Taking care of your clients

Clients are arguably the most valuable part of any law firm. You may have incredible knowledge and expertise, but without clients you quite simply won't have any legal matters to work on.

Customer service is the question of how you treat the clients that instruct your firm. This encompasses very practical issues – such as how quickly you deal with their matter – as well as emotional ones – such as how you make your clients feel.

It's important to remember that individuals often approach a law firm at a very emotional or distressing period of their lives. Depending on the area of law your firm specialises in, you may be supporting people at a time of bereavement, redundancy, injury, divorce or prosecution. Whatever the circumstances, they will be relying on your experience and expertise to solve their problem . . . and they'll expect you to treat them with respect, kindness and efficiency while you do it.

8.1 Why is customer service so important?

The level of customer service you provide is generally the primary reason why your firm will retain or lose clients. This will also likely determine whether or not you will benefit from client referrals.

You would have to be very well-known and respected in your particular field to retain and take on clients on the basis of results alone. Even if clients get the result they want, they'll generally also want to receive it in a way that makes them feel valued.

For example, there's a big market for budget online conveyancing services. Purchasing and/or selling property is already an expensive endeavour, and many clients will be tempted by the promise of paying far less for this service. However, even if completion is reached and the end result is generally a good one, many of these clients will hesitate to use the service again (or recommend it to their networks) if they've had to wait for ages for their emails to be answered.

8.2 What does good customer service look like in practice?

When it comes to good customer service, lawyers often think of the value and quality of the legal advice they're providing. Clients, however, tend to think in terms of the outcome or result, how they were made to feel during the process and how effectively they've been able to move on afterwards.

Because of this, good customer service needs to be more than just offering good, reliable advice. Instead, it needs to be something you consider at every level of your firm. Each process you put in place and each communication you send needs to be examined from the client's perspective.

Good customer service starts from the very first contact you have with a client, whether that's meeting them at a business event, fielding a phone call, responding to an email or answering a question on social media.

We recommend that you set out to tell clients from the outset how they can be expected to be treated. One of the major considerations here is the question of how often you will check in with them to update them on their case. Informing them early on how often you plan to do this can be a very useful exercise. Most clients will be happy with the usual set up, while some will ask for something different.

While no two clients are the same, we think it's fair to say that the majority of people have the same attitude to good customer service. If you're able to make clients feel involved, included and informed, they're less likely to have any reason to complain.

A large part of customer service is:

- responding to emails and phone calls promptly;
- keeping your promises;
- showing genuine interest in the client and their issues;
- interacting professionally and courteously;
- remaining calm, professional and respectful even in high-pressure scenarios;
- being proactive in the running of your clients' matters;
- listening attentively;
- identifying clients' objectives and priorities before you start, then developing a plan to meet these;
- ascertaining how clients want to receive communications, and how frequently;
- aiming to under-promise and over-deliver;
- ensuring bills are accurate and reflect the value of the work performed (producing a billing guide can help to show transparency in these matters);
- taking responsibility right away if something has gone awry;
- thanking the client for their instructions once the matter has come to an end.

Clients may not always recognise great legal work, but they will recognise a law firm that cares about them and makes every effort to provide high-quality service.

8.3 The initial client consultation

The first meeting you have with each client is an excellent opportunity to assess their needs and set expectations. It's essential that you're able to listen carefully to your clients in this initial meeting, as this will give you a good sense of:

- what their priorities are;
- what they're expecting from you;
- how involved they want to be;
- how they feel emotionally about the process;
- if they're going to have any special requirements over and above your usual customer service process;
- how their personality will impact on the case;
- what they would consider a good result.

The type of questions you ask in an initial conference, whether it's face-to-face, via video conference or over the phone, will help you to find answers to these questions. Over time you'll be able to develop a routine for this and will start to feel more confident about the assessments you make.

The key question to answer at this point is whether the expectations the client has are impractical, unrealistic or even impossible. A careful balance of listening and asking questions will give you the information you need to decide whether the client and their matter are right for you to take on.

This is a careful consideration, as it may be that you feel a client's expectations are too unreasonable and you will not be able to meet them. In these cases, it's worthwhile attempting to explain the realities to the client to see whether they will reconsider these expectations. If they do, you may well be able to move forward together. If not, it's likely you'll need to turn down their instructions in order to save yourself a great deal of stress!

Once you've explored what a client needs and expects from you, the next stage of an initial consultation is to make clear what you're able to offer them and how you'll be able to meet their needs. Being explicit about this early on will help your clients to know what to expect from you – and when. A proposed timeline can be helpful at this point, as well as some guidelines on how and when clients can contact you.

8.4 Client care letters

Once you and your client have agreed to work together, the next stage is to send out a client care letter in whichever way your client prefers to receive correspondence. This document should be tailored to each client's matter and include all the information they'll need from you during the course of your work together.

This is a very traditional method of doing business, but it's survived because it's a great way to provide important information right at the point of instruction. Though there's no formal requirement to do this, we believe it's a valuable facet of how a law firm takes care of its clients. Providing a well put together client care letter can also help to protect your firm from unfair allegations of insufficient information or inadequate customer service.

The best client care letters are drafted in a user-friendly way with the client in mind. They shouldn't be filled with complicated legal language, be too long, be too generic or be difficult to read (e.g. small text or dense paragraphs).

Rather, a good client care letter should include:

- a summary of the work you'll be doing on the client's behalf;
- contact details for all personnel the client might need to get in touch with;
- details of your opening hours and any out-of-hours services you offer;
- expectations on how regularly you will contact clients;
- clear instructions for any actions the client needs to take and/or information they need to provide;
- an expected timeline for the work being completed;
- clear information about fees and billing;
- your responsibilities as a law firm;
- the responsibilities of your clients;
- a checklist of the next steps.

You may also want to refer to the Law Society's practice note on client information requirements, which includes valuable guidance on writing both client care letters and terms of business documents (**www.lawsociety.org.uk/support-services/advice/practice-notes/client-care-letters**).

8.4.1 Fee and billing information

It's important that your customer care letters include information on costs that is clear, easily accessible and in an appropriate form to the client. Not all firms do this, but we think it's important as it can show transparency and help to build trust.

You may find it beneficial to include:

- whether the work will be charged at a fixed fee or on an hourly basis;
- a breakdown of the fixed fee (if relevant);
- the relevant hourly rates and an estimate of the time to be charged (if relevant);
- an explanation of the factors that may affect the final number of chargeable hours (if relevant);
- whether hourly rates or fees may increase during the retainer period;
- any expected disbursements and the likely timeframe for these;
- if there is potential liability for any other costs;
- whether you have a right to exercise a lien over papers for unpaid costs.

8.4.2 Making responsibilities clear

It can be helpful for everyone if all responsibilities are made clear at the beginning of the process. Some of these responsibilities may seem fairly obvious, but there can be real benefit in getting them down in writing.

For example, your responsibilities as a law firm might be:

- to work on all client matters to the very best of your ability;
- to treat clients with respect at all times;
- to advise clients of any relevant changes in the law;
- to advise the client of any circumstances or risks you are aware of/consider to be reasonably foreseeable that could affect the outcome of the matter.

The clients' responsibilities might be:

- to provide clear, timely and accurate instructions;
- to provide all required documentation in a timely manner;
- to safeguard any documents that may be required for disclosure.

Again, though all of these things may seem obvious, taking the time to include them in a client care letter can reassure clients that you take your responsibilities seriously and encourage them to do the same.

8.5 Terms of business

There are actually no regulatory requirements for law firms to provide clients with their terms of business. However, we believe it's good practice to do so. This helps to ensure everyone knows what's expected of them and from other parties.

Unlike the client care letter, this is usually a static document that won't change from client to client. Though we wouldn't recommend putting these terms actually into the customer care letter, we do think it is beneficial to send out a copy alongside it.

Your terms of business will usually set out details of:

- the standard of service clients can expect;
- information on professional indemnity insurance and what cover clients are entitled to;
- any clauses that limit the liability of the firm;
- how bank account details will be verified to protect against fraud;
- data protection and GDPR issues;
- storage of documents and any related costs;
- confidentiality and disclosure;
- any relevant outsourcing of work and how this might affect clients;
- how files are audited and vetted;
- the process for terminating the retainer;
- client due diligence the firm will undertake;
- financial arrangements with clients;
- your firm's complaints policy.

Though, again, there's absolutely no legal requirement to do this, it's standard practice to ask clients to sign and date a copy of the terms of business. This acts as evidence that they've read and understood them, both for your own peace of mind and as potential evidence for any complaints in the future. You may want this signature to be done on a hard copy of the document, or you may want to encourage clients to sign it electronically.

8.6 Setting and managing client expectations

Even if you do a very thorough job of setting and managing client expectations during the initial client consultation and in your client care letter, this aspect of the job is far from over.

You will need to check in with your client at regular intervals during the process to make sure their emotions and expectations have not got out of alignment. The solicitor–client relationship is ever-evolving, especially during lengthy cases. It's also important to consider that many of your clients may have never worked with a legal professional before. It's your responsibility to manage the client's expectations during the process to ensure they remain realistic – even when the process is completely unpredictable.

It's likely that you've dealt with a client with unrealistic expectations during your time in legal practice. This might manifest as them constantly calling to ask for updates or by challenging the number of billable hours they've been charged for. No doubt you'll know that these kinds of problems can end up costing you a great deal of time and energy; it's far better to be proactive about keeping expectations in check before you get to this point.

8.7 Balancing professional and empathetic behaviour

It's important to always remain professional, but it's equally important to use your personal empathy. As a legal professional, you're used to the legal process; many of your clients will not be. They are likely to be going through a stressful and emotional time, which can give rise to volatile or erratic behaviour, especially while navigating entirely new legal territory.

You'll need to take clients as you find them and try to be understanding of their behaviour. Of course, you'll need to set boundaries for how you expect to be treated by clients, but you may need to assess these on a case-by-case basis.

As a law firm owner, you'll need to find a balance between professional and empathetic behaviour. This will involve acting as an impartial, trustworthy advisor, but also being able to give reassurance, and letting clients see your humanity and your belief in their case.

8.8 Fees

Ultimately, the fees you charge as a law firm will have a big impact on which clients choose to retain you. The cost of services is a bigger consideration for some clients than others. An appropriate hourly rate for you and your staff will depend on a multitude of factors, not least who your target clients are and what they might be prepared to pay.

It's important to talk about the costs of your service and make them clear right from the outset. Not only will this often make clients feel more comfortable as they know what to expect, it will also reduce the likelihood of complaints later on should clients get a bill that's larger than they were expecting.

8.8.1 Hourly rates v. fixed fees

Whether it's better to charge on the basis of fixed fees or an hourly rate is a long-running debate within the legal industry.

Traditionally, law firms would charge on the basis of an hourly rate. This rate would be set by the firm on the basis of the expertise and experience of each individual lawyer. The client would then be charged this rate for each hour that the lawyer had spent either directly giving them legal advice or working on their matter.

In recent times, there's been a drive towards offering fixed fees for certain services instead. This is when a law firm calculates how much each service (e.g. writing a will, drafting a lasting power of attorney (LPA) or securing a divorce) would usually cost, then translate this into a fixed fee they then offer to all clients.

It's worth noting that you don't have to choose one price strategy and stick to it. Most law firms will use both hourly rate and fixed fee prices for different services, depending on what makes the most sense. You could also allow clients to opt to set a cap on their fee, whereby you ensure that billable hours don't exceed a certain number.

Being flexible about how you offer costs will allow you to ensure that your clients' interests are being met, while still ensuring that you make a sustainable profit on the legal services you're providing. Whichever combination of strategies you decide to move forward with, make sure you've fully taken into account the value of your work as well as the cost of covering overheads and expenses.

The argument for hourly rates

Using hourly rates as the basis of charging for legal services might seem the most sensible, at least from the perspective of the lawyer. Effectively, we are selling our time: time spent meeting with clients, time spent drafting their documents, time spent representing them in court and time spent settling their matters.

What it costs lawyers to complete a client matter depends on how long it takes. This is generally managed by recording time accurately; most lawyers break their time into six-minute units then round these up and total them into an invoice.

The real benefit of this type of charging is that there's no guesswork in it for us. We can be confident we've charged for the exact amount of time we've spent on a matter and therefore that we've been properly compensated for the work done.

However, this does result in clients being conscious that the clock, and thus the meter, is always running! Critics also say that charging by the hour is inefficient, opaque and open to misuse.

The argument for fixed fees

In many areas of legal practice, clients are becoming more and more price sensitive. This means that for many, the traditional way of billing is no longer satisfactory. Clients often want to know at the outset what the cost of their legal matter will be.

Fixed fee billing can be a good solution in these situations. It's common for wills, divorces, conveyancing services and LPAs to be offered on a fixed fee basis. In potential litigation, the initial letter of claim is often prepared on a fixed fee basis.

Lawyers are sometimes unsure about offering fixed fees, especially for matters that are likely to be unpredictable. Though you might enjoy a healthy profit on a straightforward matter that all goes to plan, this profit could be significantly reduced if the matter is held up by unforeseen issues.

If you do decide to offer fixed fees – which is often a lot more attractive to clients – it will be important to think carefully about what level to set those fees at. It may make sense to set them at what would've been an average hourly rate for the task, as this will allow the bigger profit from more straightforward cases to balance out the smaller profit from unexpectedly complicated ones.

8.8.2 Regulatory requirements for fees

Your regulator will have rules and requirements for how you manage billing and payments. It's important to make sure you're fully apprised of these and that you regularly review and update your billing processes in line with these.

The Law Society published a practice note on price and service transparency in November 2019 (**www.lawsociety.org.uk/support-services/advice/practice-notes/price-and-service-transparency**). This is a very useful resource to refer to when establishing billing processes.

SRA Transparency Rules

The SRA Transparency Rules came into effect in December 2018. They are designed to ensure that clients have all the information they need to be able to make an informed choice of which legal practice to instruct.

The rules require all regulated law firms (including freelance solicitors) who advertise that they offer certain services to publish information on their costs for these services. These services are set out in Table 8.1.

Table 8.1

For members of the public	For businesses
Residential conveyancing (including freehold sale or purchase, leasehold sale or purchase, mortgages, and remortgages)	Debt recovery (up to £100,000)
Probate (uncontested cases with all assets in the UK)	Employment tribunals (defending claims for unfair or wrongful dismissal)
Motoring offences (summary only offences)	Licensing applications for business premises (new applications or varying existing licenses)
Employment tribunals (claims for unfair or wrongful dismissal)	
Immigration (excluding asylum applications)	

In addition to publishing prices for these services, the rules also require you to make clear:

- what services are included within the quoted price;
- any services not included in the price that clients might reasonably expect would be included;
- details of the experience and qualifications of the legal professionals who will carry out the work;
- what the typical timescales and key stages of the matter are.

All this information must be published in a prominent, easy-to-find location on your website. If your law firm doesn't have a website, you must ensure that this information is readily available upon request in another format, e.g. a printed factsheet.

SRA mandatory requirements for billing

In addition to the transparency rules, the SRA also has a list of other mandatory requirements in relation to billing and payments (**www.sra.org.uk/solicitors/guidance/transparency-in-price-and-service/**):

1. You must provide price information prominently, in a clear and understandable format.
2. You must specify whether or not prices include VAT.
3. You must make clear exactly what is included within the displayed price. This is important with both hourly rates and fixed fees in order to avoid any confusion.
4. You must set out the basis for your charges alongside your published range of costs. This includes hourly rates and/or any other factors that will determine the final cost.
5. You must explain if the delivery method of each of your services affects the cost of that service. For example, if you charge more for face-to-face meetings than telephone or video meetings.

BSB regulations

BSB rules state that barristers must publish information about the fees they charge. This will usually be on your website, though if you don't have one you will have to publish fee details in a hard copy format.

As a barrister, you will need to make clear whether you charge on the basis of a fixed fee arrangement, an hourly rate arrangement, a conditional fee arrangement or an alternative arrangement.

The rules are more stringent if you provide certain types of direct access services. This will apply to you if you work in the areas of:

- employment tribunal cases;
- financial disputes arising out of divorce;
- immigration appeals;
- Inheritance Act advice;
- licensing applications in relation to business premises;
- personal injury claims;
- summary-only motoring offences;
- winding up petitions.

Barristers working in these direct access areas will need to:

(a) publish specific hourly rate or fixed fee charges;
(b) make clear any circumstances where these fees may vary;
(c) set out any possible extra costs;
(d) state whether their fees include VAT;
(e) supply a statement of the direct access services they provide, the key stages of their work and a timescale for these key stages.

8.9 Supporting vulnerable clients

As a law firm, you're likely to work with all sorts of different clients. This will almost certainly include vulnerable clients. This is a wide category and can encompass all sorts of different issues such as disability, low literacy, mental health issues, neurodiversity, victims of crime or those who speak English as a second language.

It's important to ensure that vulnerable clients get the same high-quality legal advice and customer service as any other client. In order to do this, you're likely to need to take some extra steps to ensure that your service is accessible. This may include:

- taking the time to read through documents with your client;
- having documents translated into the client's first language;
- meeting clients in their own home rather than an office environment;
- simplifying or repeating explanations where necessary.

8.10 Client due diligence

8.10.1 Overview of due diligence checks

Client (or customer) due diligence is the process of carrying out checks to ensure your client is who they say they are.

This is important for two reasons. First, doing these checks will give you peace of mind about the security of your firm and that you're not unknowingly supporting criminal activity. Second, if your firm offers certain services you will need to carry out thorough checks by law.

The Money Laundering, Terrorist Financing and Transfer of Funds (Information on the Payer) Regulations 2017, SI 2017/692 applies to all independent legal professionals (whether a firm, sole practitioner or freelance solicitor) who:

- buy and/or sell property or business entities on behalf of clients;
- manage client money, securities or other assets;
- open or manage bank, savings or securities accounts;
- organise contributions necessary for the creation, operation or management of companies;
- create, operate or manage trusts, companies, foundations or similar structures.

This legislation doesn't apply to legal professionals who are employed by public authorities or work in-house, or to notary publics who are acting as a public certifying officer (so long as they have no substantive role in the underlying transaction).

There are also certain legal activities that are not covered by the legislation. These include:

- paying costs to a legal professional;
- providing legal advice;
- participating in litigation or a form of alternative dispute resolution;
- will writing;
- work that's funded by the Legal Services Commission.

If you're subject to these regulations, regulation 27 of the legislation states exactly when due diligence must be carried out. Careful checks must take place when:

- establishing a business relationship;
- carrying out an occasional transaction that amounts to €15,000 or more (approximately £13,000 or more);
- you suspect money laundering or terrorist financing may be taking place;
- you have doubts about the accuracy or adequacy of the documents that have been provided to you.

In the process of these checks, you will need to do three main things:

1. Verify your clients' identity with the help of a reliable independent source (usually this will be with a valid passport or driving licence).
2. Identify whether there's a beneficial owner who is not your client. If this is the case, you will need to make all reasonable efforts to verify the identity of this beneficial owner and understand the ownership and control structure of the group or organisation you're working on behalf of.

3. Assess the purpose and intended nature of the business relationship or transaction, and, where appropriate, obtain further information on this.

If you're working with a corporate entity, the due diligence process is slightly different. You'll need to obtain and verify:

1. The name, company number or any other registration details.
2. The address of its registered office and – if different – the principal place of business.
3. Which law it's subject to.
4. The company constitution or other governing documents.
5. The names of the individuals who sit on the board of directors (or equivalent managing body) as well as the names of the senior persons responsible for operations.

Finally, regulation 31 of the legislation notes that if you can't complete sufficient due diligence checks for whatever reason, you will not be able to work with the client.

8.10.2 Enhanced due diligence checks

There are certain situations where enhanced due diligence measures must be applied. These circumstances are set out in regulation 33(1) of the 2017 regulations.

Enhanced due diligence checks must be carried out for any transaction or business relationship involving:

- a person established in a high-risk country;[1]
- a politically exposed person, or a family member or known associate of such a person;
- any other situation that presents a higher risk of money laundering or terrorist financing.

There are a few different ways that you can carry out enhanced checks. These include:

- seeking additional, independent and reliable sources to verify the information or documents your client has provided you with;
- taking additional measures to better understand the background, ownership structure and financial situation of the client (and any other parties involved in the transaction);
- exploring the purpose and nature of the business relationship of all parties in order to confirm the intended transaction is consistent with this;

[1] The Law Society maintains an up-to-date list of these high-risk countries at: **www.lawsociety.org.uk/support-services/advice/articles/european-commission-list-of-high-risk-third-countries**.

- carrying out increased monitoring during the course of your business relationship, especially when it comes to the scrutiny of any possible transactions;
- checking the credit or electoral history at the address the client has provided.

8.10.3 Simplified due diligence checks

In some circumstances, the 2017 regulations (specifically regulation 37) allow for simplified due diligence checks to be carried out when you're satisfied the business relationship or transaction presents a low risk.

This might be because the client is a publicly owned enterprise, or perhaps because they're based in a low-risk geographical area.

In these cases, you may feel comfortable confirming and verifying the basic details of the client and not carrying out any further checks or investigations.

8.10.4 Further things to note about the due diligence process

Money laundering costs the UK over £100 billion each year (**www.nationalcrimeagency.gov.uk/news/national-economic-crime-centre-leads-push-to-identify-money-laundering-activity**), so it's not surprising that the government takes compliance with anti-money laundering regulations very seriously.

If you're found not to be complying with these, it's very likely that your regulator will take action against you.

In order to prevent this – and to protect your firm from involvement in criminal activity – it's important to ensure that you've carried out a thorough firm-wide risk assessment. This will include ensuring that you and your staff, if you have any, are fully aware of what's required by the legislation and that you know how to spot warning signs. Both this risk assessment and your firm's anti-money laundering process should be properly written down and reviewed regularly.

If you work with cryptocurrencies, it's worth being aware that – at the time of writing – the government is currently intending to bring these into the scope of anti-money laundering and terrorist funding legislation.

8.11 Obtaining feedback

One of the key ways to work on continuously developing your customer service offering is to make obtaining feedback part of your usual process. Doing this is the best way to understand how well you're doing and whether there are areas where you need to improve.

8.11.1 How to obtain feedback

Some clients will be very vocal in telling you about their experiences. However, clients tend to only volunteer feedback when they feel they've had a really good or a really poor experience. The more valuable feedback is often from those in the middle ground, and to get this you'll need to be proactive.

The most straightforward way to do this is to send a post-matter review form, questionnaire or survey to each client after their matter has been closed. Some clients won't respond, but others will likely appreciate that you're embracing client views and consider their feedback important. This also illustrates that your firm's primary aim is to solve their problems and fulfil their needs, not just to take their money.

It's also important to be aware that client feedback is everywhere. In addition to sending out client feedback surveys, you'll also need to do regular search engine and social media searches for the name of your firm. Collecting this will enable you to find out what people are saying about you, your firm and your brand. It's also likely to be worth your time to set up a Google Alert for your name and/or the name of your law firm. You will then receive an email whenever Google detect a new mention of you or your firm online.

If you do discover that a client has complained about your service online, you may want to contact them to invite them to tell you more about why they were unhappy. Though this might not be a very enjoyable task, it will probably be a worthwhile one. Remember: you need to be open to bad feedback in order to learn and improve.

8.11.2 Dealing with complaints

Though we should all strive for every client to be happy with our service, in reality you'll never be able to please all people all the time. Occasionally, all firms will receive a complaint. Sometimes these complaints will seem unfounded; other times you'll need to accept and own up to the fact that you've made a mistake.

Formal complaints

The first thing to remember here is that you need to make it easy for clients to make a complaint. Paragraphs 8.2–8.5 of the SRA Code of Conduct for Solicitors, RELs and RFLs require all legal service providers to establish, maintain or participate in a complaints handling procedure. Equally, Section D1.1 of the Code of Conduct in the BSB Handbook states that clients must be 'provided with appropriate information about redress, should know that they can make a complaint if dissatisfied, and know how to do so'.

This means you must ensure that you have an appropriate procedure in place for complaints to be recorded and handled. You'll need to inform clients in writing at the time of engagement (usually as part of your terms of business) about how they can complain and to whom they can do so. This should include any rights they have to complain to the Legal Ombudsman.

Informal complaints

Of course, not all complaints will come as formal letters or emails. A complaint can be any expression of dissatisfaction, such as a client phoning to point out that something has not been dealt with within the promised timescale. Though this might not need to be recorded as a formal complaint, the client is still clearly unhappy.

We'd recommend that this type of informal complaint is dealt with as promptly as possible. If it isn't, you may find the problem just gets bigger. Even if the client doesn't formally escalate their complaint, they're likely to go on to share their dissatisfaction with their networks.

Dealing with a complaint

Once a complaint has been made, it is your responsibility to ensure it is fully dealt with. This is important both for the reputation of your firm and in terms of regulatory requirements. Paragraph 8.5 of the SRA Code of Conduct for Solicitors, RELs and RFLs states that: 'You [must] ensure that complaints are dealt with promptly, fairly, and free of charge.' Section D1.1 of the Code of Conduct in the BSB Handbook makes clear that 'complaints should be dealt with promptly and the client kept informed about the process'.

In bigger firms, you may want to nominate a certain member of staff to investigate and respond to complaints. If you're a freelance solicitor, or if you have only one or two members of staff, this is likely to be your responsibility. It is a requirement for all responses to be sent within eight weeks, and these must confirm that the complaint has been fully understood, set out any action that will be made in response to the complaint and explain how this decision has been arrived at. If there's evidence of a delay or poor service, appropriate action might be issuing an apology or offering a reduction in the bill.

In the case of more serious complaints, you'll need to discuss the matter with your professional indemnity insurers before you decide on any action. If a complaint has been made that accuses you or your firm of negligence, you should never make an admission of liability without the prior agreement of your professional indemnity insurers.

Once you've concluded your firm's internal complaints procedure, the response you give to your client will need to include information about their right to complain to the Legal Ombudsman. This must include the contact details for the ombudsman along with the relevant time frame for them doing so.

Complying with the Legal Ombudsman

The Legal Ombudsman is an independent body established under Part 6 of the Legal Services Act 2007. The Legal Ombudsman exists in order to resolve service complaints about lawyers in a fair and impartial way. The Legal Ombudsman Scheme Rules (**www.legalombudsman.org.uk/wp-content/uploads/2019/03/Scheme-Rules-1-April-2019.pdf**) explain the framework for operations and the maximum amount of compensation it can order, which is £50,000 excluding interest and costs.

Individuals, small businesses, charities, clubs, societies, associations, and trusts with a turnover of less than £1 million can all make complaints to the Legal Ombudsman. They can do this within six months of a law firm's final response to a complaint.

There are some exceptions to this timescale. The Legal Ombudsman is able to investigate complaints about poor service that's occurred since 5 October 2010, so long as the complaint is referred within six years of the problem occurring or within three years of the complainant finding out about it.

Solicitors are required by paragraph 7.3 of the SRA Code of Conduct for Solicitors, RELs and RFLs to co-operate with the Legal Ombudsman in investigations about legal services. However, solicitors do not have to provide information that you could not be compelled to provide in civil proceedings before the High Court, such as information covered by legal professional privilege.

In addition to this, please note that paragraph 7.5 of the SRA Code of Conduct for Solicitors, RELs and RFLS states that you must not attempt to prevent anyone from providing information to the SRA or to any other body that exercises regulatory, supervisory, investigatory or prosecutors functions, which includes the Legal Ombudsman.

Barristers are also legally obligated to co-operate with the Legal Ombudsman.

The process of a Legal Ombudsman investigation

Once a complaint has been accepted by the Legal Ombudsman, the complaints procedure will begin. The steps of this are as follows:

1. An investigator will ensure that the complaint received is clearly defined.
2. The investigator will contact you and request information and documents regarding the complaint.

3. The investigator will endeavour to resolve the complaint informally, known as an informal resolution. If your firm agrees to an informal resolution, details of the complaint will not be published on the Legal Ombudsman's website.
4. If an informal resolution is not possible, the investigator will draft a report based on their investigation. This report is called the preliminary decision.
5. You will be able to respond to the preliminary decision if you disagree with it, though you will need to provide clear reasons for disagreeing. The investigator's report (and your response, if you've made one) will be referred to an ombudsman.
6. The ombudsman will consider the investigator's report and any responses from you or the complainant. They will then make a decision. This will be based on their opinion of what is fair and reasonable considering the circumstances of the complaint. They will give a full explanation of this decision. All cases that require a final decision will be published on the Legal Ombudsman's website for a year.
7. The complainant will be asked if they accept the decision. If they do accept it, then you will be bound by it and must follow the actions ordered. Both parties will then be banned from starting and continuing legal proceedings that relate to the complaint. As the Legal Ombudsman is a public body, the only way to challenge a final decision is to go through judicial review proceedings.
8. If the complainant rejects the decision, or doesn't respond within the given timeframe, then the ombudsman will consider the case closed and you will not need to follow any actions ordered in the final decision.

When a case is referred to the Legal Ombudsman, a case fee of £400 is payable by the law firm. This will be payable at the end of the proceedings, but may be waived if the case is settled in favour of the lawyer (this means that the case is resolved for the same or less than what was offered by the lawyer). However, this will only be the case if the Legal Ombudsman is satisfied that the lawyer took all reasonable steps under their complaints procedure to try and resolve the complaint themselves.

The case fee can also be waived if:

- the complaint is out of the Legal Ombudsman's jurisdiction;
- the Legal Ombudsman dismisses the complaint;
- the complainant abandons or withdraws the complaint (so long as the Legal Ombudsman is satisfied that you have taken reasonable steps under your own complaints procedure).

8.11.3 Making changes based on feedback

If you want to maintain high standards of customer care, you'll need to consistently listen to your clients and make adjustments to your delivery of legal services where necessary.

Being proactive in this way will help you to strive to fully meet the needs of your clients and stay ahead of the competition.

CASE STUDY 8: NEIL BROWN

Neil Brown is a solicitor and the managing director of decoded.legal. decoded.legal specialises in internet, telecoms and tech law. Neil is also a fellow of the Society for Computers and Law.

When did you launch your law firm?

I started decoded.legal in January 2016.

How much knowledge and experience did you have before you started?

I had never worked for, let alone run, a law firm! I trained, qualified, and practised in-house for 11 years. My wife had worked for a US law firm in London as a trainee, and worked in-house for six years after qualification.

That is one our core strengths: we know what businesses need because we've both been there.

What would you say is the most important lesson you learned in the first few years of your firm?

Be yourself. You've presumably started a firm because you have something to offer, and that something – whatever it might be – makes you stand out from competitors.

By all means try things. In fact, definitely try things. Stick with what works and change what doesn't. If you don't experiment, you'll never know.

And, by all means, take a look around, and see if what seems to be working for other firms might also work for you. But don't try to be another firm.

Can you tell us how you learned this particular lesson?

By worrying.

By worrying that when we gave simple, practical advice, rather than pages and pages of research with a list of options at the end, we were doing something wrong.

By worrying that we were missing a trick by preparing plain English agreements, tailored to the business's needs based on years of sector experience, rather than PLC templates with some blanks filled in. Or by suggesting that, rather than spend money on legal advice on dealing with something, they could consider making certain technical changes and avoid the situation entirely.

By worrying that being 'me' on our firm's website, and social media accounts, and in person, didn't project the 'right' image for a law firm.

In essence, worrying because we were doing something different.

I was confident that what we were delivering – risk aware, pragmatic guidance, and documents which were moulded to each client's needs – was exactly why people were coming to us. At the same time, I was worried that, because that was not necessarily the type of advice I had seen numerous other lawyers give, that I was not hitting the mark.

Reassurance came from speaking with clients. Yes, they said, this was what they wanted. And, so far, it seems to have worked, and I make a point of routinely checking with each client that we are delivering what they want.

(Sure, there are times when what they want is the detailed research note, and some options, and a conversation or two to guide them through, but typically they know when that's what they want and they ask specifically for it.)

What changes did you make as a result of this?

I started worrying ever so slightly less.

And I always, always, ALWAYS put myself in the client's position for each piece of work, each phone call, each piece of advice, and think 'were I the client, what would I have wanted out of this?' And if I'm not sure, and it's not clear from the client's request, I ask them.

In what way do you think this made you a better law firm owner?

It gives me the confidence to 'be myself' across all aspects of our business. I've lost track of the number of times people have said 'wow, you're nothing like the lawyers we used before'. And, since they typically pay me and hire me again (our model is nearly all repeat business), I'm guessing they mean it in a positive way. Hopefully.

We try stuff. Sometimes it doesn't work so well, so we try something different next time. Sometimes it does work, so we keep on doing it. Sometimes it really doesn't seem to make much of a difference either way, but I enjoy it, so we keep on doing it.

We focus on delivering what our clients want, and, wherever we can, identifying when what they say they want doesn't align with what they actually need, and checking in with them about it.

What advice would you give to a new law firm owner about this?

It's your business. Do it your way. (And keep enough money on hand to pay your bills and your next eye-watering indemnity insurance premium.)

Chapter 9

Establishing systems and processes

Establishing effective systems and processes is a vital part of preparing your law firm for success. Putting these routines in place for your business will enable you to quickly and easily handle repetitive tasks.

This might take the form of a standard new client induction procedure or a checklist to complete before you mark each matter as closed. You will also need to think about systems and processes for things including handling the firm's finances and maintaining your office space.

Systems and processes don't have to be complicated. In fact, it's usually better if they're not! Taking the time to explore the best way of doing things right at the beginning of your firm's journey can pay dividends in the future.

9.1 Why are systems and processes important?

9.1.1 The benefits of systems and processes

Systems and processes are important because they make things easier for you and your staff on a daily basis. Processes help to make sure tasks are being done in the most effective way possible and that everyone knows what's expected from each task.

Streamlining the firm's activities in this way will likely make your job easier and more enjoyable. It will ensure that you're not wasting valuable time (or head space) on repetitive tasks when you could be focusing on fee-earning. Over time, robust systems and processes will increase your profit margins.

When you develop systems and processes for your business, you will be setting a solid framework you can rely on in the future.

This will:

- reduce worries – you won't need to worry about basic tasks or compliance being forgotten once you've set up workflow systems that incorporate these;

- underpin how you deliver legal services – effective systems and processes will positively impact the client experience;
- ensure consistency – robust systems and processes will ensure your firm works effectively all the time, not just on good days.

The fundamental thing to keep in mind here is that it's your systems and processes that will keep your firm organised. This organisation is the key to running an efficient and effective business that's open to and ready for growth.

Systems and processes will ensure that you always know where things are, at what stage each file is at and that you don't waste time unnecessarily on basic tasks. They will also ensure that any staff members or consultants are able to quickly understand what's expected of them and how to effectively contribute to the running of the firm.

9.1.2 Are there any downsides to establishing systems and processes?

Though we wouldn't say there are downsides to this way of working, we do want to point out that this task is very much front-loaded. Though effective systems and processes will save you considerable time and headspace in the future, you will need to invest a fair amount of both to get them properly set up.

It's also important to remember that systems and processes aren't a check-box that can be ticked off once in your business and never considered again. Getting the right systems and processes in place is an ongoing process in itself. It will involve a fair amount of trial and error, and even when you think you've found something that works . . . it may not work as well when you have twice as many staff or five times as many clients.

Our advice here would be to not get too caught up in making systems and processes 'perfect' right from the outset. You could spend a week designing the perfect client intake form before you launch your firm, but you may well not gain a full understanding of what information the form should collect until you've taken on a dozen or more clients. *Be prepared to change and adapt as you go.*

If you're right at the start of building your firm, you may not think there's much point in going through this exercise. When you're doing everything yourself it may not seem like a good use of time to write things down as formal systems and processes. However, trust us when we say this *is* likely to be a valuable exercise.

Writing things down and formalising them as you go will mean you have a solid framework in place for when your team gets bigger or your client numbers rise. It will also save you a lot of time when your first member of staff does start, as you will have a ready-prepared 'how to' guide to get them started.

9.2 What should you consider when introducing systems and processes?

When you begin to experiment with systems and processes, we recommend you think carefully about these five factors:

1. Simple is often best.
2. Flexibility is vital.
3. The task of creating processes can be delegated.
4. Processes need to be scalable.
5. The task needs to fit the process, not the other way around.

9.2.1 Simple is often best

Some of the best systems and processes are the simplest ones. Not all tasks require specialist tools or software. Especially in the beginning, you'll likely find the simplest answer is the best one.

For example, if your firm handles matters for dozens of clients every month, it might be appropriate for you to invest in some all-singing-all-dancing case management software. However, if you're only working with two or three clients per month, you might find that a large whiteboard above your desk will help you keep track of things perfectly well.

9.2.2 Flexibility is vital

You and your staff are not robots. If you set in place systems and processes that are too rigid, you're all likely to get frustrated. There will always be circumstances or clients that don't fit the mould; you'll want to be able to adjust your systems and processes accordingly.

It's also important to encourage staff to use their own initiative and creativity. This won't be possible if you've made your firm's systems and processes inflexible. The danger of inflexible processes is that staff will become so accustomed to following them exactly that they'll lose sight of the reasoning behind them and will no longer be able to identify when something needs to be changed or adapted.

You'll also want to be able to make bigger changes to the way your systems and processes work as time goes on. For example, you might be the only person who manages the firm's finances in the early months or years, but if and when you delegate this task to an accountant, you'll need to be able to adjust your systems and processes to suit.

9.2.3 The task of creating processes can be delegated

If your law firm has staff, you'll be able to delegate the task of creating systems and processes. Giving each person the responsibility for certain systems and processes can ease the burden on you and help to encourage fresh ideas and innovation.

If you decide to work in this way, make sure you discuss as a team what you're hoping to achieve with your new or refined processes to ensure everyone is fully onboard and understands what's expected of them.

9.2.4 Processes need to be scalable

It's likely that your business will grow and change significantly within the first few years. With this in mind, you'll need to build processes that are designed to be scalable as your workload increases and/or your team numbers grow.

Having these scalable systems and processes in place will help you to ensure that you keep service and client satisfaction levels high, even during periods of high-growth.

9.2.5 The task needs to fit the process, not the other way around

This is perhaps one of the most important considerations here. Don't fall into the trap of letting the systems and processes dictate how you do things! The process needs to fit how you want to work, not the other way around. If you're using a tool or piece of software you have to work around, it's probably not the right tool.

Instead, aim to start with the objective and then work backwards. Building the entire process around the objective will help you achieve the task faster and more efficiently.

9.3 What processes do you need and how should you design them?

When you set out to design systems and processes that are right for you and your firm, our advice is to let go as much as possible of those you were expected to follow at your previous firm.

You're likely to be setting up a very different firm than the one you left. It will be younger, and therefore more modern. It will also probably be smaller (for the time being, at least). It may have a different service offering, target market or style of customer service. Though some of the processes you're used to may be appropriate for your new firm, in most cases there will be a way of doing things that's better suited to your new circumstances.

All systems and processes should start from a place of understanding of the nature of your firm. Consider the vision and mission statement you have put together: what sort of firm have you set out to create?

- Will you be a forward-facing firm, or more traditional?
- Will you be endeavouring to maintain a small carbon footprint?
- Will you have additional team members?
- If you do have team members, will they be working on-site or remotely?
- Will you be utilising as much technology as possible?
- Will you be offering a certain level of service to your clients?

The answers to these questions will help you to start to understand what type of framework your law firm will require. For example, if you want to cut carbon emissions and go paperless, you'll need to create digital processes that make this possible. Equally, if you plan to work with remote team members, you'll need to make sure that client files and management information are stored in a way that they can be securely accessed from anywhere.

If you're not sure where to start with systems and processes, our advice would be to look at the very basic things you do every day. For example:

- How should initial email enquiries be dealt with?
- How should incoming post be processed?
- How will appointments and meetings be arranged?
- What is the right process for opening a client file?
- What are the things that need to be done before a file is closed?
- How will you store both open and closed files?
- What is your process for sending and chasing up invoices?
- How will you track important data?

Ultimately, any system or process you implement must have two main objectives:

(a) to make a task easier for you;
(b) to improve the experience for your client.

It might help to consider which systems and processes you need in terms of the following headings, which we expand on below:

- managing administration;
- handling office practicalities;
- IT and practice management software;
- file storage;
- client matters;
- accounts and billing;
- human resources (HR);
- compliance and security;
- health and safety;
- marketing;
- risk assessments and emergency planning.

9.3.1 Managing administration

Administration usually refers to any activities related to the running of a business, such as paperwork or finances. If you're running a law firm, you'll also have administration that's related to the running of each matter or case.

The administrative burden that comes with running a legal business can be mind-boggling. In addition to managing the everyday business and client-related admin, you'll also need to keep on top of the demands and compliance tasks placed upon us by regulators.

Administration is classic 'busy work'. You could very easily keep yourself occupied with these sorts of tasks from morning to night, but this would be unlikely to move your business forward or bring in any actual paid work. It's important to be clear on which administrative tasks are necessary, which can be delegated to members of staff or contractors, and which don't actually need to be done at all.

As the business owner, your time will be much better spent on fee-earning work or on bringing new clients in. It's rare that an administration task genuinely needs to be done by you, or even someone who is physically present in your office. In order to ensure that your business is sustainable and that you have space for growth, you'll need to delegate essential administrative tasks to other members of your team, whether they're employed staff or virtual workers. So long as you have effective systems and processes in place, you'll be able to do this safe in the knowledge that tasks will be completed exactly as they should be.

When you first launch your firm, it will likely be very easy to manage your administration yourself. This is for three reasons:

1. You may not have much fee-earning work to do, so will have plenty of time.
2. The simpler your systems (as they're likely to be in the beginning) the less associated admin there is.
3. It'll all still be a novelty.

These three factors will change over time. Even if you genuinely enjoy administrative tasks, they're likely to start to lose their appeal over time.

As your firm starts to get busier, your time will become more and more valuable. You will need to explore how you can safeguard your time for important client matters. If you're not ready to take on additional staff, or if that isn't something you have plans for at all, you'll still be able to delegate administrative tasks. Virtual assistants, freelancers and contractors can all be fantastic resources for this.

A flowchart for tackling admin

If you're struggling to manage your administration workload, you might find this flowchart useful. It will help you to determine whether the task really needs to be done, and, if it does, how it could be handled.

Table 9.1

Is the task really necessary? Ask yourself: is it essential for customer care or compliance? Is it helping you to build your client list or improve your services? Is it necessary for organisational purposes? Is it something that still works for your firm? Is it just busy work?
If no: Let it go and find something more useful to do with that time.
If yes: Is there a better way of doing the task? Ask yourself: are you doing it the best way? Or are you just doing it the way it's always been done? Is the process flexible enough? Is it taking more time to do than it should? Is it fiddly or frustrating? Do you have all the tools you need to effectively do the task? Are all the steps of the task necessary? Do you have technology or software already in place that might make this task easier? Could the task be fully automated? Is there a simpler way?
If yes: Can the task be delegated? Ask yourself: do you need to be involved in the process at all? Could someone else record the information/fill in the form/deal with the enquiries/authorise the payment? If you do feel you need to be involved, could you hand over responsibility for the majority of the task and just approve it at the end?

9.3.2 Handling office practicalities

In addition to managing your actual fee-earning work and the associated administrative tasks, you may find that there are additional office practicalities that need to be managed.

What these look like will vary greatly depending on the type of workspace you have.

If you work from home . . .

If your business is based at home, office practicalities probably won't be too much of a concern for you. Yes, you'll need to make sure your desk is tidy, your office is clean and the fridge is stocked, but these are things that would happen as part of your usual housework routine anyway.

However, there will still be some factors to consider here. You'll need to make sure you're fully prepared in terms of office consumables such as stationery, branded goods and printer cartridges. Instead of having to go out to purchase these items as and when they're needed, you may want to consider whether it would save you time and headspace to set up a subscription service instead.

If you work from a co-working space or serviced office . . .

If you work from a managed space, the majority of your office practicalities will be handled by the management team. This is the major benefit of choosing this kind of workspace over a more traditional office set-up.

Of course, you'll still need to manage office consumables as mentioned above. Depending on the particular set-up of your workspace, you may also need to think about snacks, lunches and hot drink supplies.

If you have traditional office premises . . .

This is where you'll really need to start thinking about office practicalities and how they can best be managed. This is likely to need quite a shift in your mindset if you're moving from a home office or managed office.

Don't underestimate the importance of setting up processes to manage these practicalities. Investing some time right at the beginning to consider how these things can most effectively be done will likely save you a great deal of time in the future.

The practicalities you'll have to consider include questions such as:

- Who will clean the office?
- Who will make sure office consumables are stocked up?
- Who will make sure there's milk in the fridge?
- Who will wash the dishes?
- Who will accept responsibility for deliveries?
- Who will answer the phone?
- Who will top up tea and coffee supplies?

The answers to these questions should not all be you! Unless you're the firm's only member of staff, you should be delegating most – if not all – of these jobs.

Even if you are a sole practitioner, you don't have to do all of this yourself. Engaging a cleaning firm or setting up regular deliveries are easy ways to reduce some of this pressure.

9.3.3 IT and practice management software

Whether or not your firm has an office is likely to be less important in terms of productivity than what kind of digital set up you have. This is an ideal place to bring in systems and processes, as there are so many ways that technology can make your daily work life easier.

We're lucky to have so many different options in terms of software and applications. However, it can be tempting to invest in far more than you need!

When setting systems and processes, you'll need to think very carefully about what you need from technology, and then explore the different options that are available for achieving your outcomes. It makes more sense to do things this way around, rather than just exploring what's on offer and what other firms are using, as you'll then be sure you're only opting for software you really need. Too many software options can complicate your systems and processes and stop them from being streamlined and efficient.

We suggest you formalise the digital tools you'll use in each situation. This can simplify things and make sure everyone is on the same page. It can also prevent you from having to make a decision every time the circumstance arises, as you'll already have a process in place.

For example, it may be helpful to create a digital process for:

- **Making appointments:** Which calendar software will you use for appointments? Who will have access to make appointments? Will you allow clients to see meeting availability/book themselves in on your website?
- **Meetings held via video chat:** Where will you set meeting reminders? How will you collect the client's username/other credentials? Which video-call platform will you use as standard?
- **Sharing key reminders and information between team members:** Will you use email for this, or is there a more effective way to communicate? Could an application such as Slack make it easier for everyone to be up-to-date? Would a firm WhatsApp group be a simpler option?
- **Maintaining subscriptions:** Which digital subscriptions will be necessary for your firm? (E.g. HM Land Registry or Certainty National Will Register). Where will subscription details be stored? Will you set digital reminders for updating and renewing memberships?
- **Sending out paperwork digitally:** Will you send paperwork digitally via email rather than in the post? How will you manage electronic signatures? Where will digitally signed paperwork be stored?

- **Managing casework:** Will you invest in case management software? Can you afford to be tied in to a long contract? Is there a simpler way you can manage casework digitally? Could free or inexpensive task management software work for you instead?

9.3.4 File storage

The traditional process of file storage is to have a bank of filing cabinets somewhere in your office. Some law firm owners still prefer this – but there are some significant limitations to this.

Many law firms now aim to have an entirely digital file storage system, though – depending on the area of law you practice within – it may not be possible to go completely paperless.

Considerations for physical file storage

Only keeping physical copies of files is likely to have some downsides and limitations. Printing absolutely all files to store in this way would take up a lot of space, which would not be very practical for most home offices or in co-working spaces. There are also environmental concerns for this.

Physical file storage could be a problem if you were unable to access your usual workspace for a period of time. For example, how would you manage if your office building was inaccessible due to unexpected maintenance work or an unprecedented situation such as the COVID-19 lockdown? You also need to be aware that you could lose all the files if anything happened to your file storage area, such as a fire or flood.

If you believe that physical file storage is still the right option for your firm, we strongly advise you to make sure you have a digital back-up.

Certain types of law firm will need to store original documents for clients. This will usually be copies of wills or lasting powers of attorney (LPAs). If this is something your firm is going to offer, you'll need to ensure that you have ample file storage space.

We'd also recommend setting a process in place to scan and save digital copies of all documents. This would mean that you were able to reconstitute certified copies of documents should anything happen to the originals.

Managing electronic file storage

You'll need to consider how you'll manage the storage of electronic files, either as an accompaniment to physical storage or as an alternative.

Each time you open a new file on your computer, you'll need to determine where to save it. Setting yourself a framework for this will make things easier every time you need to save a file and every time you need to open one.

Formalising the framework of where certain files are saved and what naming convention you use will make sure that your digital files are consistent and properly organised. This will also make it far easier for multiple people to work with the same group of files on a shared drive without having to constantly ask each other where to find certain documents.

It's also vital for you to consider the security measures that are in place for accessing these files. Presumably your computer or laptop itself will have a password, but you may also want to set up access passwords for any sensitive folders or documents. You'll need to think about whether all staff should have access to all documents via a shared drive, or whether you want to make files available to only the personnel who are involved with them. We'd also suggest that you implement the option to wipe hardware remotely. This could be invaluable if your laptop is lost or stolen.

We'd recommend having a risk-assessment meeting with an IT professional to ensure that your files are stored as securely as possible.

Cloud-based storage

In addition to saving electronic files to your computer's own hard drive or an office shared drive, you may also want to consider the possibility of cloud-based storage. This can be beneficial for two main reasons:

1. It can make files available to you and your team members wherever you are, whatever computer you're using.
2. It will act as a back-up to protect files should anything happen to your computer.

If you decide to set up a cloud-based storage system, you'll need to put processes in place for managing this. Just as you would with files on your own hard drive, you'll need to formalise rules for how files are named and what order they're stored in.

You'll also need to ensure that all cloud-based files are safely and securely stored; you may want to consider two-factor authentication if you're dealing with particularly sensitive files. Again, we'd recommend consulting with an IT professional to make sure the system you choose is a secure option.

Another big consideration for cloud-based storage is the question of how your files will be transferred there. You'll need to put systems and processes in place that will ensure that the files that need to be saved in the cloud make it there.

You could handle this by:

(a) saving all files to the cloud;
(b) having clear procedures for which files should be saved in the cloud;
(c) setting up an automatic upload of files.

Should you aim for a paperless office?

In recent years there's been a big drive towards the idea of a paperless office. This can be a great option both in terms of the environment and for keeping your office more streamlined and minimal. It can also help to save money on postage and to ensure that the systems and processes you create are more fully scalable.

It's hard for established firms to achieve this ideal, as they generally have such a big volume of paperwork already. The benefit of being a new firm is that you can make the decision to be paperwork-free right from the start.

If you would like to be paperless (or as paper-free as possible) make sure you set up your systems and processes with this in mind.

You will need to create processes for:

- sending documentation digitally;
- holding only digital copies of client files;
- sharing digital files with staff members;
- scanning any paperwork that comes in right away, then shredding and recycling the originals.

9.3.5 Client matters

Systems and processes are just as important for how you manage case work and client matters as they are for more administrative tasks.

Your firm should aim for consistency: all clients should benefit from the same great service. Establishing well thought out systems and processes will help you to ensure that this is the case.

To understand which systems and processes are required, you could start by taking one of the more straightforward client matters you deal with and breaking it down into individual tasks.

For example:

1. Responding to an initial enquiry.
2. Making an appointment for an initial client meeting.
3. Collecting the client data you need to open a file.
4. Taking client instructions.
5. Sending out a client care letter and terms of business.
6. Completing legal work related to the matter (this stage will, of course, need to be broken down into much smaller tasks, depending on the kind of matter it is).
7. Sending final documentation.
8. Calculating and sending a final invoice.

Once you have a sense of all the stages involved in each matter, you'll be able to see where there are repetitive tasks that could be made easier by establishing systems and processes.

A good starting-point for this might be to draft standard letters for each stage of the process and to organise these in a logical way. You could use a numbering system for these standard letters to make them as easy to find as possible.

If you're a litigation practice, we'd also recommend implementing systems and processes for allocating key dates. You'll have to carefully consider whether you need a full case management system for this, or whether you can use a free phone or desktop task management application.

9.3.6 Accounts and billing

Ensuring that your firm is paid for the work you do is obviously very important. Many business owners find this side of things overwhelming – but setting up practical systems and processes for this can help reduce the strain.

Your main objectives for accounts and billing processes will need to be:

1. Sending out clear, easy to understand invoices in a timely fashion.
2. Keeping track of invoices and whether or not they've been paid.
3. Sending polite reminders for unpaid invoices.
4. Processing and recording payments.
5. Paying any invoices you're sent promptly.
6. Tracking expenses and receipts.
7. Regularly balancing your books.

Just like any other area of your business, once you've broken this down into small tasks you can start to build a framework for managing them. Make decisions on who will be responsible for completing these, when they need to be done and what tools will be needed to support this.

For example, there are some excellent options for affordable business accounts software online. Something like this will help you to keep track of business spending as well as create and send invoices of your own.

You might decide that the most effective way to manage accounts and billing is to pay invoices as soon as you receive them and send them as soon as each client matter is closed. Alternatively, you may want to diarise a weekly finance hour where you deal with any invoices or closed client matters from that week all at once. Or, of course, you may decide that you'd rather outsource the whole thing!

Whichever type of working makes the most sense for you, formalising these routines will help to make sure nothing gets missed.

9.3.7 Human resources

When your law firm is ready to take on staff, you'll need to begin developing HR systems and processes. We suggest you take some time to put these in place before you take on your first team member, as it'll likely make the process much easier.

In the first instance, you'll need to consider:

- developing an on-boarding process;
- how you'll manage staff training and continuing professional development (CPD);
- how you'll keep track of staff hours, holidays and sick days;
- how you would deal with misconduct or complaints;
- how you will manage payroll.

Again, this is an area it might make more sense for you to consider outsourcing. HR professionals have a great deal of specialist knowledge. There may be no financial benefit to you managing all of this yourself when you would be better off focusing your time on fee-earning work and paying an HR consultant to work on your behalf.

9.3.8 Compliance and security

Compliance and security is a big area of concern for law firms. On top of general legislation that applies to all businesses, such as the GDPR, you will also be subject to additional legal-specific regulations, many of which will be determined by your regulatory body.

It's really important for all law firm owners to ensure that they have a good general knowledge of what's expected of them in terms of compliance. Once you have this understanding, you'll then have to put systems and processes in place to ensure compliance tasks become a natural part of the daily routine of your firm.

You'll need to consider how you'll manage compliance and security processes such as:

- **Digital data security:** Will files be accessible on the cloud? Who will have access to documents? Would it make sense to password-protect certain documents? Are you using the most secure digital storage options possible? If using the cloud, have you checked how the tools you're using affect the ownership of documents?
- **Access to physical files and documents:** Where will hard copies be stored? If you work from home, do you have space for this in your home office, or will you need to store them in another area of your home? If you have a co-working space or shared office, will you need to invest in secure storage space to keep hard copy documentation in? How will this be organised so that nothing is lost? Will filing cabinets be locked? Who will have access to the keys?
- **Data protection and GDPR:** What kinds of client data are you storing? Have clients consented to you holding this data? How will you provide

clients with a copy of all their data if they request it? How often will you revisit your firm's data and GDPR policy?

- **Data protection and remote working:** Have you considered how working from your laptop, tablet or phone might put you at risk of breaching the Data Protection Act? Have you put policies and guidelines in place to make sure client data is treated correctly even when staff are working remotely?
- **Anti-money laundering:** Will any of the services you offer be subject to money laundering legislation? What kind of checks will you do to mitigate the risk of money laundering? When will you check clients' ID? How will you manage these checks if you don't plan on meeting with clients face-to-face? Will you use a third party organisation or tool to make this easier?

We understand that compliance tasks can feel overwhelming, especially at the beginning. The goal here is that your systems and processes will keep this under control and make it much easier to ensure all compliance and security boxes are being carefully ticked.

If you are feeling overwhelmed by this, please do remember that the processes you have in place need only be proportionate to the current situation of your firm.

9.3.9 Health and safety

As a law firm owner, it will be your responsibility to make sure that everyone who comes into your workspace is safe. This is set out in the Workplace (Health, Safety and Welfare) Regulations 1992, SI 1992/3004.

If you work from home on your own, this is likely to be far less of a concern than if you manage your own office with a team of staff and regular client visits.

Wherever you work, you'll need to make sure your premises are well-maintained and looked after. You'll also need to be aware of any problem spots, such as steep steps, and make sure staff and visitors are notified accordingly.

If you have a small firm, you'll need to keep a first aid kit easily accessible on the premises. Larger firms will need to have a first aid kit and a dedicated first aider.

You will need to conduct a risk assessment for your workplace and have a health and safety policy in place.

9.3.10 Marketing

You're likely to need to spend a good deal of your time on marketing and advertising. It's very easy to get caught up in this, and you may find you are investing more time in this area than you realised.

In addition to managing the time you're spending on marketing, you'll also want to make sure that what you're doing is an effective use of that time. Ideally, you need to make as much of an impact as you can with the smallest time investment possible.

To do this, you'll need to work extremely efficiently. And efficiency, of course, requires smart systems and processes.

Consider setting a framework for things such as:

- how often you post on your business' social profiles;
- what type of content you should share;
- how much time you will spend engaging with other social users;
- how often you or your staff will attend networking events;
- what you expect from staff when they are out representing your firm;
- what your brand guidelines are;
- how you will advertise online;
- what kind of traditional publications you will consider advertising in.

9.3.11 Risk assessments and emergency planning

There are all sorts of things that could happen in your business that you probably don't want to think about. Though it may feel uncomfortable, taking the time to tackle risk assessment and emergency planning when things are good is something you may well be grateful for in the future.

A well-prepared firm will have a plan in place for whatever eventuality might come up, including:

- fire;
- flood;
- theft;
- power cuts;
- boiler breakdown;
- computer viruses;
- phone outages;
- computer breakdown;
- staff illness;
- emergency building maintenance;
- plumbing problems.

The systems and processes you put in place for these eventualities don't need to be complicated. It could be as simple as putting together a list of suppliers and contractors that staff could get in touch with if there was a problem. You may also want to put a plan in place for what might happen if everyone needed to work from home for a certain period.

It's important to consider what would happen to the business if you were unwell or incapacitated. This is a key consideration whether you're leading a team of staff or whether you are a sole practitioner.

- **For firms with staff:** Would your staff know who you would delegate responsibility to? Who would be able to access secure client files, banking or management information?
- **For sole practitioners:** Who would be able to notify clients about your absence on your behalf? If you'd be relying on a spouse or partner to do this, would they know where to find a list of who to get in touch with?

Whatever the size or type of law firm you run, we'd suggest taking some time to ensure that you have an appropriate will and LPA in place in case of these eventualities. You may also want to consider the possibility of 'buddying up' with a trusted legal professional with the agreement that you would both step in to help should anything happen to the other.

Nobody wants to think too carefully about the risks of running a business, but taking the time to put plans in place for these eventualities can be a very valuable exercise. Not only will this mean there's something in place for if you do find yourself faced with disaster, you may also find it reassuring to know this is the case.

Risk assessments for anti-money laundering regulation

The SRA requires all firms that are subject to the Money Laundering, Terrorist Financing and Transfer of Funds (Information on the Payer) Regulations 2017, SI 2017/692 to have a risk assessment in place in relation to this.

Regulation 18 of the legislation sets out the requirement for a firm-wide risk assessment policy for this as well as for individual client or matter risk assessments. This regulation also states that self-employed barristers and BSB entities who work within the scope of the regulations must take reasonable action to identify and assess the risk of money laundering and terrorist financing.

Your policies should take into account the size and nature of your practice, as well as the type of clients you usually act for.

You should also make sure that your risk assessment is up-to-date with the latest SRA guidance and addresses the risk factors named in the money laundering regulations.

These risk factors are:

- who your firm's customers are (including whether you work with politically exposed persons (PEPs));
- the countries and geographical areas you work in;
- the services your firm provides;
- the kind of transactions your firm engages in;
- how you deliver services.

There's no rule that says you must use a specific format or template for your risk assessment. However, you may find it helpful to use a template as a starting point, as this can help to make sure nothing vital is missed. You'll also want to refer to the SRA's most recent guidance on this (**www.sra.org.uk/solicitors/guidance/ethics-guidance/firm-risk-assessments**).

9.4 Creating a process manual

The task of formalising systems and processes across the board for your firm is a big one. You shouldn't underestimate how much work this is likely to entail . . . but you also shouldn't underestimate how valuable the finished framework will be.

9.4.1 Benefits and uses of a process manual

Once you've developed your systems and processes and got them all in writing, we suggest you put them all together to create a process manual. This will be a complete guide on how things are done in your law firm, which will be useful in a number of ways:

1. Team members can refer to the process manual when they need to know how to do a certain task. This will save time in the long run as you and other more senior staff won't have to answer questions about processes all the time.
2. The process manual can play a key role in any disaster recovery plan (see **Chapter 16**) you have for your firm, as it will contain all the information an individual would need to step in to someone else's role.
3. A process manual can help to reduce insurance premiums.
4. A process manual can help to demonstrate compliance.
5. A process manual can play a key role in the on-boarding process of new staff.

9.4.2 Things to remember about your process manual

It's important to remember that your process manual is a living document that will need to be updated regularly. As processes change and develop, this will need to be reflected in the manual. It will only be a useful resource if it's current and up-to-date.

With this in mind, we suggest you make it clear to everyone in the team that ideas and opinions on all processes in the manual are very welcome. You may also want to invite all members of staff to contribute to it; guidance on processes is likely to be most useful if it's been put together by the person who generally carries out that process. Delegating in this way can also make the mammoth task of putting the manual together more manageable.

You'll want to make sure the process manual is easily accessible to everyone who might need it. We suggest saving an electronic version of the document in a location that's accessible to the whole team. You may also want to have a printed copy available, though this might not be practical if it's updated regularly.

We believe that putting together a complete process manual is an excellent way to remind yourself to continually think about improving systems and processes. This can improve the experience of your clients as well as the working experience of yourself and your team members.

Remember: the best businesses adapt as they go according to the changing needs of their clients. Your process manual should be no different.

CASE STUDY 9: PETER WRIGHT

Peter Wright is a solicitor and the managing director of Digital Law UK Ltd. Digital Law UK Ltd specialise in online, data and cyber law. Peter is also a board member of the Law Society and an author.

When did you launch your law firm?

It was officially recognised by the SRA at the beginning of 2014.

How much knowledge and experience did you have before you started?

I had 10 years' PQE and had worked in high street, large national and multi-national firms. I had no experience working for myself, but my wife, who is an American qualified attorney, did. She had opened and run her own firm in the States for over a decade, had been a consultant for others who wanted to start firms and had written a manual for the American Bar Association on how to open and run a law firm. Her knowledge and experience were a big help.

What would you say is the most important lesson you learned in the first few years of your firm?

One that my wife warned me about but I had to learn for myself (as she said she did as well) was that I should stick to the area of practice I had chosen for my firm.

Can you tell us how you learned this particular lesson?

I took on a collections dispute as a favour for a client of ours as it seemed straightforward and I had done that type of work in the past. Although it was ultimately successful, it was far from straightforward as there were court errors that took a very long time to resolve and required me to research and call on other colleagues to figure out the best way to solve them. I spent way more time on this matter than I should have and it created tremendous stress. I had not started the firm with any intention of conducting any contentious work and this experience confirmed that original decision had been the correct one. Never again!

What changes did you make as a result of this?

I developed a clear scope of work that we would take in for fee earning.

We've always had a very clear brand based on the type of work that we handle, but when we launched our new brand in 2018, the website and marketing collateral doubled down on the message in terms of what we are here to do. From that point we have been much clearer with clients from the outset regarding the work that we will handle ourselves and the work that will be referred out or handled in partnership with external specialists.

The only exception to this now is when we take on pro bono cases that our apprentice solicitors can learn from which can be supported by our other niche firm colleagues.

In what way do you think this made you a better law firm owner?

It has reduced my stress tremendously. I am a better firm owner and boss to my staff because I am not having my focus pulled away from the primary work our clients need.

What advice would you give to a new law firm owner about this?

Ask for help. It can be very lonely and we often feel as solicitors that we cannot show 'weakness' by admitting we do not know something. As a law firm start-up, you will need to ask for help from colleagues and organisations that are set up to help law firms and small businesses.

Chapter 10

Managing the firm's finances

It's not possible to run a successful law firm without having a strong understanding of how business finances work. This is an area that can be hard to get to grips with, as it's something you likely had very little to do with when you were employed.

In fact, the financial aspect of being a business owner or sole practitioner may be one of the most difficult adjustments you'll need to make. Instead of a pre-agreed salary simply landing in your bank account at the end of each month, you'll be responsible for ensuring that money comes in and out of the business in a manageable and sustainable way.

In order to do this, you'll need to ensure that you have an excellent grasp of your budget.

10.1 The importance of making (and sticking to) a budget

We won't skirt around the issue: finances are a make or break factor in business. This is true whether you're in your first few months or whether you've been in business for decades. Ultimately, if you can't bring in enough money to cover your necessary outgoings and living expenses, your law firm is not going to survive.

10.1.1 Why have a budget?

Setting a budget and sticking to it can help you keep a tight handle on your finances and ensure that things are going in the right direction. With a budget, you'll have a much clearer understanding of:

(a) what you can afford to *spend* on insurance, utilities, equipment, software, office premises, personnel, marketing, etc.; and
(b) how much money you need to be *bringing in* to meet your minimum business costs and standard of living.

With a clear budget in place, it will be much easier for you to make informed decisions about spending and re-investment in your business. It will also help you to determine the level of fees you need to be charging and how many clients you will need to engage each month.

10.1.2 Producing a budget and cash flow forecast

You will have produced an initial budget and cash flow forecast as part of your business plan (see **3.4**; there is an example budget and cash flow forecast in the **Appendix**). These documents show your projected income and expenditure for your first year in business. This initial budget will be a useful document to work from in the first instance, though it's completely normal to have to adjust and adapt it as you go.

Once you come to the end of your business' first 12 months, you'll be able to look back at the real figures from this time (rather than just the forecasted ones) and use this as a basis for setting a cash flow forecast and budget for the following year.

When you set out to produce a cash flow forecast, you'll need to consider:

- your previous year's figures (if you have them);
- that in your first year your expenses may well be greater than your income;
- factoring in your own withdrawals from the business.

What tools will you need?

Budgeting may well be a task you dread, but there are tools available that can make it a much less daunting prospect.

In the first instance, you may want to start with something as simple as a spreadsheet application. We've said it before and we're not against saying it again: simple is often best, especially in the early days.

If you want to take things up a level, you could look into using specific business budgeting software. There are some inexpensive options on the market that can substantially reduce the work required to summarise and analyse financial data.

Even if you use sophisticated software to do the analytical stages of producing a budget for you, it's worth noting that you'll still need to go through the same careful thought process to produce the data to be entered into the application in the first place.

10.1.3 Considering contingencies and seasonal patterns

It's important to aim to stick to your budget. In order to do this, you'll need to build your budget with contingencies built in.

Generally, you would do this by setting a maximum spend limit for each area in your business (think marketing, software, staff, consultants, consumables, etc.) and then ear-marking a contingency fund on top of this.

Though this is really important, it can be hard to do this in your first year of business. Your contingency fund might need to come from pre-existing savings, or perhaps a portion of any business funding you received. In future years, we recommend you ensure you pay into a contingency fund when things are good in order to mitigate unexpected expenses.

These could include things like:

- having to repair or replace broken digital equipment;
- an unexpected increase in utility costs;
- having to pay an excess for an insurance claim;
- covering your own living expenses during a period of low income;
- having to cover necessary repairs to your workspace;
- enduring an unexpected period of low business.

With this in mind, we also think it's important to consider that your budget needs to have a seasonal pattern built in. You're unlikely to be equally busy during an entire 12-month period – some times of year are usually associated with quieter periods. You'll need to make sure that your budget accounts for this and that there won't be any nasty surprises (or, at least, as few as possible!).

10.1.4 Regular reviews

It's important to review your budget and cash flow forecast regularly. You may want to do this monthly, perhaps when you perform monthly bookkeeping reconciliation tasks. This will allow you to see in real-time how you're performing in comparison to the forecast, and if any areas of spending need to be reined in or reassessed.

Assuming your budget allows for it, you may want to get professional advice on your budgets and cash flow forecasts. This can help to ensure your firm is flexible and robust enough to withstand changing financial circumstances and market conditions.

Effectively managing your cash flow and budget is a vital exercise for staying in business. Doing this will show how well you're meeting you goals and targets and will allow you to take corrective action if it's needed.

This process is also vital for minimising financial risk and showing a true picture of how your firm is performing monthly, quarterly and annually.

10.2 Billing and invoicing

It may be a cliché, but the phrase *time is money* is never more relevant than with law firm billing and invoices. After all, as discussed in **Chapter 8**, as legal professionals we are essentially charging for our time.

As a law firm owner, you need to be fully on top of this aspect of the business. Whatever type of billing cycle you decide to use, it's really important that you stick to it. No one else is going to remind you about this: your clients are unlikely to chase up your invoices!

Quite simply, the longer you delay sending an invoice, the longer it'll take for you to be paid. Work in progress (WIP) needs to be converted to invoices on a regular basis in order to bring cash flow and revenue to the firm. It's no good knowing you're owed for ongoing work if your bank account is empty when bills need to be paid. Cash flow is vital and you need to ensure you manage this proactively.

10.2.1 Effective billing and invoicing

Once you have set good systems and processes in place, it should be reasonably easy to stay on top of this process.

We recommend that you:

- **Endeavour to be as descriptive as possible on invoices:** Remember that clients are often not as familiar with legal terms as you. For example, rather than listing 'drafting pleadings' on an invoice, 'drafting defence and counterclaim' is likely to better illustrate the value of the work. This should lead to less confusion about fees.
- **State payment terms clearly on your invoice:** Your invoice should tell clients when you expect to be paid and give them all the information they need to be able to do so. Make sure you include your account number and sort code on your invoice so clients don't have to ask you to provide this separately.
- **Make it easy for clients to pay:** The easier it is for clients to pay your invoices, the quicker they're likely to do so. You may want to consider setting up facilities for taking payments on your website, over the phone or in person via a card payment machine.
- **Automate payment reminders:** Most invoicing software applications will allow you to set up automated reminders for overdue invoices. How regularly you set these reminders is up to you and will probably be a case of trial and error to find out what your clients respond to best.
- **Consider taking payment up front:** Many law firms now ask for payment up front. This may be 100 per cent of the total for fixed fee matters, 50 per cent of the total, or perhaps just a deposit or retainer for work that's billed on an hourly basis.

In order to ensure that invoicing and billing practices run as smoothly as possible, this will need to be reviewed on an ongoing basis. It's important to keep track of how many days it usually takes for you to collect payment on invoices. Accountants often refer to this period as either 'debtors days' or 'lock up'. Ideally, you will have the shortest 'lock up' period possible.

You may want to consider whether it makes sense for your business to charge interest on late payments. It's perfectly acceptable to do this, so long as this is set out clearly in your terms of business documentation. We'd also recommend adding a reminder about this on your invoices. If you're considering this for business-to-business contracts, you may want to refer to the Late Payment of Commercial Debts (Interest) Act 1998, which can be used to add statutory interest to outstanding payments above bank base rate.

However, you may decide that the additional administration required for this just isn't worth it. The relevant interest payments may be too small to bother, and many late-paying clients simply won't agree to pay it.

10.2.2 Recording time

Capturing and recording time effectively could very well be the difference between a firm that is performing well and a firm that is not.

As any lawyer who is familiar with this process knows, it takes discipline to record time immediately – or as soon as possible – after a task has been completed. If you don't stay in the habit of doing this, trying to recreate time entries after the fact often results in imprecise billing.

In many cases, this can result in fee earners under-billing, as they may forget many of the smaller tasks they've done. Though it may not be a big deal to have forgotten a six-minute task here or there, if this is done consistently it can quickly add up to a more significant loss.

Alternatively, you may find that fee earners recreating time entries can *overestimate* time spent on client matters. Though this doesn't mean the firm is losing revenue, it does mean that clients are being billed an amount that isn't commensurate with the actual legal services rendered. This could result in a breakdown in trust between a firm and its clients.

Creating a time recording policy

We recommend that you put together a time recording policy to ensure all the recording that takes place in your firm is consistent. This is just as important for sole traders as it is for larger firm owners.

In order to do this, you will need to consider questions including:

- When should time be recorded?
- What tools will be used to record time?
- Will you need to be connected to the internet in order to use recording tools?
- Which administrative tasks will you consider 'chargeable' and 'non-chargeable'?
- Will you charge for a whole additional unit of time if, say, less than a minute of that time unit has been spent?

10.2.3 Considering value-based pricing

There's a school of thought that says that pricing should be based not on how long it takes a legal professional to complete a job, but on what the value of the job is to the client. This is particularly relevant to legal work that's done in order to save clients' money.

For example, a deed of variation would be valuable to a client as putting one in place would likely save them a significant sum of money on inheritance tax. Instead of charging based on the hours of work the legal professional has put into a document like this, what if they charged a percentage of the clients' savings?

10.2.4 When should you bill your clients?

Traditionally, all legal professionals would invoice their clients once the case or matter was concluded. Though this is certainly a simple way of doing things, it's not always practical.

The problem with this model of invoicing is that you won't have any income from a case or matter until after it's completed. This may not be too much of a concern for smaller matters that will be concluded within a matter of weeks. However, if you're involved in much longer-term matters or cases, it could be months – or even years! – until they're fully concluded.

There's also the question of whether or not you should complete time-consuming work entirely on trust. Especially with new clients, you may not feel confident putting in a lot of hours without taking some form of monetary deposit.

You may wish to address these two concerns by adopting a slightly different billing model. Some law firms now ask for 50 per cent of the cost of work on account before they start. This can work well when you're offering services at a fixed rate.

If you're working with longer-term contentious matters or cases, you will want to carefully consider how you'll manage this side of things. Your clients will probably welcome this, as it's likely to be easier for them to pay for your services in instalments rather than to receive one large bill at the end of the proceedings.

You could choose to bill on a monthly basis for any hours recorded during that month. Alternatively, you could accept a sum of money on account, and work until this money is used up. If the matter is not yet concluded, you would then take more money on account to cover the next work period.

Using a loan company to fund contentious cases

Contentious cases and litigation can be difficult for law firms to navigate financially. Typically, clients will not expect – or have the means – to pay until their case is concluded. This can be a problem for legal professionals as it's not unusual for cases to take a year or more to get to this point.

There are options to consider in these circumstances. Some finance companies will now fund contentious cases on the client's behalf, which means the legal professional could be paid upfront. However, the client would have to be thoroughly advised on the nature of the loan and any associated interest costs before this was decided on as an option.

10.3 Cash flow

When we talk about business finance, we talk a great deal about cash flow. There's a key reason for this: a healthy cash flow is absolutely vital in business. Whether or not your law firm has easy access to cash will determine its financial health and how likely it is to survive and grow.

10.3.1 What is cash flow?

Though very important, the concept of cash flow is actually a very simple one. Essentially, having a sustainable cash flow is ensuring that there is more cash coming into your business than there is going out in order to ensure a healthy balance at all times.

Cash flow is not always the same thing as having plenty of client work. It's perfectly possible to be rushed off your feet with client work and yet not have enough money coming in to maintain cash flow.

This is more likely to happen for law firms who are:

(a) working on longer-term client cases or matters such as litigation or probate and are not invoicing clients for work done on a monthly cycle;
(b) not invoicing promptly for work done and not consistently chasing up invoices.

10.3.2 What is working capital?

Another term that's important to understand in the context of cash flow is working capital. Working capital refers to the difference between your firm's current assets and its current liabilities. For example, working capital is the money in your business bank account, minus any rent costs, tax payments, staffing costs, etc.

Working capital is important as this is the money your firm has at its disposal to pay its day-to-day expenses. This is the money you can consider investing in marketing or spending on consultancy or contractor fees.

10.3.3 How do owner drawings affect cash flow and working capital?

The money you, the owner, withdraw from the firm is usually referred to as owner drawings. How common it is for you to do this will likely depend on how your business is structured. If your firm is a limited company, you will generally pay yourself a regular salary (discussed at **10.4.3**). However, if you're a sole trader, you will likely take regular owner drawings from the business in place of this.

It's important to understand that owner drawings affect your firm's cash flow and working capital. The drawings you make in any period should never exceed profits and should always be kept within the amount of actual cash that's being generated.

Obviously, you will need to cover your own living expenses, but do be careful that you're not taking money out of the business that will be adversely affecting cash flow sustainability. A cash flow forecasting application – along with advice from your accountant – can help you work out the amount you can withdraw from your business each month. If you're not happy with this amount, you will need to consider what variables you can change to increase this amount.

10.3.4 What about VAT payments?

If your business is VAT-registered, you'll need to charge VAT on top of your fees. You will then collect this VAT on behalf of the government and file a quarterly VAT return, whereby this money will then be collected in by HM Revenue and Customs (HMRC). The threshold to register for VAT is taxable turnover of £85,000.

It's good practice to separate the 20 per cent VAT payments from your usual income as soon as possible. This money should never be considered as part of your working capital. If it is, you may well run into problems at the end of the quarter when the money is due in and you no longer have it.

10.3.5 The benefit of adopting a cash accounting approach

Broadly speaking, you can keep track of your firm's financial performance by way of two different approaches.

1. **The accruals approach:** When you measure accruals, you are measuring all the income for your firm, whether or not it has actually been received. This means you are recording the financial benefits of all work in progress and completed work. Though this can be a useful metric, there's a danger that it won't accurately represent what's in your bank account!
2. **The cash accounting approach:** In this approach, income is only recorded once it actually arrives in your bank account.

Most small businesses operate on a cash accounting basis. This helps you to be better aware of cash flow and how to maximise this. It also ensures that you're making decisions on owner withdrawals or salary considerations based on your actual working capital.

As your firm grows and is more able to invest in tools and software, you may want to consider buying into financial software that can easily highlight where your firm is in terms of both of these financial approaches. Being able to access this data regularly is likely to be beneficial for your firm.

10.4 Salaries and fee earning expectations

In most law firms, salaries account for the biggest chunk of expenditure. This is likely to be true for you whether you're heading up a firm with a dozen staff or whether you're a freelance solicitor. In both cases, the total salary you will need to pay your staff and/or yourself is likely to be the firm's biggest monthly outgoing.

With this fact in mind, it's really important to make sure you fully understand what the total salary costs will be in your firm each month and how you're going to ensure you meet these costs – even if the only salary you'll be paying is your own.

10.4.1 The difference between fee earning staff and non-fee earning staff

Within a law firm, there are two key types of staff. The first type is fee earning staff: defined as legal professionals who take on paid matters for clients. The second is non-fee earning staff. These are generally administrative and support staff that help in the overall running of the firm.

An appropriate number of fee earners is obviously vital for the success of a firm However, non-fee earners are also very important. A sustainable law firm will endeavour to reduce as much as possible the non-fee earning work that needs to be done by fee earning staff. Administrative staff such as personal assistants (PAs) and secretaries are fantastic resources for this, as are more specialist professionals such as those who work in marketing or HR.

How big your firm is will obviously be the decider for how many non-fee earning staff is the right number for you. Whether you're a two-person team or a 200-person team, do keep in mind that it's important to ensure a correct balance between the two. The fee earners will need to bring in enough income to cover their own salaries as well as that of the non-fee earners.

It was once generally accepted that a law firm should have one secretary for every fee earner, but this is no longer necessarily the case. It's not unusual for firms to have up to 10 fee earners for every administrative assistant. Where the right balance lies for each firm will depend on factors including:

- what kind of work the firm is doing;
- how much automation is involved in the process;
- how matters are billed;
- what fee-earning targets are in place.

10.4.2 Fee earning expectations

The number of fee earners you have in your business will determine how much income you are able to bring in. Traditionally speaking, each fee earner was expected to bring in three times their own salary over the course of the year.

This would be used for three purposes:

1. One-third to cover their own salary.
2. One-third to go towards the firm's overheads (including premises and the salaries of non-fee earners).
3. One-third would be profit for the firm.

However, this is another traditional formula that many law firm owners have reassessed. Though some smaller firms still work on this rule of three, other firms now expect each fee earner to earn four or five times their own salary.

Setting targets for fee earners

In order to ensure that each fee earner brings in a sustainable income, most firms put targets in place. These targets usually relate to how many billable hours are logged per day. If you decide to use this as a model, it's important to consider how many billable hours each fee earner will need to complete in order to bring in three (or more!) times their salary.

For example, if each fee earner is given a target of seven billable hours per day over 44 working weeks producing 220 working days per year, this would equate to a total of 1,540 billable hours per year.

Of course, a target of seven hours is likely to be achievable in a bigger firm with plenty of administrative support. In a smaller firm where fee earners are having to do administrative tasks themselves, the time this takes will need to be accounted for. Many firms set a target of five or five-and-a-half hours of billable hours per day, which allows for time spent on administration and firm meetings.

Targets can be really helpful even for start-up law firms and sole practitioners. Having a target for the number of billable hours that need to be recorded in order to hit your yearly forecasted income can help keep staff motivated and on track.

If you're a sole practitioner, or even if you're the director of a bigger firm, it might make sense to set your billable hours target on a weekly basis rather than a daily one. This will help to allow for the fact that some days might be more focused on tasks related to growing the business rather than simply working within it.

In order to be effective, targets need to be two things:

1. **They need to be aspirational.** You want to inspire and encourage your fee earners (or yourself!) to work to their full ability.
2. **They need to be achievable with the hours your staff are contracted for.** It would be unreasonable to ask fee earners to notch up eight billable hours a day if you're only paying them for seven.

Just like all other aspects of your law firm, targets should be monitored, reviewed and adjusted as necessary. You will also need to consider how these will be enforced. You might aim to address this in monthly or quarterly staff review meetings. Or perhaps you could link how well staff are meeting fee earning targets to whether they receive a bonus or annual pay increase.

Alternatively, you could consider a more technological approach: some firms use case management software that doesn't allow fee earners to log off until they have notched up the required billable hours for the day!

10.4.3 Paying yourself a salary

You will, of course, need to make a living from your business. How money comes out of the business and into your personal bank account will mainly depend on the business structure you've chosen.

If you're a sole trader, you'll be able to easily make owner withdrawals from the business as and when working capital allows.

If you're the director of a limited company, you'll have the option of paying yourself a salary (just as you would any other employee) and/or taking dividends from the company. The most tax efficient way of doing this is likely to be a mix of both.

The benefits of paying yourself a salary are that:

- You'll be able to access the benefits of the national insurance (NI) scheme, including sick pay, maternity pay and accruing years on your pension (so long as you're paying yourself above the lower earnings limit) (**www.gov.uk/government/publications/rates-and-allowances-national-insurance-contributions/rates-and-allowances-national-insurance-contributions**).
- You'll benefit from your personal tax allowance.
- Salaries are an allowable business expense, so this will reduce the amount of corporation tax the business will need to pay.

In order to pay yourself a salary, you'll need to make sure that your business is registered as an employer with HMRC. You'll also need to ensure that you're complying with all payroll management responsibilities set out under HMRC's Real Time Information (RTI) rules. Your accountant will be able to advise you on all of these regulations and which ones are relevant to you and your firm.

How much should you pay yourself as a salary?

It's generally not recommended that you pay your full living costs through a director's salary. This is for tax efficiency reasons. Instead, you may want to pay yourself a low salary that allows you to benefit from your personal tax-free allowance and NI benefits, while also ensuring that you or your company don't have to pay any NI costs for your salary.

This would mean paying yourself a low salary, probably in the region of £8,000 per year. This would be above the Lower Earnings Limit – which would give you the benefit of accessing NI benefits such as sick pay, maternity pay and accruing years towards your pension – but below the NI primary and secondary threshold – which would require you to pay employee NI contributions as well as employer NI contributions.

What about dividends?

When your company makes a profit, you can choose to use that profit to give a dividend to shareholders. In this context, 'shareholders' simply means the owners of the company. If you're the sole owner of the company, any dividend you issue will be just for you.

The benefit of paying yourself in this way is that there is a lower personal tax to be paid on dividends. Essentially, money that comes to you as a dividend will be subject to less tax than money that comes to you as part of a salary (assuming this salary is over and above your annual tax-free allowance).

10.5 Holding client money

As legal professionals, we have the honour of being trusted to look after our clients' money. This is a responsibility that needs to be taken extremely seriously. If a lawyer was to fail to keep money that was entrusted to them safe, this would have far-reaching consequences for their clients, the reputation of their business and for the wider reputation of the whole profession.

More than 7,000 law firms in England and Wales hold money on behalf of clients (**www.sra.org.uk/risk/outlook/priority-risks/client-money**). There are protections in place (such as a firm's own professional indemnity insurance or the SRA's Compensation Fund) that cover eligible financial losses for clients. However, the result of a potential loss of client money would not just be financial.

10.5.1 Why do law firms hold client money?

It's common for solicitor firms to hold client money, though barristers are not allowed to do this. Client money is defined as any cash, cheques, drafts or electronic transfers that are received and held by a firm in the process of them providing legal services.

Examples of this include:

- client damages that have been awarded as part of a personal injury matter;
- mortgage funds that a lender have sent to a legal professional;
- money that's being held to pay nursing home fees for a client where the solicitor has been appointed as a Court of Protection deputy;
- any money a client has sent to cover fees (or unpaid expert fees) that have not yet been billed for.

10.5.2 Where should this money be held?

Many law firms who regularly do this sort of work operate a separate client bank account. This means that money they are holding on account for clients is kept completely separately from their firm's main business bank account.

If you're working in an area of law where you'll need to routinely hold client money, you'll almost certainly be required by your regulator to maintain a separate client account. You'll also need to be audited each year in accordance with the SRA Accounts Rules.

The only exception to this is Rule 2.2 of the SRA Accounts Rules 2019 (which came into effect in November 2019). This regulation states that while you can hold and receive client money without a client account, this can only be for advanced payment for fees and unpaid disbursements that are incurred by you on behalf of your client and for which you are liable. In order to do this, you will need to ensure that your client has been given sufficient information about where their money will be held.

Could you outsource the handling of client funds?

There's a growing interest in the idea of outsourcing the task of handling client funds to a third party. This is covered in Rule 11 of the SRA Accounts Rules 2019, which allows firms to use third party managed accounts.

According to Rule 11, if your client is using a third party managed account, your firm will essentially not be holding or receiving client money themselves. This can reduce some of the pressure of compliance in this area, and may be a good option for new firms, smaller firms, or firms who only need to hold client money occasionally.

Third party managed accounts could potentially reduce risk for law firms. With this in mind, it may be the case in the future that professional indemnity insurance costs could be reduced as a result of using them. If this was the case, this is a method which would become more widely used by the profession.

10.5.3 Keeping client money safe

It's never been so important to take precautions to keep client money safe. The growth of cybercrime and phishing scams mean that you must stay vigilant at all times. Though certain types of legal professionals might be more of a target than others (such as conveyancers and so-called 'Friday afternoon fraud', which involves tricking buyers into sending house purchase monies to a fraudster's bank account rather than the law firm's client account, and typically takes place on a Friday as this is when most completions are made, and gives the fraudster the weekend to avoid detection) this is something that everyone needs to guard against.

In order to protect client money, you'll need to ensure that you give your firm's client account details at the start of the retainer and tell the client that these will not change during the course of your work together.

Make sure clients know that they should:

- not transfer money to any bank account that doesn't match the details you gave them;
- clarify any instructions or notifications of changes with you personally by telephone;
- speak to you by telephone before and after they send any money (this allows you to confirm that the transaction request is genuine and that the money has arrived safely).

These requirements and safety precautions should all be set out in your client care letter or terms of business documentation that you send out at the beginning of each working relationship.

10.6 Audits

Regular audits should be a key part of your financial strategy. They can help to avoid complaints, financial mismanagement and fraud, but they're often avoided as they're so time intensive. However, setting aside the time to do this will often reveal whether your processes are effective, and whether there are any under-performers in the firm.

In addition to the inherent value of regular audits, these will also be a requirement of your regulatory body and are something that professional indemnity insurers will want to see as part of your firm's risk management/reduction strategy.

10.6.1 The difference between internal and external audits

There are two key types of audit: internal and external. Though they share a name, these two functions are actually quite different.

Internal audits are undertaken by you or your staff members. Though these may include looking at financial details, they're mainly concerned with internal structures and processes. The aim of an internal audit is to ensure that your business is working as effectively as possible, and that there aren't any compliance issues that are being regularly overlooked. As the person, or group of people, doing the audit is already a member of your firm, they will not be expected to have any special training or qualifications.

External audits are different in a number of ways. Probably most importantly, they are carried out by a qualified professional who is not a member of your firm. This external auditor will be mainly concerned with looking at your business's finances, not your general working practices. An external audit would not usually be done more than once a year and would primarily be looking for discrepancies or losses within your firm's financial records.

10.6.2 What should an internal audit include?

In order to be as effective as possible, an audit needs to be a thorough and explorative process. This practice is also referred to as a file review.

For each client, you will need to consider:

- **Matter opening:** Have anti-money laundering and ID requirements been complied with? Was a conflict check carried out? Was a risk assessment undertaken? Was a client care letter sent out with a copy of the firm's terms of business?
- **Service delivery:** Are the client's instructions accurately recorded? Were they followed? Was the matter handled efficiently? How quickly were client communications responded to?
- **Billing and invoicing:** Was time accurately recorded? Has this recorded time all been billed for? Have you billed at the correct hourly rate? Was the invoice prepared correctly? Was the invoice sent on time? Was a billing guide sent out with the invoice?
- **Matter closing:** Was the client notified that their case was closed? Are there any outstanding monies to pay or return? Could the file have been closed earlier?

An audit such as this will reveal what's working well and if there are any areas that need to be addressed. Undertaking a regular internal audit will provide you with the opportunity to rectify any deficiencies that are keeping your firm from operating at its best. This should be regarded as time very well spent!

10.6.3 Should you do an external audit?

External audits are often done because they're required. Depending on your business structure, this may be something you would need to consider. You may also need to go through an external audit if you are applying for certain types of accreditation, such as Lexcel accreditation.

Even if you aren't required to have an external audit, you may want to do this for two key reasons:

1. If you want to have a full health check of your business's finances but don't think it would be an efficient use of your time or skills to do this yourself.
2. If you're concerned about possible discrepancies in your finances and that someone within your firm might be responsible for this.

An annual external audit can be a very useful tool to have in your arsenal of financial controls.

CASE STUDY 10: SHAZIA MALIK AND COSMA VENTO

Shazia Malik and Cosma Vento are the founding partners of V&S Solicitors LLP. V&S Solicitors work within a large range of legal areas including civil and commercial litigation, insolvency, debt recovery, employment, intellectual property and EU competition law. The firm has a team of dual-qualified solicitors and works with clients across the UK and Italy.

When did you launch your law firm?

We launched V&S Solicitors on 31st March 2009.

How much knowledge and experience did you have before you started?

Both of us came from City backgrounds (private practice and in-house) and between us we were qualified in three jurisdictions (England, Italy and New York). Collectively we had about 20 years' experience in areas such corporate, commercial, employment and cross-border transactions.

Whilst our work experience had equipped us with the skill set required to be lawyers with immense knowledge in our respective areas, running a business on a daily basis is not something either of us had expertise in when our firm was established.

What would you say is the most important lesson you learned in the first few years of your firm?

The most important lesson we learned in the first few years of running our business was that having an up-to-date business plan is essential. You can be the best solicitor in your chosen field, but without continually reviewing your business plan your firm may not survive the first three years.

A business plan will cover an array of topics including an analysis of your firm's unique selling point (USP) in comparison to competing firms, how you will manage your cases and how you will market your firm. However, the most imperative part of the business plan, from our experience, is the financial section.

A thorough understanding of the finances and constant planning with regards to revenue and expenses is crucial; the life of your business may depend on it. We quickly learned that we must know, at any given moment, the current financial situation of our firm and be able to recognise factors that may affect it in both the short and the long term. Needless to say, the circumstances surrounding this are ever evolving and, therefore, we inadvertently learnt to be adaptable.

Can you tell us how you learned this particular lesson?

A few years after inception, we wanted to make some financial investments with regards to our firm. These would have generated substantial income in the long term. However, had our financials not been reviewed periodically this investment would not have been possible.

By this point in time we had moved offices to the heart of the City and the businesses of some of our long-term clients had unfortunately closed down. It was a chance conversation with a solicitor at another law firm just six months after we incorporated that made us realise that our business plan, and the financial section in particular, needed to be amended after almost any change in our expense or revenue stream. This may seem obvious, but it is so easy to get caught up with the 'day job' of being a solicitor and neglect other areas of managing a law firm. This almost happened to us.

What changes did you make as a result of this?

As a result of our realisation, we made a point to review our business plan quarterly at the absolute minimum and, as mentioned above, immediately after any event that would cause an impact to our financials (no matter how insignificant it seemed). To be honest, this is not the most thrilling of tasks as it requires a substantial amount of time and effort to conduct such an exercise. Even at the time, we made the decision to stay on top of all financial changes instead of delaying their review, but it wasn't until a few years later that we truly appreciated the value of making this change.

In what way do you think this made you a better law firm owner?

We felt more in control of our situation and found this conducive to better future planning of the firm. Having an enhanced understanding and awareness of all the financial aspects of the firm allowed us to set realistic short-term goals in order to achieve our long-term goals. It also meant that even if there were teething problems in the beginning, we were equipped with the foresight of knowing where we were heading and how to get there.

This knowledge gave us a sense of comfort that 'winging it' just wouldn't have been able to.

What advice would you give to a new law firm owner about this?

Running a successful law firm is not just about having lots of clients and billing them. Yes, to the outside world maybe that is how the fruitfulness of your law firm is measured, but in truth the reality is very different. Of course, this is a key element to any business, but remember that it's just the top layer of your law firm.

In order to achieve a wonderful top layer and to do so efficiently and productively, an immense amount of 'behind the scenes' work must take place, not only at the outset but also on an ongoing basis. Even though it's not visible to the naked eye, you cannot disregard the foundations when building a beautiful dwelling. It provides you with a stable and reliable structure that will not come tumbling down like a house of cards at the first sign of wind.

We've found that everything works from the bottom up, so if the base is comprehensive, solid and thoroughly thought through, this filters all the way up to the top and makes everything else run more smoothly.

Chapter 11

Making technology work for you

It was once possible to start a law firm with absolutely no thought of computers, websites or digital marketing. This is no longer the case. Every start-up firm will need to have given a good amount of thought to their digital strategies and processes, even if their aim is to run a more traditional firm.

There's obviously huge scope here as to how much you and your firm are prepared to embrace technology. There are a myriad of opportunities for those who want to run more virtual-facing firms, though even those who want to be more focused on in-person interactions will likely need to utilise many of these.

11.1 Why technology is important for a law firm

The internet has only been publicly available since the 1990s, but since then it has changed our personal and business lives beyond recognition. We now rely on digital tools from pretty much the moment we wake in the morning; it's how we communicate with each other, how we research things, how we seek to access new services, and how we order anything from basic necessities to luxury goods.

Though there are always downsides to new innovations – the number of emails that pile up in your inbox each day might feel like a burden – online tools offer the promise of flexible ways of working and communicating. Harnessing these can make your life easier and your clients happier. They can also exponentially increase your firm's bottom line.

Ultimately, technology is a fantastic resource for saving time and money. Making the most of digital tools within your law firm can save you hundreds of hours and thousands of pounds a year, but to do this you'll need to ensure you have the right set up.

And herein lies the first challenge: getting to a point where you have worked out which devices, applications, case management systems and online tools work most effectively for you can involve a lot of trial and error.

11.2 Using technology in your firm

If you previously worked in a large law firm, you're likely to have had very different experiences with technology than you will in your start up. Previously, you may well have had access to IT support. You will also have used specific software packages.

Over time you will have become used to these resources and may well have used them more-or-less on autopilot. You'll know how to use the majority of the tools within them and have probably become adept at doing things very quickly. Because of this, it might seem natural to try and replicate the technology you used in your old firm in your new one.

If this is your current thought process, we invite you to reconsider. For one thing, your fledgling law firm will be in a very different position to your previous one. The digital set-up in your previous firm is unlikely to be exactly the right choice for where your current firm is now.

Instead, it will be a very useful exercise to go right back to basics and consider how to set up technology in your firm in the most beneficial way.

All firms are different and there is no one-size-fits-all approach here. Instead, we recommend starting with the basic foundations that will elevate your routine tasks and administration.

11.2.1 The basics

Every law firm will need to have basic technological building blocks in place in order to survive in the modern world.

This is true even if your vision for your firm is for it to be more traditional with an emphasis on face-to-face interactions. You will still need to use technological devices to complete work and manage client correspondence.

Though we can't give you a complete blueprint for where to start, we have put together a list of questions to ask yourself. Working through this list and answering each question should give you an outline for your firm's digital foundations:

- **Hardware:** Will you use a desktop computer or a laptop? Will you opt for PCs or Macs? What operating system will you need? Will you also invest in tablets?
- **Broadband:** Will you need to invest in a separate broadband package for your business? Or will you be able to use what is already in place in your home or co-working space? Have you tested the available broadband speeds? Will they be sufficient for your needs? Will you need to upgrade to fibre optic broadband? Will you need to install a lease line? What are the best deals available for if you do need to invest in a new contract or upgrade your current one? Are there any offers or flexible contracts available?

- **Telephones:** Do you already have a landline phone number, or will you need to request a new one? Will you have the landline phone number going directly to a physical landline, or will you permanently redirect it to your mobile? Will you use a standard phone line, or will you use a voice over internet protocol (VOIP) system? Will you use a landline phone number at all or just advertise your mobile number? Will you invest in smartphones for your employees?
- **Printing and scanning:** How often will you need to print, copy or scan documents? Will you have a big enough workforce to require a professional printer/scanner on contract? Will you be able to do everything you need with a simple home office model? How much can you budget for the equipment itself, as well as regular replacement ink cartridges? Could you find a local business who offer IT support who would be able to advise you on the right solution for you?
- **Word processing software:** What software will you use to create documents on your computer? Some PCs will come with a Microsoft Office package built in, but others will not. Consider whether you want to pay for desktop applications such as Word and Excel or think about whether there is a more inexpensive option. You may want to choose to buy a subscription to use Microsoft One Note in your browser. If you want to keep costs down, you could consider alternative free options such as Google Drive or Open Office.
- **Document storage:** How will you store electronic files? Will you be using web-based or computer-based word processing software? How will you structure your files and folders to make documents easy to find? Will you implement a naming convention for individual files and documents?
- **Legal software:** Do you need case management software right away? Could you use a simpler method for the first few months? If you do think you need one now, do you have a clear enough idea of what you need? Could you get software recommendations from other legal professionals who have a similar firm to you? Does the legal software you're considering have a long contract term? Could you make use of a free trial? Could you find a more flexible option, especially if you're not yet confident it's the right software for you?
- **Accounts software:** How will you keep track of your business income and expenses? What sort of software will you need to do this? Will the software you're considering be compatible with the shift towards making tax digital? Will any legal practice management software have accounts tools built in? Or will you have to choose accounts software that is compatible with your existing software? Could you start with a simple, inexpensive package until you need something bigger? Could you ask your accountant for advice?

What do you have available already?

One of the most sensible ways to determine how to use technology in your new firm is to consider what you have already and whether that could work for you.

For example, if you already have a PC with Microsoft Office package installed on it, it's likely that this will be all you need to begin with. This would mean you already have a word-processing tool (Word) along with spreadsheets (Excel), presentation software (Power Point), an email program (Outlook) and possibly a database tool (Access). Investing in alternative software when you already have this available might not be the best use of your initial business funds.

We suggest you spend a bit of time researching and experimenting with what you have. You may find that your existing hardware and software is actually up for doing the job you have in mind for it – certainly in the early days.

This isn't to say that you should continue using the same old software forever. The way you use technology in your firm should, of course, be reviewed and changed from time to time, just like everything else. But what you need when you start out is likely to be far simpler than what you may wish to explore a year or two down the line

11.2.2 Further opportunities

If your vision for your business is to run a modern, forward-facing firm, you'll likely want to look at further technological opportunities. These are likely to be particularly important if you plan to do a lot of your work remotely, or even if your plan is to run a fully virtual firm.

- **Video conferencing:** How do you plan to hold virtual meetings? Will you use free video call tools, or will you consider investing in paid video conferencing software? Does your computer have a good enough webcam and microphone built in, or will you need to invest in separate hardware for this? If you will be maintaining an office with a meeting room, will you equip this with video conferencing and presentation equipment?
- **E-signatures:** Will you be asking clients to sign documents electronically (where legally appropriate)? If so, what software tools will you provide for them to do this with? Is the solution you've found sufficiently streamlined and professional?
- **Cloud computing:** Will you be saving electronic documents to the cloud? Will you be doing this for back-up purposes? Or will you need to do this so that you, team members and clients can access documents from wherever they are in the world? What will be the best way to share documents and resources with your team? Could you get advice from an IT specialist about how to set this up?

- **Virtual receptionists:** Will you always be able to answer the phone yourself? Even if you can, would this be the best use of your time? If you can't get to the phone, how likely would your clients or potential clients be to leave a message? Would a virtual call answering service be a good solution for you?

One of the best ways to spot new opportunities for digital innovation in your firm is to consider what parts of your daily work routine you don't really enjoy doing or don't consider yourself to be very good at.

Once you've identified one of these tasks, ask yourself:

- Could it be delegated to someone else in your firm or to a contractor?
- Could technology help to make it easier and more manageable?
- Could the task be completely automated?

These questions will help you determine whether you could benefit from some additional digital experimentation.

11.2.3 How long will it take to get the digital side of your office established?

Once again, there's no one-size-fits-all answer for what kind of digital set up your firm will need. How you use technology, who will be involved and the tools you'll need in place is likely to develop into a strategy organically as your firm gets established. This, of course, will then need to be reviewed periodically.

Once you have a new piece of software/hardware/digital tool to try out, make sure you've considered all the implications of what you're trying to do. Before you sign up or download anything, make sure you remind yourself of the problem you're trying to solve or process you're trying to simplify.

An effective way to do this is to work through all the steps of the process or problem and map it out on paper. This will help you to see easily whether the new tool you have in mind will streamline the process or complicate it. You don't want to end up with the technology duplicating steps and therefore negating any time savings.

If you're still sure that the tool or software is the right solution after this exercise, you can feel more confident about getting started and investing the necessary time it will take to set it up.

You should usually expect a new digital tool to take a bit of extra time when you first implement it, both for you and for any staff members you might have. This is a natural stage of the human learning and adjustment process. Usually, you will all be able to work through this and come out more efficiently on the other side.

However, you need to remember that the end game is to make your life easier. If after four weeks of using the new system things are still taking longer or not working as promised, we'd suggest you go back to the drawing board. Most paid software packages and tools offer a month's free trial. These allow you a fairly risk-free chance to trial their offerings without committing to anything long term.

It's completely normal to go through this stage of trial and error in business. This will likely only get more common as your business grows! It's only through this kind of trial and error that your business will be able to evolve and innovate.

11.3 Offering legal services online

The idea of offering legal services online is a hot topic and will be for a long time yet. There is a great deal of discussion around what is and isn't permitted in a regulated market, but a lot of what is shared in response to this question can be misguided.

Whether you choose to offer your services face-to-face or online, the risk assessment process will be largely the same. You will need to determine:

- whether your planned services will protect the public in the way they should;
- whether you will be able to demonstrate compliance.

The reality here is that the marketplace has been irrevocably changed by the growth of the digital world. If you shy away from offering online services altogether you will likely find yourself lagging behind in what is an increasingly competitive legal field.

There will always be clients who don't like the idea of obtaining legal advice online. However, as time goes on this will no doubt shift and the normal expectation will be for online services to be readily available.

There are already numerous online legal service providers in the marketplace. Many of these are run by unregulated legal professionals (such as will writers or conveyancers), but please don't let this put you off if you are regulated.

The SRA has an ongoing conversation around looking to the future and offer regular conferences and seminars on the subject of the evolution of legal services. Many of these discussions centre around the idea of 'the unmet legal need' and how this has grown due to the vast reduction of legal aid services.

Providing legal services online may be a good option to help with this. This is because online legal services are likely to be more cost-effective for those who can't afford to work with a lawyer in a more traditional way. This would be in line with offerings being put in place by other service industries, on subjects as diverse as financial services and counselling.

More and more legal tasks can now be handled completely online. This includes applications that need to be made to governmental departments, many of whom now maintain their own legal services. It won't be long until all applications need to be completed online.

In order for your law firm to grow and flourish, it will be vital for you to keep up with these changes. It would be terrible to lose clients simply through being slow on the digital uptake, especially when the skills and expertise of legal professionals are still very much needed.

11.3.1 Selling legal templates and resources

Many of the common legal challenges are reasonably straight-forward. There's no reason why legal professionals shouldn't offer inexpensive automated online services related to these straightforward issues. This benefits the client as they can get quick, easy and affordable access to the information they need. It benefits the law firm as this is a passive income stream that can bring in limitless earning potential in return for only the initial time outlay.

In practice, this could look like offering templates for some of your most commonly requested legal documents such as:

- wills;
- parking ticket appeals;
- employment contracts;
- tenancy agreements;
- contractual or commercial agreements;
- loan agreements;
- letters of complaint.

Many legal providers charge a base fee for each template with optional add-ons. A common add-on in this context would be for a legal professional to look over the template once it's been filled in, or to add a specific clause to the document that isn't covered by the template.

You may also want to consider the possibility of charging for advice-based resources. Some legal professionals offer guides for purchase on specific legal areas such as civil claims or immigration. This could be done either in the form of an eBook or fact sheet, or you could potentially use a survey-based tool to allow the client to answer key questions about their circumstances in order to narrow down to the advice that is most relevant to them.

Of course, you would have to carefully consider any terms and conditions associated with clients using these services. Providing documents that simply need to be customised by the client does – to some extent – absolve the legal services provider from giving any actual 'advice' but you'll still need to carefully consider the scope of your services here. We encourage you to think particularly carefully about whether these offerings safeguard both your clients and your firm.

This can put some of the onus onto the client to ensure themselves that the document they've created from a template is actually fit for purpose. This will be an ideal scenario for clients in some cases, but other clients will need more support and will opt for a more personal service.

11.3.2 Chatbots and document assembly

There are ways to move some – or even all – of your existing legal services online. Doing this would still allow you to provide individual advice and support to clients but would give you the opportunity to benefit from using automation for routine process work.

If you provide non-contentious legal services, it's highly likely that you will regularly produce documents for review and approval for clients. Though these documents may well all be very similar in essence, many clients will still see the value of paying for an experienced professional to produce them.

Other clients might not see this value – or may have a smaller budget to work with – and will be interested in using an artificial intelligence (AI) service to produce their documents at a lower cost. This has clear benefits to this group of clients: they would be able to access a legal service at a price they're happy with. An AI service can also produce documents almost instantly and at any time of day, assuming they can be signed electronically and/or clients are happy to print them off themselves.

There can also be clear benefits to legal professionals to working in this manner. There will obviously be an initial financial investment to get the framework for this kind of AI service in place. You will also need to spend a fair amount of time setting it up and teaching your AI software how to respond to clients. However, once this initial financial and time outlay has been made, you'll be able to produce legal documents for an unlimited number of clients with only very limited input.

How do chatbots work?

Chatbots are AI applications that can automate routine process work. A client would enter an online chat with the chatbot, which would ask them key questions about the document they wish to have prepared. The chatbot would then collate the client's answers and enter them into the template for a legal document.

This document could then be made available for the client to print instantly, if necessary. Alternatively, they may want to pay an extra fee for the document to be looked over by a legal professional from the firm.

You could also provide a chatbot service that offers legal advice to clients. The chatbot would collect some key information about the situation in order to produce relevant legal advice. Again, clients could then choose to pay extra if they had any more questions, required advice to be more specifically tailored for them or wanted to speak directly with a legal professional.

Not all chatbots are used for legal work. There are plenty of less sophisticated chatbot applications on the market that can help clients navigate a firm's website or find answers to frequently asked questions.

These can be a useful way to provide an easy point of contact for clients on your website and help signpost them to key information without any actual time commitment for you or your staff. We will note here that many law firms have instant chat facilities on their website that are actually manned by real members of staff.

11.3.3 Is providing self-service legal services right for you?

There are plenty of companies who exclusively offer their services online. This is common in legal fields such as conveyancing or divorce, where clients are often keen to reduce their costs.

The self-service legal market is certainly growing, and this might be demoralising for you if you are trying to build a firm that's based on the value of bespoke legal advice.

It is important to consider how this movement online will affect the public perception of lawyers and what we do. Speeding up and automating processes could undermine the skill and expertise necessary in the legal field. More and more our responsibility is to educate the public about where personally tailored advice is needed, and where a standard guide will be sufficient.

If you're looking for a way to provide legal services as a fully regulated professional, it might be wise to consider how you can provide the convenience of an online platform but retain the benefit of the skill, expertise and empathy of a real person. However you're providing legal services, the customer service you provide is always going to be the market by which you attract clients who understand the benefit of paying for professional advice.

11.4 Possible pitfalls of technology

Technology can be a brilliant support for your law firm and can go a big way towards making the management and output of your firm more efficient. However, even with the most thoughtful implementation and support, there will be times when it just doesn't seem to be working in your favour.

In these circumstances, we suggest that you step back from the problem and take stock. Ask yourself:

- Is it a software or hardware issue that needs fixing?
- Are your tools all fit for purpose?
- Could you or your staff benefit from additional training?
- Have you rushed into a purchase?
- Could you benefit from specialist IT support?
- Is the process you're using really working for you?
- Are you aiming for flexibility or perfection? (Hint: the first is likely to be best.)

Some possible pitfalls of technology, which we explore below, include:

- increased expectation from clients;
- navigating cyber security concerns;
- letting the technology dictate your processes;
- forgetting about the human connection.

11.4.1 Increased expectation from clients

Early predictions about technology were that it was going to make our lives easier and give us all far more free time. Unfortunately, this isn't quite how things have panned out! Instead, the time we have saved by adopting technology has been ploughed back into the concept of increasing productivity.

Technology has contributed to the raising of client expectations. Communication is so quick and easy that clients often expect their messages to be responded to as soon as possible, even if they're sent outside of normal business hours.

There's also the issue of the huge amount of information that is available online. This means that clients are likely to have more information about the legal area you're supporting them in than ever before. This can be helpful in some circumstances, but in others it can lead to added confusion as clients may not understand why you are adopting a different approach than they have read about online.

How should you address these expectations?

Today's law firms need to work to set expectations for their clients right at the beginning of their working relationship. Some of the ways you will do this will be very simple – such as clearly stating what times of the day you are able to respond to messages and how quickly you will endeavour to do so.

Other ways to manage expectations might be a bit more labour intensive. Some law firms find it helpful to produce their own factsheets or guides to send out to clients at the point of instruction.

These resources can be a useful way to enlighten clients about the ins and outs of the legal process they're going through and address any common misconceptions. Taking the time to share this information can help clients to have more reasonable expectations about the length of the legal process and what the outcome might be.

11.4.2 Navigating cyber security concerns

Cyber security is obviously an area that every business owner needs to take seriously. This is especially important for law firm owners who are likely to be using digital means to store privileged or confidential information, or to manage financial transfers.

Despite this, it's not uncommon for a lot of what has been written on this subject to be bordering on scaremongering. You will need to use common sense to assess what the likely risk is for your firm and to put secure – but proportionate – checks in place to counteract this.

Aim to educate yourself on what any real cyber security risks might be to you and what you really need to put in place in response. You may find that you would benefit more from stringent processes for checks on any financial transactions and possible phishing emails rather than spending money on digital tools for this purpose.

Take advice from IT professionals as well as other law firm owners.

Tips on avoiding phishing scams

A phishing scam is when fraudsters send emails purporting to be from someone you trust. The idea is to persuade you to hand over crucial information or money before you realise the correspondence isn't genuine.

Much of this can be avoided by remaining vigilant and training yourself and any staff members to know what a scam email might look like.

Remember to:

- never click on links in emails that look suspicious;
- always double-check the email address you're replying to: is it a genuine one, or is it ever-so-slightly different from the organisation's actual URL?
- look out for typos and grammatical issues in official correspondence – this can be a clue that they're not genuine;
- never enter password or username details in response to an email.

If you're unsure about whether or not a correspondence from an organisation or other business is genuine, we'd recommend that you err on the side of caution. Phone them on a number you've phoned them on previously (not a number given in the suspicious email!) to confirm.

In addition to this type of phishing scam, some fraudsters are now seeking to intercept email correspondence between companies and clients. The aim of this type of scam is to replace one of the parties' bank details with their own in order to benefit from the result of any transactions.

To protect against this type of scam you will need to:

1. Make clear to clients that you will never email them with updated bank details. Encourage them to call your office on a number they have used previously to confirm your bank details before they make a transfer.
2. Think carefully about how you will send your bank details to your clients. If you're doing this via email, you may want to put the bank details in a branded PDF document rather than in the body of an email. This reduces the possibility of mistakes being made due to email typos.
3. Consider how you will ask clients to send their bank details to you. Some firms prefer this to be done in person or over the phone, while others accept details by email but always phone to confirm them.

Email is one of the least secure forms of communication. Any sensitive information that's received via this method should be verified. These vital steps must be taken by everyone within your firm; make sure they're set out clearly in your process manual as well as in client care letters, and terms and conditions documentation that are sent to clients. You will also want to make clear that by emailing you clients are accepting the risk of corresponding via this method.

So long as you have these processes clearly recorded and can demonstrate that they've been followed, if you're unlucky enough to be caught up in a fraud situation you'll be able to demonstrate to your insurer that you took all appropriate steps to mitigate risks.

Is it worth investing in 'secure email'?

Some companies are now offering 'secure email' services, but you'll need to research this carefully to determine whether this is right for your firm.

The benefit will obviously be to give both you as a firm and your clients the peace of mind that all data is safe.

However, there will be extra costs associated with using this kind of email system. They can also involve a much bigger time investment. You and your clients will need to go through extra authentication processes to access each email, which can seriously complicate things.

If you're working in a field where cyber security and sensitive data is a particular concern, this might be something to carefully consider. If not, a secure email system might just represent additional expense and complication.

Cyber Essentials scheme

Cyber Essentials is a government information scheme operated by the National Cyber Security Centre. This encourages organisations to adopt good practices when it comes to the security of information.

This scheme is designed to help firms guard against the most common cyber threats. It covers all the basic things that every business should consider in this respect, including firewalls, security settings, viruses and malware, and keeping software up-to-date.

Taking part in the Cyber Essentials scheme will clearly demonstrate your firm's commitment to cyber security. The scheme is relatively inexpensive but could have real benefits for your firm.

Certification from this scheme can:

- give you tools and expertise to protect your firm from cyber threats;
- bolster your firm's risk assessment and ensure compliance;
- demonstrate your commitment to clients;
- reduce your professional indemnity insurance premium.

It's also well worth noting that if you plan to bid for government contracts that involve the handling of certain sensitive and personal information you will be required to be Cyber Essentials certified.

11.4.3 Letting the technology dictate your processes

Whatever technology you choose to use in your law firm, it's really important to make sure you remember that you are in charge, not the tech! It's easy to fall into the trap of letting your digital tools mould your processes, rather than the other way around.

If a certain digital tool makes you do a task in a way you wouldn't do it otherwise, you'll need to carefully consider whether there's a better digital tool out there for you.

Before you even consider signing up for a new application or tool, think carefully about why you think you need it. How do you think it will support you?

Will it make things:

- easier?
- more streamlined?
- quicker?
- more client friendly?
- more professional?
- more up to date?

Our advice is to ensure that each piece of software or digital tool you commit to is in line with your general vision for your business.

11.4.4 Forgetting about the human connection

Despite all the digital tools we now have at our disposal, the law is still very much a service business that's heavily reliant on human connection. A successful law firm needs to have staff who are able to show empathy and understanding at what could be a very stressful time for clients.

It's really important to remember the importance of developing a professional relationship with clients: both in terms of directly person-to-person and the more general relationship your client has with your firm's brand.

Human connection is important, and this is often what will represent good value to your clients. Developing a strong professional relationship is also more likely to encourage clients to bring repeat business and recommendations.

11.5 The future of legal technology

The technology industry is extremely fast-moving. Many of the tools that we will be using to provide legal services in five or ten years haven't even been developed yet.

Though it's impossible to predict the full extent of the future of legal technology, there are a few innovations that are starting to gain attention: predictive coding for disclosure; and online court.

11.5.1 Predictive coding for disclosure

Predictive coding (also known as technology assisted review) is the practice of using a piece of software to digitally review a group of documents in order to syphon relevant information. This would usually be used to quickly review a large number of documents in order to collect information to be used (usually) during the course of a litigation matter.

Predictive coding for disclosure is often more consistent than manual human review, although it still requires a fairly big input from a lawyer in order to train the software to recognise and locate relevant search terms in order to highlight any information that is relevant to the case.

The current legal standpoint on this is that it's been ruled acceptable to use this kind of technology in cases where there is an adequate cost/benefit analysis in place.

11.5.2 Online court

Though many lawyers are now very familiar with the process of e-filing documents for court, most lawyers who are involved in litigation will still need to visit a physical court.

However, there are some fields where this is slowly changing. One key area that is considering adopting an online court model is civil disputes.

In the past the justice system has been inaccessible to many individuals or small businesses who wish to make smaller claims. This is because the cost of taking a matter to court would be far higher than the actual sum in dispute.

An online court could help in this situation as it would be far more accessible in terms of cost as it wouldn't necessarily need lawyer involvement. This doesn't mean that lawyers would be barred from the whole process, just that they would be expected to provide legal advice earlier on in the proceedings, and generally at a fixed cost.

Online courts have also been utilised in situations where it's not possible for people to gather in person, such as during the COVID-19 pandemic.

CASE STUDY 11: MELISSA FISH

Melissa Fish is a solicitor and the founder of Paper & Chain, a media business affairs boutique. Paper & Chain provides business affairs services to audio-visual content creators. Melissa and her team of consultants all work from home as the firm is built on a model of flexible working.

When did you launch your law firm?

Paper & Chain was launched in the spring of 2019.

How much knowledge and experience did you have before you started?

Before I launched, I had amassed over a decade of experience as a solicitor at a City law firm advising clients in the media and entertainment sector on rights issues and how to develop, finance, produce, exploit and acquire audio-visual content across all media platforms. I acted for and collaborated with content creators, independent production companies, broadcasters, sales agents, financiers, studios and distributors, at both an international and a domestic level. I had also experienced what it was like being 'client-side' during in-house stints at Discovery Channel and Warner Bros earlier on in my career.

Throughout these years of servicing media clients and listening to their needs, I realised there was a more efficient, economic and collaborative way to deliver the same expertise. And so, Paper & Chain was born!

What would you say is the most important lesson you learned in the first few years of your firm?

Not every great meeting will convert into an instruction. Use your time and energy in the most productive way to increase your chances of winning work. Focus on what is within your control and try not to dwell on what isn't, especially the 'what ifs'.

Can you tell us how you learned this particular lesson?

In the early days I had some really positive meetings where it seemed as though I was a shoo-in for the work. I'd start planning and resourcing to accommodate the massive influx of work promised . . . then when the work didn't materialise, I'd spend more time and energy obsessing over what went wrong. The reality is that there are so many competing variables that affect whether you get instructed for a project or not. Some will be within your control but the vast majority will not.

What changes did you make as a result of this?

I stopped spending energy on the 'possibility' of an instruction and instead used that saved time constructively to either attend more meetings with new contacts or focus on existing clients.

In what way do you think this made you a better law firm owner?

Any way you can make your business more efficient is an advantage; time needs to be spent where it will reap the most rewards. These experiences made me focus on the best way to utilise my time and the importance of retaining a positive mental attitude.

What advice would you give to a new law firm owner about this?

I would advise seeing every meeting as a positive step, whether an instruction follows it or not. Making new contacts, hearing about their challenges and learning about their businesses gives you important information that can only benefit you and help you achieve your goals.

There have been so many times when I almost didn't attend a meeting because I thought it would be fruitless, only to then be onward introduced to someone in that person's network that won me a new client.

So, have as many meetings as possible and enjoy the process of connecting rather than concentrating too much on the outcome. Spending any time prepping for work that hasn't come in yet – or wasting energy concentrating on the reasons why it didn't – is not productive.

Chapter 12

Employing staff

There are so many different reasons to start a law firm. Some of you may be setting out with the intention of building a firm that will be a major player in the industry. Others will want to take advantage of the new freelance solicitor regulations to take more control over their working life.

Wherever you fall on this spectrum, sooner or later you're likely to reach a point of wanting some support. In many cases, this will mean taking on traditional employees . . . but it doesn't have to. There are many different ways of accessing additional support for your business. The key is finding the one that works best for you.

12.1 When is the right time to take on staff?

When you started your law firm, your first objectives were probably something along the lines of getting some clients, bringing in some money and enjoying the freedom of running your business.

Over time, these objectives will start to shift. The more successful you are with your marketing and customer service efforts, the more work will start to come in. If this trajectory continues, you'll likely reach a point where you'll need help to service the work and/or handle administrative matters.

12.1.1 Things to consider

Like most things in business, there's no single formula to tell you when the right time is to take on staff. However, there are a few red flags to look out for:

- You're so busy with administrative tasks you're struggling to get anything else done.
- You've been neglecting your marketing and advertising efforts completely.
- You've started working longer hours and your work/life balance is nowhere in sight.
- You've been ignoring calls or emails from clients.

- You've been actively turning away work.
- Your customer service is slipping.
- You're feeling completely overwhelmed.

Though the answer to all of these predicaments might be to bring in extra support, the best support for each circumstance is likely to be different. There are multiple different ways that you could address these issues.

They include:

- hiring an additional legal professional;
- hiring an administrative assistant;
- hiring a paralegal;
- taking on the services of a specialist contractor (e.g. marketing, digital media, HR, copywriter, etc.);
- signing up for a virtual assistant service;
- taking on additional legal consultants.

Whichever way you decide to bring someone new on board, hiring is a big investment in your business. This investment generally will bring a return, but it's not likely to do this right away.

12.1.2 Hiring for a permanent position

How you feel about hiring a permanent member of staff will generally depend on your initial vision for your business.

If you imagined yourself at the helm of a large law firm, you may well feel excited about taking the first step towards this. However, if you planned to work from home alone indefinitely, you might not be able to think of anything worse!

You'll also need to be aware of whether or not you're legally entitled to employ staff. Limited companies and limited liability partnerships (LLPs) can employ staff, as can sole traders and partnerships. The main consideration here will be if you are a freelance solicitor under the new regulations, as freelance solicitors are not allowed to have any employees.

Recruitment can be daunting whatever stage of business you're at. Hiring your first ever member of staff will be particularly so. Not only are you not likely to have any experience in this area, you may also feel very aware of how closely you'll be working with your new employee and how important it will be for you to be able to work well together.

Advantages and disadvantages of permanent employees

There are, of course, advantages and disadvantages to hiring for a permanent position rather than outsourcing.

Table 12.1

Advantages	**Disadvantages**
Will be available all the time	Might be unaffordable in terms of wages
Will always be 100 % focused on your firm	Might be unaffordable in terms of extra taxes
Will contribute to your firm's brand	Will create additional administration and compliance tasks
Will take a lot of pressure off you	You may prefer to work alone
Will be good company in the office	May require a suitable work space
Won't have any conflict of interests	
You'll be able to share sensitive client information with them	

Initial considerations for hiring staff

Hiring your first member of staff will no doubt bring up a host of other considerations. The first will be a matter of cost: do your business's finances allow you to do this now? Equally, you'll need to consider where the new member of staff will work. If you're currently working from home, do you have an appropriate space for another person? Or will you need to consider moving to an office space? If neither of these are a good option for you, could you work out a system for your new employee to work remotely?

You'll also need to ensure that you have fully briefed yourself on the legal and compliance aspects of having an employee.

You will need to:

- register with HMRC as an employer;
- get employers' liability insurance;
- ensure that you'll be complying with the national minimum wage;
- look into whether you will need to enrol your employee in the workplace pension scheme;
- set up a payroll system;
- prepare to pay employer's NI contributions;
- see whether you are eligible for the NI employment allowance;
- ensure that you understand what your employee will be entitled to in terms of sick pay, holidays, parental leave, redundancy pay, etc.

Once you've made a decision about who to hire, you'll then need to:

- ensure they have the right to work in the UK;
- put them through a Disclosure and Barring Service (DBS) check (previously called a Criminal Records Bureau (CRB) check);
- send them a written employee statement and contract of employment.

Writing a job description

Before you begin recruiting in earnest, we suggest you set aside some time to write a thorough job description for the role (or roles) you're hoping to fill. This will help you to clarify your requirements and get a complete sense of the skills and attributes the successful candidate would need to have.

We will note here that a common pitfall of this stage of recruitment is to find that you're asking far too much in return for the salary you're prepared to offer! Make sure you keep your plans realistic. Your first employee is unlikely to be able to do absolutely everything you don't like doing! Though it may be tempting to increase the salary offer in line with what you're asking for, this might not be a manageable solution long term.

Of course, though it can be helpful to have an ideal candidate in mind, you will need to be flexible. When you put together the job description, do note which attributes/skills are essential, and which would just be a benefit.

For example, you may have decided the ideal candidate would have five or more years of experience. Is this non-negotiable, or would you be prepared to forego this for a candidate who seemed a perfect fit in terms of personality? You may find that someone with less experience on paper will fit into your team more easily as they could be more prepared to learn and adapt.

It's often said that it's more important to recruit for attitude rather than skills. It's unlikely that you would be able to change an employee's general attitude or behaviour, but you would be able to teach them new skills.

Should you consider contract-to-hire?

If you need to hire a legal professional but are unsure of this initial commitment, you might want to think about recruiting for a contract-to-hire position. This would essentially allow you to set a trial contract period of perhaps a few months before you would then commit to a long-term hire.

This would be helpful for two key reasons:

1. It would allow you to test things out and confirm that there really would be enough ongoing business to cover the cost of a new hire.
2. It would give you a chance to confirm that the legal professional you've hired is the right fit for you and your firm before anyone signs a permanent contract.

12.1.3 Is there another option? Using contractors, freelancers and virtual assistants

You may decide that a permanent employee isn't the right choice for you. This may be because you're not sure you have the business income to cover it yet, or it may be because you're a freelance solicitor and can't legally employ anyone.

If this is the case, there are still plenty of options for bringing other people on board to support your firm.

Of course, there's absolutely no reason why your firm shouldn't have a mix of different types of employees. Permanent staff members, contractors, freelancers and virtual assistants can all work brilliantly together.

Outsourcing

The practice of outsourcing means that you transfer work that would usually fall to someone within a business to external vendors. These external vendors can be located locally, domestically or anywhere in the world.

This practice is growing in popularity for all businesses, not just legal firms. However, it's proving to be an excellent option for law firms seeking to minimise costs and maximise their flexibility.

Common kinds of work to outsource within a law firm include:

- administration;
- initial preparation and drafting of contracts;
- dictation;
- legal secretarial services;
- telephone answering;
- proofreading;
- research;
- diary management;
- book-keeping;
- document review;
- filing for Companies House;
- due diligence checks;
- IT support;
- marketing;
- graphic design;
- social media work;
- website management;
- copywriting;
- HR work;
- recruitment.

Outsourcing tasks like this can lead to huge cost savings when compared to hiring in house staff to do them. Doing this can also save significantly on recruitment and training costs.

Using a virtual assistant

Virtual assistants (VAs) are one of the most common outsourced professionals for law firms to rely on. Law firms can often be inundated by minor administrative tasks. Though these are vital to keep work going, they're not likely to be the best use of your skills or experience. VAs are an excellent choice for firms who would benefit from the services of a personal assistant (PA) but don't have the capacity to hire someone permanently.

A VA works remotely and handles many of the same tasks that a PA, receptionist or secretary would handle. This can significantly increase the efficiency and profits of your firm, as the time you gain from not doing menial or repetitive tasks such as answering the phone, setting up appointments or transcribing notes can be used to focus on fee earning work. You may even be able to increase your capacity for more work just by hiring a VA.

Though VAs can be incredibly useful and cost-effective, to tap into these benefits you will need to invest a bit of time in training your VA. The better your VA knows your firm and how you work, the more useful they will be able to make themselves. Though it may seem like a headache to go through this initial training period, it will save you a lot of time in the future.

Using consultants

Consultants are legal professionals who work on a self-employed consultancy basis. They are usually former partner-level professionals with a specialist field of knowledge. They often consult for their former firm, although many also advise people, businesses and other organisations in their specialist area.

Using a consultant, or team of consultants, is an attractive option. They generally offer an efficient and affordable way to get the legal assistance you need on an ad hoc basis. There's no way that a small to medium firm could have a permanent specialist employee for every legal issue they're likely to come across. Instead, maintaining a roster of consultants would allow you to tap into this knowledge as and when you needed to.

Consultants can also be a useful resource during overwhelmingly busy periods. You could outsource certain matters to a consultant in order to avoid turning away clients during a particularly busy time. This may be a good option to have in place if, for example, you expect the higher number of clients to be seasonal rather than a permanent consideration.

Maintaining client confidentiality

If you're using outsourced staff, you'll need to take extra steps to ensure that client confidentiality is maintained. This may be more of a concern depending on which type of professional you are outsourcing to. For example, a copywriter or marketing professional is unlikely to be working with sensitive client data. However, a VA or consultant legal professional almost certainly would be.

The best way to do this is to ensure that any outsourced members of staff sign a confidentiality agreement. You will also need to inform clients that aspects of their legal services will be outsourced – we'd recommend including a clause to this effect in your terms of business.

There are also some regulatory requirements to keep in mind here.

Paragraph 3.5 of the SRA Code of Conduct for Solicitors, RELS and RFLs makes individual solicitors accountable for outsourced work and requires you to 'effectively supervise work being done for clients'.

Equally, Rule C20 of the BSB Handbook emphasises personal responsibility rules and makes clear that though there's nothing to prevent you from outsourcing tasks to qualified individuals, you would remain personally responsible for such work. In these cases, the outsourcing rules in Rule C86 must be complied with.

Rule C86 includes requirements that:

- your obligation to clients are not altered;
- you remain responsible for compliance;
- any third parties are subject to the same obligations as you regarding: confidentially, compliance, personal data and inspections by the BSB.

12.2 Navigating the recruitment process

Recruitment can be a very time-consuming process. It can also be quite overwhelming, especially if you get a large response to your job advertisement.

There are two ways to manage this. You can either keep everything in-house and manage the recruitment process yourself, or you can choose to use the services of a recruitment consultant.

12.2.1 Keeping recruitment in-house

The main benefit of keeping things in-house is that it's a cheaper option. This might seem more sensible if you're trying to stick to a budget on this.

Equally, if you have a large professional network and are confident you can source a suitable employee by drawing on this, you may not feel that a recruitment consultant is necessary.

If you do choose to manage the recruitment process yourself and won't be drawing on your existing network, we'd advise you to think carefully about where to advertise. The sort of job you are recruiting for will have a big impact on this.

If you're looking for a legal professional or paralegal, you'll probably want to advertise on a specialist law industry job website. However, if you're recruiting for an administrative role, you may want to consider using a more general job website.

You'll need to make sure you're prepared to set aside time to:

(a) answer questions about the role over the phone and via email;
(b) read through all job applications;
(c) shortlist quality applicants to interview.

You may find that once you've done all of this, the extra time (and stress!) would've been well worth the cost of the recruitment consultant's fee.

12.2.2 Using a recruitment consultant

We'd recommend that you use a recruitment consultant with specific experience in recruiting for the legal sector. Putting in the time to choose a recruitment professional you trust and feel happy with is likely to be a wise investment, especially if you expect to be recruiting more people in the future.

The more open you are with the recruitment consultant about what kind of business you have and what kind of staff you're looking for, the better prepared they'll be to find a candidate to suit.

Once you've confirmed the job description with the recruitment consultant, they'll then start putting together a shortlist of candidates for you. You'll then be able to review these and decide which, if any, you would like to interview.

If you do choose to use a recruiter, we'd advise you to respond quickly to their messages. If they send you a CV that interests you, you'll want to act right away to avoid the candidate being interviewed by another firm.

12.2.3 Managing the interview stage

How you feel about the interview stage may well depend on whether you were ever part of an interview panel at your previous firm. If you have experience in this, you'll likely feel more prepared for leading this process yourself. If not, you might want to call in some extra support. Your recruitment consultant would be a good start here, if you're using one.

Our advice for this process is:

1. Be as transparent as possible – about the type of work the successful

candidate will be doing, the brand and culture of your firm, the working hours, the location, the salary and any potential bonuses. Once your new employee starts, you don't want them to be surprised about anything!
2. Develop an interview process that has a clear way of scoring candidates against the criteria from the job description. Your recruiter (if you're using one) will be able to help you with this.
3. Though an interview naturally needs to be reasonably formal, you're likely to get the truest picture of each candidate by creating as relaxed an atmosphere as possible.
4. Ask questions with the aim of assessing whether the candidate would be a good fit for your firm, how competent they are, if they will get on well with clients and what their value would be to your business. Focus on these positives rather than trying to catch anyone out.
5. If you want to move forward with one of the candidates you interview, we'd recommend making them an offer as soon as possible. However, it's sensible to discuss this with the recruiter (if you're using one) before you say anything to the candidate. This is because the recruiter may know if the candidate is holding any other offers, and if the salary offer you're preparing to make is in the right ball-park.
6. Once you've made an offer and the candidate has accepted, you'll need to take up their references and do all necessary due diligence.
7. Assuming all is well with the candidate's references and other checks, you'll need to send an offer letter and a contract of employment as soon as possible.

12.3 Legislation in recruitment and selection

The Equality Act 2010 came into force in October 2010. This legislation was intended to provide a simpler, more consistent and more effective legal framework for preventing discrimination. This is something you will have to ensure you're following throughout the recruitment process, and indeed in all dealings with future employees.

The 2010 Act replaces previous equality legislation including:

- Equal Pay Act 1970;
- Sex Discrimination Act 1975;
- Race Relations Act 1976;
- Disability Discrimination Act 1995;
- Employment Equality (Religion or Belief) Regulations 2003, SI 2003/1660;
- Employment Equality (Sexual Orientation) Regulations 2003, SI 2003/1661;
- Employment Equality (Age) Regulations 2006, SI 2006/1031;

- Equality Act 2006, Part 2;
- Equality Act (Sexual Orientation) Regulations 2007, SI 2007/1263.

The 2010 legislation covers all the same groups that were protected by these previous pieces of legislation. These groups are now called 'protected characteristics'. These protected characteristics cover:

- age;
- disability;
- gender reassignment;
- marriage and civil partnership;
- pregnancy and maternity;
- race;
- religion or belief;
- sex;
- sexual orientation.

It is illegal to discriminate against any of these protected characteristics during the recruitment process. If a candidate believes you have chosen not to hire them on the basis of any of these characteristics, they would be able to report you to the Equality and Human Rights Commission (ECHR).

12.3.1 Types of discrimination

There are many different ways for discrimination to occur. These include:

Table 12.2

Direct discrimination When someone is treated less favourably because of a protected characteristic they have or are thought to have, or because they associate with someone else who has a protected characteristic.	**Indirect discrimination** When a rule, condition, policy or practice that applies to everyone particularly disadvantages people with a shared protected characteristic. This can be justified if you can demonstrate the rule is a 'proportionate means of achieving a legitimate aim'.
Discrimination by association Direct discrimination against someone because they associate with someone who has a protected characteristic.	**Perception discrimination** Direct discrimination against someone because they are perceived as having a protected characteristic, even if they actually don't.

Victimisation	Harassment
When an employee or candidate is treated badly because they have previously made or supported a complaint/ grievance under the Equality Act 2010, or because they are suspected of doing so. There is no protection for those who have made a complaint maliciously or supported one they know to be untrue.	Unwanted attention or unpleasant behaviour experienced by an individual as a result of them possessing a protected characteristic.

If you're unsure what is covered by each protected characteristic, this brief guide may be helpful to you:

Table 12.3

Age People of all ages can be protected in this way. For example, people are protected against discrimination for being 'too old' as well as being 'too young'.	**Disability** This is defined as a physical or mental impairment that has substantial and long-term effects on an individual's ability to carry out everyday activities.
Gender re-assignment Transgender individuals are protected, whether or not their transition is being medically supervised.	**Marriage and civil partnership** Those who are married or in a civil partnership are protected from discrimination on this basis.
Race In the context of the Equality Act 2010, race as a protected characteristic refers to skin colour, nationality, and ethnic or national origins.	**Religion and belief** Individuals are protected on this basis regardless of which religion or belief system they subscribe to. Not following a religion or belief system is also protected.
Sexual orientation This protects those who identify as LGBTQ+.	**Pregnancy and maternity** Women are protected against discrimination on this basis during the course of their pregnancy and maternity leave.
Sex In the Equality Act 2010, sex can mean either male or female, or a group of people like men or boys, or women or girls.	

12.3.2 How should you navigate this as an employer?

As an employer, it's important to be well-versed in all types of discrimination and protected characteristics so as not to inadvertently breach any legislative requirements during the recruitment process.

You will also need to continue to comply with the Equality Act 2010 throughout all ongoing dealings with staff members.

As an employer, you may find it helpful to:

1. Audit all your existing employment policies.
2. Audit all other policies and procedures.
3. Identify any areas where they may be risks of non-compliance.
4. Ensure that all staff are fully aware of their obligations under the Act and have undergone relevant training.
5. Proactively implement anti-discrimination policies and practices.
6. Monitor employees to ensure they are implementing measures effectively.
7. Continue all of this as an ongoing process.

12.4 Inducting and training staff

12.4.1 Induction

When you welcome new members of staff to your firm, there will need to be a clear induction process to get them settled and ready to start work.

Even the most experienced professionals will need some support before they are able to start fulfilling the role you've recruited them for. They may well have previously worked in firms that are similar to yours, but they haven't worked in *your* firm before, so they will need some time to become familiar with your workflow and processes.

You might want to:

- Create clear processes for setting up virtual accounts, file access, payroll, etc.
- Make sure all compliance regulations have been met.
- Ensure new starters get a full tour of the office and where everything is kept.
- Provide a 'digital' tour to ensure new starters are familiar with where and how virtual files are stored.
- Provide new starters with a copy of your firm's process manual and explain how to use it.
- Ensure that they have been briefed on health and safety protocols.
- Make sure new staff members have been added to any relevant staff email lists and calendars.
- Ensure that new starters are familiar with all the software packages your firm uses.
- Make sure new starters have been given a copy of all relevant policies, and that they have read and understood them.
- Provide keys or access codes when necessary.

Many firms find it helpful to produce a checklist for everything that needs to be covered with a new starter. That way you can be sure that each new member of your team is given all the information right at the beginning of their employment.

12.4.2 What about ongoing staff training?

Part of the responsibility that comes with being a legal professional is the requirement for continuing education. As a manager, you will need to ensure that you give all your staff – not just fee earners – frequent opportunities to access training.

This might take the form of regular in-house training for all team members. This could be run by you, another member of the team or a third party trainer. Alternatively, you may want to take advantage of external training courses. These could be in person or online.

Conferences are often excellent sources of training for both you and your staff, and will offer further opportunities to network.

Don't be afraid to think outside the box when it comes to promoting training and continuing professional development (CPD) in your firm. In addition to the more traditional CPD opportunities, you could consider encouraging your staff to:

- attend webinars;
- listen to legal podcasts;
- contribute to industry publications, both print and online;
- present their own seminars;
- explore teaching opportunities.

There are compliance requirements in terms of ongoing training for both barristers and solicitors. These are set out in Part 4, Section 3 of the BSB Handbook and the SRA's continuing compliance regulation.

12.5 Taking care of your staff

Sir Richard Branson was once quoted as having said 'train people well enough that they can leave; treat them well enough that they don't want to'.

Once you've found the right staff, it's really important to make looking after them a priority. Not only will this create a positive environment in your workspace, it will also help you retain staff, which is a lot more cost-effective than hiring new ones. It's also important to understand that the better you look after your staff, generally the better they will look after your clients.

12.5.1 Offer a competitive salary and benefits

One of the most obvious ways to treat your staff well is to ensure that you are offering fair and competitive salaries. Additional benefits can also help on this front. Some employers seek to offer things such as bonuses, private medical insurance, interest-free season ticket loans or death-in-service benefits. Other simple measures such as providing refreshments and snacks in the workplace can also have a big impact.

This can be a key way to attract employees to a role initially. However, in order to maintain this over time, you will need to ensure there are plenty of opportunities for staff members to progress.

You will also need to understand that competitive wages aren't enough on their own to keep your staff on side. So long as staff members are being fairly compensated, they're much more likely to be motivated to stay based on how your firm makes them feel rather than what you're paying them.

12.5.2 Make everyone feel part of the team

For many individuals, feeling as if they are truly part of the team will be just as important as the renumeration they receive. Make sure you give members of staff plenty of opportunities to contribute to things such as:

- making processes more efficient;
- developing new services or products;
- planning events;
- improving customer service;
- growing the firm's vision.

Regular team-building exercises can also go a long way towards ensuring everyone feels connected. This doesn't have to be anything expensive or complicated: setting aside half an hour on a Friday afternoon to share coffee and a cake can be very effective.

You may also want to encourage employees to have regular lunches together. Depending on the budget of your firm, you may be able to cover occasional meals out or takeaways for these events, or you may want to ask everyone to bring in something to share.

12.5.3 Offer praise and recognition

It's absolutely vital to make sure you give your employees praise and recognition – so long as it's deserved, of course!

Praising team members for work they've done particularly well is an effective way of making them feel appreciated, as is offering regular recognition.

There are many different ways to offer recognition. You may want to:

- celebrate successes (for both individuals and the team as a whole);
- give a mention in your newsletter or on social media profiles;

- acknowledge when staff have gone over and beyond or have had to deal with a particularly difficult matter, perhaps with a small token such as flowers or chocolates;
- hold an annual awards event;
- conduct annual appraisals;
- develop an 'employee of the month' type initiative;
- offer bonuses, either on the basis of meeting targets, completing exceptional work or at regular times of year, such as Christmas.

Of course, there's another key way to offer recognition to your employees, and that's to ensure you have a transparent promotion structure and that you encourage employees to work towards this.

If you have legal professionals on your team who have been qualified for three years or more, have you considered promoting them to senior fee earners? You may also want to consider the value of inviting legal professionals who have been qualified for eight or nine years to become salaried or equity partners. On the other end of the spectrum, if you have administrative staff who you think would make excellent fee earners, could you consider offering them funding towards the courses they'd need to be able to do this?

Don't shy away from discussing an employee's potential with them. It's much more likely to make them feel recognised and appreciated than it is to make them want to leave and take their skills elsewhere!

12.5.4 Think outside the box for additional staff benefits

Not all staff benefits have to have a clear monetary value. You may find that your staff really appreciate less obvious benefits.

You could consider:

- marking staff birthdays and/or work anniversaries;
- giving staff time to do charity work;
- offering sabbaticals in return for continuous service.

12.5.5 Get to know your staff

All staff like to be given encouragement in their work. You'll be far better placed to understand how each member of staff would like to receive that encouragement if you've taken the time to get to know your staff.

If you don't take the time to get to know staff, and don't compliment or praise them when appropriate, it's likely they'll ultimately lose enthusiasm. This would result in your team becoming accustomed to settling for doing the bare minimum, which would be bad news for your firm over time.

12.6 Managing staff

How involved a law firm owner is with general staff management will generally depend on the size of the firm. If you're the owner of a small law firm, it's likely you'll also act as line manager for most, if not all, members of the team. In a bigger firm, the owner might be more remote and only focus on the management of the management team itself.

However many members of staff you're responsible for managing, you must do this well in order to avoid bad feelings and quickly catch developing problems. Your staff will want to be managed well – not micro-managed – and will want to receive feedback and support in achieving their career goals.

Of course, there are a lot of competing demands when it comes to running a law firm. You may feel that managing staff shouldn't be a priority, but this is absolutely not the case.

12.6.1 Managing staff for the first time

Being a successful manager requires completely different skills than being a successful lawyer or a successful business owner. Many of the law firm owners we know would cite good management skills as the hardest things to master.

If you've never done this before, we would very much encourage you to seek some training yourself on this. You might want to consider taking a training seminar or workshop, some of which may be subsidised, or perhaps reading some books on the topic if that's all your budget allows.

All staff members are individuals and will likely react best to slightly different ways of working. Your job as a manager is to build a team who are able to bring out the best in each other – and in you – and to ensure that they have everything they need to be able to work as productively as possible.

As a starting point, we recommend that as an employer you strive to be one key thing: approachable.

12.6.2 Aim to be an approachable leader

It may once have been common for employers to adopt a strong and inflexible leadership style, but things have very much changed in this respect. Rather, most managers now find greater success in making themselves approachable. Many firms refer to this as having an 'open door' policy. The idea here is that staff should feel like they can come to you at any time to discuss ideas, concerns or issues.

One of the key factors of approachability is ensuring that you listen to staff members. This is something you may do often with your clients, and there should be no difference for your employees. Sometimes you will agree with your staff and sometimes you will not, but it's important to develop a trusting environment where everyone feels they can raise their thoughts, ideas and concerns.

One of the key arguments for being an understanding and supportive manager is that you absolutely want your employees to feel they can be honest with you. If a mistake has been made, it's vital for them to feel comfortable telling you about this. This will allow mistakes to be corrected before they become far bigger issues.

It's also worth noting that the more you work towards building genuine, trusting relationships with your staff, the more they're likely to use this as a guideline for their own relationships with other staff members and clients.

12.6.3 Make sure you have reasonable expectations

No matter how great a fit your team is or how well you seek to manage them . . . it's impossible to keep everyone happy all of the time. If this is what you're aiming for: stop.

All you can do is endeavour to do your best by your staff. In return, you can expect them to do their best in their role.

12.6.4 When management really isn't right for you

If you really struggle with managing your team, there are ways to address this. Training is really important here, but you also have the option of bringing in reinforcements.

Having the support of an HR professional can be invaluable. This could be on an outsourced basis or in-house, if you have the capacity.

This may well seem like a big financial investment, especially if you're in the early stages of running your business. However, if management is something you find very stressful and time-consuming, professional support is likely to be well worth the outlay.

12.7 What happens if things go wrong?

It is very difficult to effectively manage staff. This is a complex role and you almost certainly won't get it right all of the time. There will also be incidents where staff make mistakes or actively make choices that are not in the best interest of the firm.

The trick is to recognise that frustrations and difficult circumstances will always occur, but that you should aim to minimise these as much as possible. You will also need to have policies and procedures in place for incidents as and when they occur.

12.7.1 Know when to give in

No matter how carefully you manage the recruitment process, and how well you seek to train and manage your staff, sometimes things just won't work out as you had hoped.

If this happens, you'll need to learn from the experience and seek to move on as quickly as possible. It's important to listen to your instincts on these matters: if you have a feeling that someone isn't right for your firm, ask the questions you need to ask to get a full understanding of the situation.

It might be tempting to ignore these sorts of problems for a while in the hope that they will work themselves out. Before you do this, consider the costs. Salaries are likely the biggest overhead your firm has. If you ignore these issues for a month, two months or even longer, the salary you are paying that member of staff will just add up.

This may involve a very difficult task such as having to dismiss someone or accept their resignation. Both these eventualities are likely to feel uncomfortable and will also create additional work in the short-term. However, you will need to trust that the right situation has occurred and that the extra work you're putting in now will save you from the potential of a great deal more work in the future.

12.7.2 Have robust procedures in place

From time to time you're likely to have to deal with mistakes or issues of misconduct. These sorts of issues can be really difficult and unpleasant to deal with.

The best way to approach this is to put robust procedures in place to deal with wrongdoing before it happens. Ideally you would be able to work with an HR professional to put these procedures in place. If not, we suggest taking advice from other law firm owners about the policies and techniques that have worked best for them.

If you don't address these sorts of issues properly, the situation often escalates. You could even end up leaving yourself in the firing line for not handling the issue appropriately or in accordance to employment law. This could be very damaging to you and your firm in terms of financial cost and in terms of your own mental wellbeing.

12.7.3 Focus on prevention

You'll likely find that it's far better to proactively work towards preventing things going wrong than it is to sweep up the damage afterwards. This is a far more effective and low-stress strategy!

You may want to:

- hold inclusive team meetings;
- schedule one-to-one catch ups with each team member (do these regularly, not just if there are any concerns);
- develop a clear and comprehensive company manual;
- have proper employment contracts and review them regularly.

CASE STUDY 12: ANNA NEWPORT

Anna Newport is a solicitor and the director of law firm Newport Land and Law. Newport Land and Law specialises in conveyancing, property law and private client law. They are based in West Yorkshire and manage a flexible and remote team who work with clients throughout the UK.

When did you launch your law firm?

I launched Newport Land and Law with my husband in March 2017.

How much knowledge and experience did you have before you started?

I'm a bit unusual in that I started my career as a legal secretary and worked in a variety of departments as a floating secretary before an employer spotted my potential and put me through my degree. By the time I qualified I was already running my own department; I'd seen from the other side of the desk how to do that successfully.

I've worked in residential and commercial conveyancing plus private client law – so have more range than most – but when I set up Newport Land and Law I had never run my own business or been a partner at a firm. I knew how to run a firm from the bottom up but not how to run it from the top down. It's fair to say there were a lot of known unknowns, and a heap more unknown unknowns that I've discovered along the way.

What would you say is the most important lesson you learned in the first few years of your firm?

If you make a mistake, ask for help straightaway. Our industry has a culture of shame, meaning offices up and down the country are piled high with rugs under which have been swept a great many mistakes. Under a rug (or in a locked filing cabinet or a shredder) is not the place for a mistake – out in the open is where you want it so that it's unlikely to be repeated.

I am determined that my firm will operate with a culture of honesty and not blame – quite the opposite of what I've experienced throughout most of my career. I encourage the team to talk openly about things that don't go right so that we can learn together about how to do better next time. I never want anyone to be too frightened to admit to a mistake or worried about the consequences. There's precious little in this world that can't be fixed with paper: either the kind we write on or the folding kind.

Can you tell us how you learned this particular lesson?

The way mistakes are handled is something I've observed throughout my career. Seeing people sweat about the consequences of their most recent mistake instead of trying to deal with it has stuck with me for a long time.

It's a nonsense to think that any lawyer can go through their whole career without making a mistake or landing a claim, so facing up to mistakes and learning from them is the healthiest – and most prudent – thing to do.

For example, I recently forgot to update a policy after the reminder emails from the SRA went into my junk folder. When I realised, I rang them straightaway and gave a clear timescale of when I would have the updated policy to them. Having initially worried about the consequences, I was met with a very reasonable and understanding response. Much better than if I'd chosen to ignore the mistake and hoped it would go away!

What changes did you make as a result of this?

As a fast-growing firm we're still setting up the infrastructure needed to support the team. We have already started recruiting for more office and practice management support as our current part-time person – fabulous as she is – can't possibly get through everything in her hours.

I've also always been particular about policy and procedure, but like many people started with off-the-shelf versions. We've since slowly honed each process and procedure to fit our remote and flexible working model.

How we have done that has been the most important part. We approached changes to each process or policy through conversations with the team and with curiosity as our mindset. We asked ourselves, and them: Does the policy fit with our ethos? Does it enable people to work efficiently and effectively, or is it hindering that? Does it have our clients' interests at its heart, or can we change things to make it more client-centred?

I view the policies and procedures we have as the foundations on which we're building the firm. Get these right and you can layer on the right people, knowing you have a stable base to support them.

In what way do you think this made you a better law firm owner?

The thing I wanted most when I set off on this crazy ride was to build a firm that really and truly cares about its clients, not just one that writes trite paragraphs about the concept on a website. I also wanted to create a firm which really works for its consultants and makes sure they are well cared for. Our new adapted policies and procedures really help achieve that, and the clarity they provide is better for everyone involved.

The last three years have shown me the difficulties of balancing regulatory responsibilities and the values I hold dearest. It's not impossible to achieve, but it takes constant adjusting, like it would if you were in charge of a huge tanker. Just a one- or two-degree variation from the end-point can take you a long way off course, and while I hesitate to use an over-done journey analogy, I do believe that small adjustments make a huge difference in the long term.

What advice would you give to a new law firm owner about this?

Be crystal clear on your values and keep these in mind when considering both the big-picture strategy stuff, and the minutiae of how you achieve it. Both are equally important and a mismatch in one area will have a massive impact on whether or not you are being true to those values.

I would also reassure anyone starting a new firm that it is possible to be different. Regulation has changed to allow us to set up different structures, alternative business structures and the like, so use that to create the company you always wanted to work for.

My final piece of advice would be to know what you want before you set off. Every year we create one-, two-, three- and five-year plans. The detail gets hazier as the timeline gets longer, but we know where we're heading, and that gives us the confidence to make the right decisions to get us there.

Chapter 13

Wellbeing and work/life balance

There are so many things to juggle as a business owner. We've spoken about many of them during the course of this book: employees, processes, marketing, customer service and your accounts. Of course, that's not to mention the actual legal work and billable hours you'll be taking on! As if this wasn't enough, many of you will also have plenty of other responsibilities to contend with outside of your firm.

When you run your own business, it's tempting to dedicate as many hours to it as you can. We understand this: of course we do! Your law firm is your vision, your creation, your baby. You will want to put your heart and soul into ensuring its success, even if this means you're taking away time you would usually dedicate to other areas of your life.

Though this may feel like the most natural way to approach running a business, doing this can often turn out to be counter-productive. If you'll allow us to take the juggling metaphor a little further: the only way all the balls will stay up in the air is if the person doing the juggling is able to keep going. If the juggler gets too tired or overwhelmed, all the balls will fall back to earth.

Ultimately, we all need to take care of ourselves if we want our businesses to grow and flourish. If you're not on top form yourself, over time you will start falling behind with your responsibilities and your firm will almost certainly suffer as a result.

13.1 What's at risk?

If you don't make any special effort to support your own wellbeing as a business owner, it's highly possible that this could come to blindside you in the future. This is true whatever stage you're at in business.

This could manifest in any number of ways:

- a general feeling of being overwhelmed;
- a decline in your physical health;
- a decline in your mental health;
- a lack of creativity;
- a lack of motivation;
- boredom with your business;

- an inability to maintain your vision;
- indulging in unhealthy behaviours.

It's important to be mindful of the fact that you could reach a point where your personal wellbeing comes to a head. This could feel very much like hitting a wall and not being able to continue moving forward with your business.

Reaching this position is by no means a necessary part of running a business. The trick is to keep close tabs on your health and mental state and understand when you can afford to keep pushing ahead and when you need to stop to give yourself a breather.

In terms of long-term growth, it's far better to put measures in place to give yourself the rest you need than it is to keep pushing yourself until you can't push anymore. If you do find yourself hitting a crisis of wellbeing, it may well be very difficult to get yourself up to speed again.

13.1.1 Are lawyers more susceptible to burnout?

No one chooses a career in the law because they think it will be an easy ride. The industry places very high expectations on us, starting with our rigorous training. The academic and intellectual demands that are placed on us require us to work long hours as a matter of course, concentrate at a high level for long periods of time, and demand perfection from ourselves and those around us. As our careers continue, we are faced with high workloads, intense competition, pressured environments and competing demands.

The law is not the only industry that makes these kinds of demands. However, we do think it's fair to say there are unique challenges and pressures that come with being a lawyer.

Research shows that those of us in the legal profession are more likely to turn to alcohol and drugs as a coping mechanism. Indeed, the figures suggest that 15–24 per cent of lawyers will suffer from alcoholism at some point during their career (**www.theguardian.com/society/2011/nov/13/doctors-lawyers-alcohol-addiction**). We suspect you don't need us to tell you that this would not be a very sustainable method of keeping your law firm afloat.

13.1.2 What can you do to prevent this?

It's important for everyone to make time for their own wellbeing. However, we believe this is particularly important for those of us running businesses within such a high-pressure industry.

When you run your own firm, you will need to take steps to create an organisation that will work for you, not the other way around. Part of this will be ensuring that the processes and systems you implement ensure that everyone within the firm is able to maintain a healthy work/life balance.

Working as the owner of a firm is different than working as an employee. You will need to adopt an entirely different mindset and be prepared to experiment with different ways of doing things.

Adjusting to a process of working smarter, not harder, is a gradual process for everyone. You'll probably find that your ability to do this successfully will develop in stages. By this we mean that you should expect your success rate will go up and down . . . though hopefully it will remain on an upwards trajectory!

Speaking of upwards trajectories, most business owners hope that their businesses will grow year on year. If this is the case for you, the way you work and engage with what goes on in your business will need to change, too. For example, if you're taking on more work each year, you will not be able to be as involved and engaged in each project or piece of work in your fifth year of business as you were in your first.

Whatever motivation you had for starting your own firm, we're reasonably confident that it wasn't to continually work harder year on year. This wouldn't be enjoyable or sustainable, and it wouldn't give you much scope for enjoying the rewards of your success.

Be realistic about what you expect from yourself and your firm

Being a lawyer is a very serious job. Not only do we have to be very conscious that we are dealing with people's lives, we are also held to very high standards by our peers and regulators.

With the pressure put on us from third parties (as well as the pressure we pile on ourselves), it's easy to start berating yourself when something hasn't quite gone to plan.

Of course, what you need to remind yourself of here is that lawyers aren't magicians or superheroes. You will not be able to solve every problem that comes your way, nor will you be expected to. Rather, all you can aim for is to do your very best for each client.

You've read already about how important it is to manage your clients' expectations. What you may not know yet is that you will also have to do some significant work towards managing your own. However much of a perfectionist or conscientious professional you may be, you will need to reign this in somewhat when it comes to how matters progress within your firm.

Remember:

- You will not always be able to achieve the outcome you want to achieve for a client.
- You will not always be able to prevent staff from making mistakes.

- You will not always be able to predict what will happen in any given situation.
- You will not always be able to afford to put the best solution in place.
- You will not always be able to persuade the clients you want to instruct you.
- You will not always be able to make the right decision.

The better you're able to come to terms with all of this, the better you will be able to focus on the bigger picture. Building a successful law firm is a long journey: try to embrace it for what it is. If you lose yourself in too many small details or occurrences along the way, you won't be helping yourself, your clients or your family.

Make sure you celebrate your achievements

We think it's important for everyone's peace of mind to spend a little time looking back at how far you've come. It's easy to fall into the trap of constantly looking to the next thing without fully appreciating or celebrating each achievement in your business.

It can be really helpful to start a practice of noting down any milestones or achievements you've hit. This could be things such as:

- number of clients worked with;
- small hurdles that have been overcome;
- cases that have been won;
- business developmental goals you've surpassed.

Not only is it great to have this information easily accessible during regular goal-setting sessions, looking back at this can also be really helpful at times when you need a mental boost.

In addition to making sure you're keeping track of these milestones, don't forget to celebrate them! This is important in terms of creating team spirit and unity within your firm, but it's also great for everyone's mental health. This is just as true if you're heading up a large team as it is if you're working alone as a self-employed barrister or freelance solicitor.

Everyone needs to take time out every now and again to celebrate what they're doing right. How big or small you make your celebrations is completely up to you. Perhaps you'd enjoy celebrating with homemade cakes in the office, or perhaps you'd prefer an early Friday finish. Whatever works for you and your team is great, so long as everyone (yourself included!) feels appreciated.

13.2 Working smarter, not harder

Being strategic about how you plan and manage your workload will give you the best chance of achieving a work/life balance that works for you and your loved ones.

When we talk about working smarter, we do *not* mean putting pressure on yourself to work towards unrealistic timescales or overwhelming yourself with never-ending to do lists.

Rather, we'd suggest focusing on planning your workload strategically. The most effective way to do this is usually to narrow in on your priorities: what do you need to get done that day, that week, that month or that quarter?

Writing short daily or weekly 'to do' lists that are based on these priorities will help to ensure you are focusing your efforts in the most useful places and are not getting caught up in busy work. Setting aside a regular time to reassess these priorities and ensure that they're all still relevant can also be a good use of your time.

13.2.1 Avoid being a busy fool

Not every client or opportunity will be right for you and your business. It can be very tempting to say yes to everything, especially in the early days, but this is rarely the right choice. Being busy is not the same thing as being successful.

Taking on clients or opportunities that don't really fit in with your goals for your firm may bring in some short-term benefit, but in the long-term you're likely to look back at these and see them for what they were: distractions.

It is a real skill in business to know when to say no and not to be afraid to say it. Business owners need to let go of any guilt they may feel about this and focus instead on what they have to gain. After all, saying no will not only save you time, it will also allow the person you are turning down to move on and talk to someone else who might say yes.

13.2.2 Be a master delegator

The simple truth of the matter is that you cannot do everything yourself. You are a human being, not a machine, and forcing yourself to manage absolutely everything yourself is likely to be a recipe for burnout.

Part of the beauty of being your own boss is that you can build a daily work routine that you love. There will likely be some tasks in your business that need to be done personally by you, but most will not. Be honest with yourself about what really needs to be done by you, which tasks you really enjoy, which you dislike and which ones take up more of your time than you can justify. Keep the ones you need to do and the ones you enjoy, and work towards delegating the rest.

Who you delegate tasks to will depend on the structure of your business. You might have a member of staff or two who are perfectly placed for this, or you might want to do some research into how you could create a virtual team using outside contractors. Either way, have faith in the team you have put together and trust them to take on their share of the burden and responsibilities of your firm.

Of course, delegating a task isn't always the end of the story. Even when you've passed a task onto someone else, it might be tempting to micro-manage how they do it. The only likely outcome from this is that you will frustrate your team and yourself and probably remove all the benefits of delegating the task in the first place.

Whatever you do, don't just conclude that the task would've been done better if you'd done it yourself. This is a trap and will likely result in you failing to delegate in future! Instead, if there really was an issue with how your team member handled the task, consider looking into:

- how you communicated expectations;
- whether there was sufficient documentation in place to help with the task;
- what tools were available;
- whether additional training is needed.

Delegating tasks effectively is a really important part of safeguarding everyone's wellbeing at work. Not only will it help you to maintain a more sustainable workload, it will also help your team to feel useful and appreciated.

13.2.3 Do not multitask

There's a belief that the more tasks someone is doing at any one time, the more effective they are. Though this is certainly a long-standing belief, it's also a complete misconception. Scientists have determined that every time we are distracted from a task, it takes an average of 23 minutes and 15 seconds to properly get back to it (**www.fastcompany.com/944128/worker-interrupted-cost-task-switching**). It may make you feel more productive to flit from casework to a HR issue to your emails and back again, but in reality all you're doing is making yourself less effective.

In order to really make the most of the work time you have available, we recommend that you focus on just one thing at a time. We have more than enough distractions to deal with in our daily lives without actively increasing them.

You may want to take this a step forward and actively work towards minimising distractions, especially when you're focusing on your most important work.

It might be helpful for you to:

- **Batch work:** Challenge yourself to batch similar tasks together at certain points of the day. You might block-out specific times for responding to emails, returning phone calls, paying invoices or writing content for social media.
- **Turn off notifications:** New emails and messages can be very distracting when you're trying to focus on important work. You may find it helpful to turn off notifications on your devices during these times.
- **Ask staff not to disturb you:** Your employees might be used to asking you questions whenever they come up. It might be helpful to have set times when you ask them not to disturb you, unless something is really urgent.
- **Invest in some noise cancelling headphones:** If you find yourself regularly getting drawn into conversations in the office (or into household conversations if you work from home), you might find that a pair of noise cancelling headphones help you to maintain better concentration.
- **Carefully plan your workspace:** Some people find that they can get easily distracted by case notes or other documents that are sitting on their desk. If this is an issue for you, you may find that designing a more minimalist workspace makes a big difference to your concentration.

13.3 Stress management

Stress is a very normal part of the human experience. Some jobs are undoubtedly more stressful than others, and being a lawyer probably falls fairly high on the rankings for this. As a lawyer, you're likely to find yourself being pulled and pushed in different directions by clients, staff, regulators and other professionals, all on a daily basis.

Though stress is normal and is often actually helpful in terms of motivation and productivity . . . there is a limit to this. Like everything, we need to make sure we are properly moderating how much stress we're taking on. If you don't do this, you could easily find yourself being overwhelmed by it. And when you get overwhelmed with stress, it's impossible to function at your best.

The thing about unhealthy stress is that it can permeate into all aspects of our lives. Stress at home or in a personal relationship could result in you making poor decisions at work. Equally, an impossibly stressful work day could lead to tensions building at home.

Though there's no way to completely cut out all stresses (we humans have an impressive ability to always find *something* to worry about), you can work towards getting a better handle on how you keep your stress levels manageable.

In order to keep you and your wider firm running at full capacity, you will need to take some steps towards developing stress management techniques. Some of these will be concerned with actually implementing processes, checks, balances and habits. Others will be more to do with small mindset shifts that will help to set healthy expectations for you and the people around you. Some steps to consider are:

- control your perfectionism;
- make small changes first;
- surround yourself with a team you can trust;
- let go of the little things;
- recognise the power of self-care;
- prioritise a good night's sleep;
- reach out to family, friends and other business owners;
- take holidays (and enjoy them!);
- embrace it: stress is not always the enemy.

13.3.1 Control your perfectionism

Many business owners struggle with their perfectionist tendencies on a daily basis. Obviously you will want your business to be as successful as possible, but be wary of finding yourself stuck in an 'all or nothing' approach.

If you allow yourself to believe that something has to be absolutely perfect for it to be worth doing, you're likely to end up in a paralysis of inaction. You won't be able to move forward with the job at hand if you're too caught up in the idea that a result that's anything less than absolutely ideal would be a failure.

Ultimately, there is no such thing as perfect. It's unlikely that you would ever be 100 per cent happy with any piece of work. Continually striving for this is likely to lead you down a very clear path to burnout. Rather, it's better to focus on doing your best, completing each task and moving on to the next one.

13.3.2 Make small changes first

From time to time all business owners feel like things aren't going their way. When you find yourself in this mindset, it's easy to feel that the only way out is to do a full 360 degree turn and completely change everything. Trust us when we say this is almost never necessary!

The more you get caught up in the idea that big changes are needed, the more you're likely to feel powerless and overwhelmed. Instead, we suggest you consider making small changes. Even the smallest of changes can, over time, transform your business. They can make your workload more manageable, your daily tasks more enjoyable and your firm more profitable.

Perhaps you're frustrated with the cumbersome process of opening a file and never being able to find the information you need to carry out anti-money laundering checks? You could consider delegating the whole process, spending a bit of time refining how files are stored, or asking clients to fill out the forms themselves.

Perhaps you feel like you're working as hard as you can but your profits aren't increasing? You could consider making a small increase to your charging rates or conducting a review of your overheads.

Perhaps you feel you spend too much time giving free advice to clients without them then going on to instruct you? You could ask for a financial commitment from prospective clients earlier, set clearer professional boundaries about how much free advice you'll offer or consider putting together some free downloadable resources so this doesn't take up your time.

In all three of these examples, any of the small solutions given would likely make a marked cumulative difference to your workload *and* your mindset over a few months.

13.3.3 Surround yourself with a team you can trust

The kind of team you endeavour to build up around you will depend on the kind of law firm you plan to run. There is no perfect blueprint for what your team should look like, it all depends on what is right for you and your firm.

Your team might be:

- a traditional group of office-based fee earners and administrators;
- a group of diverse legal consultants;
- a group of virtual contractors;
- a group of other business owners you can rely on for advice and encouragement;
- a mix of all or some of the above.

Whatever your team happens to look like, they will play a very key role in supporting your wellbeing. Not only is the right team likely to contribute significantly to how profitable, successful and sustainable your law business is, they will also help to keep things fresh, manageable and enjoyable.

We do want to emphasise, however, that building the right team around you will almost certainly take time. It's almost impossible to build the right team on the first try. Rather, you'll need to reassess, remove and replace as you go.

The people who come and go during this period will help you to refine your understanding of the type of people you need in your team. They will also help you to practice and improve your management style!

In terms of building a team of other business owners you can turn to for advice and encouragement, don't be afraid to reach out to the people who inspire you. Many other business owners will be willing to share their experiences with you. Networking groups and professional associations can be a good place to start these types of conversations, and social media is also a fantastic resource. Do make sure that you're also willing to share and help other business in return. If you want other people to lean on, you'll need to be prepared to prop them up too!

13.3.4 Let go of the little things

Almost everyone has the tendency to get caught up in small annoyances. There are plenty of these to contend with when you run your own business. The trick here is to develop the ability to recognise when something *is* a small annoyance rather than a real problem.

Ask yourself:

1. Will you remember it in a year?
2. Is there anything you can do about it?

If the answer to these questions is yes, the best course of action is usually to focus your energy on moving forward with a solution.

If the answers to these questions is no, the best course of action is usually to focus your energy on letting the annoyance go. This isn't always as easy as it sounds, but it can help to throw yourself into a task you can do or to revisit recent achievements instead.

Though we do believe taking care of smaller details is vital to the success of a law firm, there's a big difference between taking care of small details (e.g. ensuring all stages of your customer experience are up to scratch) and getting caught up in small annoyances (e.g. giving yourself a hard time because you can't get a paragraph to line up properly on your website).

It's important to make sure that you don't get so caught up in small annoyances that you become disillusioned or lose sight of where you're headed. There are all sorts of things that might not go to plan from time to time. Don't let them overshadow your satisfaction in all the good stuff you've made happen.

13.3.5 Recognise the power of self-care

It's far easier than it should be to overlook the importance of taking care of yourself. While you're busy keeping your business afloat, taking time out for yourself might see like an indulgence. However: this is far from the truth!

We all need to invest time in caring for ourselves, especially if we want to stay healthy, alert and full of ideas.

Popular self-care practices include:

- eating healthily and staying hydrated;
- exercising regularly;

- meditation (there are many great apps to help with this, for example Headspace);
- taking time out for hobbies;
- enjoying fresh air;
- reading;
- listening to music;
- spending quality time with loved ones.

Many people have a self-care routine for the evening, but you don't need to confine these kinds of activities to outside traditional working hours. After all, one of the major benefits of running your own business is having the flexibility to build your own schedule.

You may want to build self-care activities into your normal daily routine. Something as simple as setting aside a proper lunch break with a proper meal could make a big difference and would be a great way to set a healthy example for any staff you have. If your law firm does have staff, you could also consider introducing self-care practices for the office. Again, this doesn't need to be anything complicated or intensely time-consuming, it could be as simple as properly entrenched lunch breaks for all, a weekly coffee and chat hour or regularly taking your team meetings out into the fresh air.

An important component of self-care is to pay attention to your health – both physical symptoms (e.g. headaches, muscle tension, chest pain, digestive problems, heart rate, difficulty breathing, insomnia, clenched jaw, low immunity, etc.) and mental/emotional symptoms (e.g. feeling overwhelmed, easily angered, depression, panic attacks, etc.), as well as getting check-ups and health checks (e.g. blood pressure, coronary, stress hormone, etc.).

If you find it difficult to commit to making time for self-care activities, we suggest you try diarising them. Formally blocking out this time in your calendar will remind you that these practices are just as important as attending meetings and returning client calls. Self-care time provides a vital opportunity to look after yourself and reflect; it shouldn't be something you only do when there's nothing else more pressing.

Remember: you wouldn't ordinarily cancel a client meeting to go swimming; don't cancel your planned swimming session to fit in a last-minute client meeting! Your wellbeing is just as important as your client's.

13.3.6 Prioritise a good night's sleep

Speaking of self-care, sleep is often the unsung hero of this. It's vitally important to make sure you're getting a sufficient amount of sleep, but many people don't make sure this happens.

There are all sorts of reasons why our sleep might be affected for reasons outside of our control (such as young children, sleep disorders or anxiety).

However, there are plenty other controllable reasons why you might not be getting enough sleep. It can sometimes be tempting to stay up late working in order to try and get ahead with work. However, doing this would be a perfect example of short-term gain causing long-term problems.

Getting between seven and nine hours of sleep each night has been proven to improve the health of your heart, to reduce stress, to improve your memory and to make you more alert (**www.verywellhealth.com/top-health-benefits-of-a-good-nights-sleep-2223766**).

Essentially, the better you sleep, the better you're likely to be able to deal with whatever's thrown at you the following day.

13.3.7 Reach out to family, friends and other business owners

It can be incredibly valuable to talk through worries and stresses with other people. You might have supportive family members or friends who are happy to fulfil this role for you. If not – or if you're looking for a more experienced perspective – it will likely be well worth your time to seek out other business owners to talk to.

You don't need to limit yourself to only speaking to other law firm owners. You will likely also get some excellent support and perspective from other business owners.

If you feel you would benefit from talking through your stresses but aren't sure who to turn to, you might want to consider finding a coach or counsellor to speak to instead. These services can be hugely valuable, and they're not just for people who are already struggling with their mental health. Many business owners find it hugely beneficial to have a safe space to talk about these things in and doing this can help to prevent you experiencing problems in the future.

13.3.8 Take holidays (and enjoy them!)

Most business owners love spending time working in – and on – their business. When this is the case, it can be easy to forget how important it is to spend time away from it.

Taking a holiday from your business from time to time is vital if you want to maintain your enthusiasm. Remember: you will need just as much time off as other people.

When we say a holiday, we don't necessarily mean you should be regularly jetting off to exotic places. Though getting away can be a really valuable way to gain headspace, you can often benefit just as much from spending some time at home away from work. Of course, wherever you go it is important to try and take some *real* time off. As the owner of the firm you will always need to be reachable for emergencies, but you should be able to delegate or put a hold on the vast majority of your usual tasks for at least a few days.

However you choose to spend your annual leave, taking proper time out to recharge and enjoy yourself will help you to focus on your core values and your original vision for your business. It's important to take time to remind yourself why you started your business in the first place and what you wanted to achieve. Spending some time sitting with these fundamental considerations will likely lead you to come up with some fresh ideas that could well have a profound and positive effect on the overall health of your firm.

13.3.9 Embrace it: stress is not always the enemy

If you decided to start your own business in the hope that it would be less stressful than working as an employed lawyer . . . you've probably already discovered that was a rather futile aim! There is absolutely no escaping the fact that running a law firm is stressful.

However, it's important to recognise that stress itself is not the enemy. A healthy level of stress is the body's natural biological response to dealing with stimuli. It's actually a form of 'good' stress that we're experiencing when we feel excited, exhilarated or motivated.

Stress becomes dangerous when we experience it at a level that's too much for us to handle. This is usually referred to as chronic stress and can often build up on us when we repeatedly find ourselves in stressful environments without giving ourselves any restful time out.

We live in a culture where being 'busy' has come to be prized very highly. As a result of this, we often get caught up in running around and filling up our calendars to the brim, simply because that's what we believe success looks like. It's unsurprising that the next step in this trajectory is to start to feel stressed and overwhelmed.

If you're feeling this way, it might be worth trying to take a mental step back from the situation and looking at it from another perspective. Are you really stressed because of the job at hand, or could it be more to do with your perspective?

Often, the 'bad' stress we feel can be turned into 'good' stress with just a slight change in focus. It can be helpful to aim to concentrate on the actual task or situation at hand rather than how you feel about it. To do this you will need to cultivate a practical mindset: what can you do with the skills and resources you have?

Positive thinking (and reminding yourself of all your strengths) can be an effective way of turning bad stress into good stress that will motivate you to move forwards and get the job done.

13.4 Maintaining a healthy firm

When we talk about health and wellbeing in business, it's important to note that you can't just think about this on a personal level. You and your team members may have all taken steps in your own lives to promote self-care and good mental health, but this won't be enough to keep your whole firm healthy.

As a business owner you have a duty not only to maintain your own wellbeing, but also to cultivate a work environment that promotes this for everyone. Just as you personally are unlikely to perform at your best when you're not looking after yourself, the same is true for your staff.

It's really important to build an office culture that places equal importance on self-care and a sustainable work/life balance as it does on the usual markers of productivity and output. Like almost everything in business, you will need to go through a period of trial and error to find the ideal balance here.

Some ways to maintain a healthy firm are:

- check in with your staff;
- promote cohesion;
- provide signposts to mental health resources;
- develop an effective internal communication strategy;
- create a culture of working reasonable hours;
- carefully consider targets;
- accept that this is an ongoing learning curve;
- appreciate the link between a healthy environment for staff and the financial health of the firm.

13.4.1 Check in with your staff

One of the first things to consider within the question of building a healthy firm is how you will effectively check in with your staff, as well as any consultants or contractors you work with.

Formalising regular one-to-one meeting with all staff members will give you a chance to find out how everyone is feeling about their workload and their place in the firm, as well as whether they are under any extra pressure outside of work. If you're able to pick up on niggling issues quickly, you'll be far better placed to put a solution in place before those niggling issues turn into big problems.

Not everyone will feel confident having this kind of chat with their employees. Indeed, you may not feel that this is one of your strengths. If this is the case for you, you may want to consider outsourcing the task to an HR professional.

In many cases it's actually more effective to have these regular staff check-ins completed by an HR professional. Not only will they have the training and experience to be able to deal with concerns appropriately, they'll also have a healthy level of distance from the situation. Staff will be able to raise issues without worrying about offending you, and you'll be shielded from any potentially uncomfortable conversations.

13.4.2 Promote cohesion

There is a real benefit in ensuring that you regularly bring your whole team together. This promotes cohesion and encourages all members of staff to feel like a valued part of the bigger whole.

There are numerous different ways that you could facilitate this sort of cohesion. What works for your firm will depend on factors including size and personality. Very formal group activities are unlikely to go down as well if your firm generally has a more casual work environment, and vice versa.

Team building exercises and group training can work well in this sense. As can occasional celebratory meals (such as at Christmas or after a large matter has concluded). You might also want to consider giving a small nod to staff members' personal milestones such as birthdays or marriages.

13.4.3 Provide signposts to mental health resources

One of the easiest ways that you can help to promote wellbeing in the workplace is to ensure that you signpost your team members to some of the excellent metal health resources that are available for legal professionals.

You could do this by putting information physically on a noticeboard in your office, or you could include it in a staff handbook or shared drive.

Organisations who offer resources for legal professionals include:

- **The Law Society** (**www.lawsociety.org.uk/contact-or-visit-us/helplines**), which runs a number of helplines providing practical advice and assistance to solicitors and employees of solicitors. This includes the Practice Advice Service (offers support on legal practice), the Professional Ethics Helpline and Lawyerline (guidance on client care and handling complaints). The Society's Pastoral Care Helpline also exists to offer support on a more personal level.
- **LawCare** (**www.lawcare.org.uk**), which offers emotional support, information and training to the legal community.
- **SBA the Solicitor's Charity** (formerly known as the Solicitors Benevolent Association) (**www.sba.org.uk**), which helps solicitors and their families who are in serious financial need due to illness, accident, redundancy or other adversity. It can provide grants and secured interest-free loans as well as support and advice.

- **Solicitors' Assistance Scheme** (**www.thesas.org.uk**), which provides free confidential help and advice on any problem, whether personal or professional, for all solicitors in England and Wales, their families and employees.
- **Wellbeing at the Bar** (**www.wellbeingatthebar.org.uk**), which provides barristers and chambers' personnel with the information, skills and support they need during any difficulties in their private lives.

13.4.4 Develop an effective internal communication strategy

You're probably already well aware of how vital your firm's external communications are. They determine how you will engage with clients and other professionals, and ultimately how much work is likely to come your way.

What you may not have considered is that it's also really important to ensure that you develop an effective internal communications strategy. How you communicate inside your firm will play a key role in determining how positive and engaged staff are, and likely how productive they're able to be.

Just as all your external messaging should be consistent, so should your internal messaging. This is particularly crucial during any periods of change. Think carefully about how you will communicate updates about the business to staff. Will you establish a daily or weekly briefing? Will you send out a regular director's email? Keeping communication lines open and honest will help to promote a supportive atmosphere.

Just as you should keep lines of communication open with your staff, make sure you encourage them to communicate regularly with you. Encourage staff to share their feedback and ideas. Showing staff that you value their opinions will help them to feel valued themselves.

13.4.5 Create a culture of working reasonable hours

It's important for your staff to have a healthy work/life balance. In order to facilitate this, you will need to ensure that you create a culture of reasonable working hours. Employees that are regularly expected to work late or take work home with them are likely to feel they have a poor work/life balance.

One of the key ways to create a culture of reasonable working hours is to lead by example. If staff see you constantly staying late in the office, or if you send them work emails from all hours at home, they may well assume you expect the same from them. This is also true of holidays and annual leave. If you rarely take a day off, you might unwittingly be setting a standard for your staff.

Your team members will be far more effective if they are getting sufficient time outside of work to rest, relax and indulge in their own interests. Make sure you give them the time to do this.

13.4.6 Carefully consider targets

Targets can be a healthy and effective way to ensure everyone within your law firm is staying on task. They can help to reduce the reliance on busy work and motivate staff to work at their best.

Unfortunately, targets can also become a real point of contention. It's important to make sure the targets you are setting are achievable within the timeframe your staff are contracted to work within.

We also recommend that you carry out regular target reviews with your team members. This will help to identify if there are any issues, or if anyone feels they are being put under too much pressure.

13.4.7 Accept that this is an ongoing learning curve

It is only really in recent decades that employers have come to understand just how important it is to protect and promote the wellbeing of their employees. Many of the management techniques that are best practice now wouldn't have even been on an employer's radar 10 or 20 years ago.

With this in mind, it's important to remember that everyone is still learning on this front. If you are serious about creating a law firm that truly cares about the wellbeing of its people, you will need to commit to learning about this on an ongoing basis and adapting your practices as you go.

13.4.8 Appreciate the link between healthy environment for staff and the financial health of the firm

It's certainly not an exact science, but there's plenty of evidence pointing towards there being a definite correlation between the financial health of a firm and the wellbeing and happiness of the people within it. A study carried out by the University of Oxford showed that happy employees were 13 per cent more productive.[1]

It's simple really: when a team feel like they have a handle on their work and their mental health, their productivity is likely to increase. Alternatively, if your workforce are stressed and feeling out of control, their productivity is very likely to nosedive.

[1] Bellet, Clement; De Neve, Jan-Emmanuel; and Ward, George, *Does Employee Happiness have an Impact on Productivity?* (October 14, 2019), Saïd Business School WP 2019-13. Available at SSRN: **https://ssrn.com/abstract=3470734** or **http://dx.doi.org/10.2139/ssrn.3470734**.

CASE STUDY 13: JODIE HILL

Jodie Hill is a solicitor and managing director of Thrive Law, which specialises in employment law and human resources services. Thrive Law is also leading a national campaign to highlight the importance of supporting mental health in the workplace.

When did you launch your law firm?

I launched Thrive Law on 1 March 2018.

How much knowledge and experience did you have before you started?

None really! I had only just five years' PQE when I set up Thrive Law at the age of 29. I had never run a business or even managed a team. I had no investors and set up singlehandedly.

What would you say is the most important lesson you learned in the first few years of your firm?

The biggest lesson I have learnt is to know where your strengths lie and bring in people who can support you. It can take time to build the right team around you, but once you've got this right you can thrive.

For example, I have an office manager, a financial director, a legal cashier and a compliance team, all of whom are outsourced. The functions provided by these people are all pivotal to the firm but would be very time-consuming for me to do myself. By outsourcing these tasks to trusted professionals, I've massively increased the time I have to spend networking, being the face of the company and bringing in work, as well as supporting and leading my team.

Within six months of launching the firm I took on a marketing apprentice. For me, marketing and building our profile online is vitally important. At Thrive we live to sow equality and diversity into the culture of our firm and the firms we work with. We want to live in a world where everyone in the workplace is treated equally. To do this, we strive to ensure equality remains at the top of the agenda for our business. As we are activists for social change, all of this has to be factored into our marketing in order to get our consistent message out there.

Can you tell us how you learned this particular lesson?

Setting up a law firm is very daunting! There is so much to do and without any financial backing or other partners – it all falls to me. I have anxiety and had a breakdown the year before launching the firm, so I was very mindful of the importance of not overloading myself with pressures I couldn't handle.

What changes did you make as a result of this?

I wanted to set the foundations for the firm right from the outset, so I brought in experts where I needed them from the beginning.

Sometimes the first or even second round of people you bring into your business might not be right. Don't be afraid to move them along and keep looking for those professionals who will be the ideal fit. Especially in a small team, fit is everything. You need to be able to trust everyone who's involved.

When things weren't working out with outsourced team members, as tough as it was, we had to remove and replace until we had the quality and service level we expected.

In what way do you think this made you a better law firm owner?

Despite being a small firm, Thrive Law has the same functionality as a larger firm. This means we have been able to compete with much bigger industry players.

We pride ourselves on thinking differently and laterally to make the workplace fair for everyone. Authenticity is key in my firm too. We believe in equality; expanding our team in this way has enabled us to play our part in creating workplaces which are healthy, inclusive and free from barriers.

In 2019 we were proud winners of the 'Diversity & Inclusion' Award at the prestigious annual Yorkshire Legal Awards. This award celebrates active promotion of equality, both internally and externally, with a significant focus on identifying and removing the legal profession's barriers to entry.

In the same year we also won the Yorkshire Post's Yorkshire's Finest Excellence in Business Award in the Social Mobility category. We were celebrated by the judges for driving the company's agenda far outside the scope of a legal practice, namely our campaign around mental health in the workplace. Part of the reason we have been so successful in publicising and getting the word out about our campaign is because we chose to take on a marketing professional early on.

What advice would you give to a new law firm owner about this?

Do your homework! Start by doing a full business plan and forecast BEFORE you set up. You will need to work out what all the extra costs are going to be and use recommendations.

I also recommend that you speak to other small law firm owners and ask which outsourced professionals they work with. I'm happy to share who I work with; many other firm owners will be too. In fact, since I set up Thrive and established our core team of consultants, that same team has gone on to support other small law firms.

Chapter 14

Growth and expansion

Once your law firm is firmly established, you may feel the time is right to look into options for expanding. For many people, growth is a natural part of running a business and this may have been what you've been working towards since day one.

The concept of growth and expansion can mean different things to different people. You may understand the concept with a more traditional focus on opening additional offices or significantly expanding your team. However, there are of course many ways to grow your business and experience greater success that don't include traditional growth. This might be through achieving greater professional satisfaction, building your personal profile or achieving a better work/life balance.

If your vision for your business does incorporate growth, there are many different ways for you to achieve this. However, we do want to emphasise that growth shouldn't always be equated with increasing your bottom line.

14.1 Does your firm have the potential to grow?

It's important to remember that your law firm is just like any other business. Profitability is vital to its success, and in order to build and increase that profitability you will need to pursue sustainable growth in some way.

A great deal of this growth will stem from innovation. Most law firm owners have to really focus on innovation during the early years of running their practice in order to build a successful firm that aligns with their vision, their capabilities and the realities of what their clients want. However, once things have started to go well, many firm owners fall out of the habit of thinking in this way.

In order for your firm to have true growth potential, you will need to continue to think in terms of innovation, even when it no longer feels necessary. Continuing to explore ideas for how your firm can seek to support its clients in new ways will be a huge factor in ensuring that your firm retains its potential for growth and doesn't start to stagnate.

14.2 How do you know when it's the right time to expand?

Expansion is not always something to aim for. Growing too fast can be just as dangerous for a firm as failing to grow at all.

Having the enthusiasm and expertise for growth is not enough. There is a very complicated combination of factors to consider before you can determine that the time is right to expand.

Once again, there's no simple answer here. Instead, you'll need to look at the issue from as many different angles as possible to try to explore whether the time is right.

14.2.1 Considerations for expansion

You could start by asking yourself the following questions:

- Do you have a clear, fully fleshed out plan?
- Does your firm have the capacity to carry out that plan?
- Have you done a full analysis of the market?
- Is there demand for your proposed expansion?
- Are you ahead of your competition?
- Are you excited and enthusiastic about the expansion?
- Do you have the right people in place to make it happen?
- If you don't yet have the right people, do you have a strategy to find them?
- Are you being held back by the wrong people?
- Have you done enough research?
- Do you and your staff require any training?
- Is your business currently secure financially?
- Have you had detailed discussions about this with your accountant?
- Do you have enough time to dedicate to the expansion?
- Do you feel that you have enough experience?
- Why have you settled on one particular growth plan and not another?
- Are you currently having to turn away business?
- Have you taken advice from other professionals?
- Are you ready to make sacrifices to move your business forwards?

14.2.2 Who could you turn to for advice?

You may have spent a lot of time asking for advice in the early days of your firm. However, you may be operating under the idea that this becomes less necessary as your firm becomes more established. This isn't true, especially when it comes to the issue of growth.

If you're considering options for expansion, this is a great time to turn back to your advice networks. Your accountant is an obvious choice here, but is by no means the only person who can help. You might also want to turn to any business mentors you've picked up along the way, as well as colleagues and fellow law firm owners. It can also be really helpful to talk to the owners of businesses in other industries, especially those who have already taken some of the expansion opportunities you're considering.

No two business growth experiences will be exactly the same, but talking to others and finding out how things have worked for them will give you better insight into how to best manage the process.

14.3 What growth and expansion options could you consider?

There is far more than one way to grow a business. The path that's right for you and your firm will depend on a number of factors, not least your vision for the future.

You might want to consider starting to offer additional legal services, or branching out into a new area of practice. Equally, you might consider aiming to work with higher value clients or on higher value matters. You may also consider growing your own personal brand by seeking to join advisory boards or mentorship schemes.

Alternatively, there are a range of more traditional ways to expand a law firm that might be the right option for you, which we expand on below:

- opening additional offices;
- merging with another firm;
- buying out another practice;
- taking on additional partners or directors.

14.3.1 Opening additional offices

There are plenty of reasons why you might want to consider opening an additional office.

- You might want to expand into a new geographical area.
- You might want to offer your services to a certain demographic of clients.
- You might want to have better access to certain knowledge or expertise.
- You might want to create increased geographical flexibility for yourself.

Taking steps to open a new office could give you the capacity to increase the firm's turnover, recruit additional staff and raise your profile in a new area.

How much work will a new office generate?

Though there is certainly opportunity here, it's important to be realistic about how much additional income – and additional work – a new office is likely to generate.

You'll need to carefully consider how much of the work that might be drawn in by your new office wouldn't have been possible from your old one. This distinction is likely to be clearer if your new office will be in a significantly different geographical area than your current one. However, if you're planning to open a new office in the same city or county as your current one, this will be something you need to consider carefully.

Especially in the early days, you'll likely find that the new office will need to draw resources from your existing office. This is not necessarily an issue in the short term, though if it continues beyond an initial settling-in period it's likely to become a problem.

If your new office ended up simply draining resources and custom from your old firm, this would clearly not be a sustainable situation.

How easy will it be to build a new client base?

When you open a new office, you will also need to build a new client base. Don't assume that this will be significantly easier than when you did it the first-time round! It's true that you will already have the benefit of an established brand and far more experience, but the reputation you have earned in your existing area of business will not automatically follow you to the new one.

You will likely find that there are barriers to entry in the new area. These barriers may be very similar to what you have experienced before, or they might be significantly different. Be prepared to think creatively to find innovative solutions to new problems.

Moving forwards as a bigger firm

You may find that in some ways your new office has a quite different atmosphere or personality than your existing one. This is natural, though it's important not to allow this to foster a 'them and us' mentality.

Like many things in business, the practice of opening a new office will require you to go through a personal shift in mindset. You will need to explore the best way to manage the relationship between both offices and take the business forward as one cohesive force.

It's also important to remember that though an additional office will hopefully bring in an additional income, it will also bring in additional work. You will have double the overheads, double the staffing issues, double the compliance tasks. The larger the practice, the bigger the profit potential . . . and the bigger the potential for things to go wrong.

14.3.2 Merging with another firm

Merging two or more law practices together is a common way to expand your opportunities as a director. In the 12 months to the end of January 2020,

663 law firms (including sole practitioners, recognised bodies and licensed bodies) are recorded as having closed down. However, 21 per cent of those (a total of 136) actually merged with other firms (**www.sra.org.uk/sra/how-we-work/reports/statistics/regulated-community-statistics/data/firm_closure_breakdown**).

There are all sorts of reasons why you might want to consider merging with another firm.

- **Increased geographical reach.** You might be considering merging with a firm that already has a strong presence in a geographical location you are keen to break into.
- **Increased sector presence**. You might be considering merging with a firm in order to benefit from the practice areas or industry sectors it works with.
- **Client driven forces.** You might be looking for a way to respond to client requests to provide services in additional geographical or practice areas.
- **Financial pressures.** You may be considering a merger in order to mitigate a precarious financial position.
- **Improved market position.** You might be seeking to strengthen your position in the market by joining with another firm.
- **Improved work/life balance.** You may feel that you would enjoy a better work / life balance without having to shoulder all the responsibility for your firm yourself.

What makes a successful merger?

There are many factors at play in a merger, and there's no fool-proof way to predict whether it will be successful or not. However, there are some key things that can make a big difference here.

First, a merger is more likely to be successful if it is between two firms with similar visions and culture. It would be very difficult to bring two firms together if the atmosphere and expectations in each were competing with each other. The two firms would need to be able to find a common goal and commit to working towards it together.

You would also need to be prepared to surrender your position as chief decision-maker (or decision-makers if you're already part of a team of directors). This may come as a relief to some sole practitioners who are keen to share the heavy burden of responsibility. However, this could be an uncomfortable change if you're used to making all the decisions yourself. You would need to be prepared to make this adjustment.

What makes an unsuccessful merger?

It's not easy to achieve the careful balance that's necessary to successfully pull off a merger. Things could go wrong due to poor financial performance, cultural misalignment, the loss of key clients or because of leadership and management issues.

It's likely to be much harder to make a success of a merger if you've entered into it for all the wrong reasons. Generally speaking, mergers should only occur when there is an ideal fit, and not simply as a life raft.

How do you know if a merger is right for your firm?

If you're currently exploring whether a merger might be right for you, we suggest you take some time to think about it very carefully.

You might want to ask yourself:

- How do you feel about not being in sole charge anymore? Would you be prepared to consult with other directors before making decisions in the future?
- What's driving the desire to merge? Is it for positive reasons, or because you feel you have limited options?
- What size of firm are you considering merging with? Are they bigger or smaller than your own firm? How will this impact on your future decision-making power within the firm?
- What will the new firm be called? Will the new name include your existing company name? If not, will this be a problem for you?
- What would you be looking for in a merger partner? Do you think you'd be able to work well with the other firm's directors?
- What would your expectations and objectives be from the merger? How well do you think you would be able to achieve these?
- What does your firm have to offer? Do you have niche expertise? Do you have a valuable client base? Do you have strong leadership? Do you have particularly good processes in place?

You will need to do a great deal of due diligence before you agree to anything, even in principle. It will be important to do as much information-gathering and fact-checking as possible. However, you're also likely to need to do a fair amount of soul-searching and checking-in with gut feelings. Mergers are not an exact science: your emotions will play a very key role.

What are the first steps of a merger?

If you decide you want to move forwards in earnest with a merger, you will need to enhance the value of your firm as much as possible.

You can do this by:

- ensuring that your finances are all in order;
- collecting in fees for any work in progress;
- ensuring your professional indemnity insurance record is in order (ideally this will have no circumstances notified or claims paid);
- reviewing your firm's complaints record and disciplinary record;
- minimising any long-term commitments that could be perceived as undesirable to another practice (e.g. lengthy leases, loans, long-winded cases, upcoming staff retirements);
- highlighting your firm's goodwill (generally measured by how successfully the firm has operated);
- underscoring the firm's image.

It can also be beneficial to develop a merger marketing plan. Ideally you will want this to target enough potential firms to merge with to enable you to really explore your options.

The more firms you are able to enter talks with, the better sense you'll get of what you're looking for in a merger partner.

Getting merger offers from multiple firms will also allow you to compare and contrast any offers you are presented with.

Professional indemnity insurance and run-off cover

When two firms decide to merge, this can cause practical issues relating to professional indemnity insurance and run-off cover. This subject should ideally be covered in initial merger talks to make sure both parties are in agreement over how this should be handled.

The main concern here is whether or not one or all of the practices involved in the merger will require run-off cover. If the acquiring firm does not want to become a successor practice, then the existing firm will need to purchase the necessary run-off cover *before* the merger takes place. If this insurance is in place, the insurer would meet the cost of any necessary compensation relating to a claim made after the firm has merged.

You may decide that you are happy for your firm to become a successor practice. This would mean that your firm would take responsibility for any future claims made against any of the firms you have merged with. If you decided to do this, you would need to take appropriate insurance advice and ensure that you have been fully briefed on all the implications of this decision.

In the case of firms that are limited liability partnerships (LLPs) or incorporated practices, a successor practice will only occur if either the LLP or incorporated practice becomes a principle in the new practice, or if the new firm holds itself out as the successor.

It's important to be aware here that if a merger doesn't work out and the firms decided to separate again, any successor practice would retain responsibility for all future claims arising from all previous work undertaken.

Before any merger agreement is finalised, all parties will need to agree:

1. Who will pay the excess on matters notified to insurers pre-transition?
2. Who will pay the excess on matters notified to insurers post-transition but arising from work done by the prior practice?
3. How will any future increase in professional indemnity premiums be covered (whether generally or as a result of claims arising after the transition, but from work that was completed before the transition)?

14.3.3 Buying out another practice

Purchasing another practice is a very effective way to quickly increase the scope of your firm. When you purchase a firm, this would generally include you taking over any staff, existing work and customer lists. You would also take on any leases or other obligations the firm had.

You might choose to do this for a number of reasons:

- To give your firm a big boost in a new geographical area.
- To take on expertise and a client base in a new area of practice.
- To increase the size of your team and client base.
- To quickly buy in additional resources.

Purchasing a firm may well be a key part of your firm's strategy for growth and expansion. If this is the case, it will take a lot of time, effort, research and planning in order to get this right. Jumping into an opportunity too quickly may well be something you regret in time.

What should you consider when buying a practice?

Research and due diligence are two very important factors when it comes to the process of considering whether or not to buy a law firm.

The variables you will need to take into account include:

- location;
- practice areas;
- staff;
- annual turnover;
- premises;
- profit levels;
- work in progress;
- customer list;
- network of contacts;
- previous accounts;

- cost of professional indemnity insurance;
- value of goodwill.

The cost of buying a firm will very much hinge on the value of all these factors combined. This will likely be a lengthy negotiation between what you as a buyer are prepared (or able) to pay, and what the seller is prepared (or able) to accept.

You might want to pay particular attention to:

- Whether or not the firm has a niche practice area.
- Whether the firm have future financial projections (and evidence for these).
- Whether the team has significant experience and expertise.
- Whether the firm has strong processes in place that will enable things to keep running as planned even through a transition period.
- Whether the firm has any ongoing claims or complaints against them.
- Whether the firm has profitable work in progress.

What happens to the previous owner of the firm?

Generally speaking, there are two key options here. The owner of the firm you are buying may want to hand over the reins completely as soon as the sale goes through. Alternatively, the owner may be open to staying on as a consultant.

Both of these options have their benefits and disadvantages. You may be keen to have a clean break with the firm's previous owner and take over completely yourself. Alternatively, you may decide that retaining the previous owner as a consultant would have mutual benefits.

It would benefit you, as this would provide continuity for staff and clients of the firm, and would also enable the previous owner to make key introductions that would help you in the future.

It would benefit the previous owner, as this would mean that they would avoid the need to purchase run-off cover.

This may well be a good option for you when buying a firm where the current director(s) want to retire, or a firm that is selling-up due to financial difficulties.

14.3.4 Taking on additional partners or directors

You may reach a point with your law practice where you don't feel you can continue to handle it by yourself. This may be because you have opportunity for increased workload or because you have the opportunity to expand into new areas of practice or geographical areas. Equally, it may be because you are looking for a way to bring an injection of cash into the business and are seeking to take on an additional partner or director in return for a cash buy-in.

Making the decision to take on additional partners or directors could be an effective way to increase the scope of what your law firm can do.

The personnel you choose to add could also bring a great deal to your firm. A good partner or director will invariably bring experience, expertise, a client following, a new network of contacts and new investment.

What should you look for in a partner or director?

The ideal partner or director will be someone with skills and personal qualities that compliment yours well. This doesn't necessarily mean that you should have the same or very similar skills and personalities. Rather, you may want to actively seek out someone whose strengths fill in any gaps that are currently in the business.

While considering whether someone would make a good partner or director, you might want to consider:

- How well do you know them?
- Have you worked together previously? If so, how well did you work as a team?
- Do they share the core values of the firm?
- How much respect do you have for them and their expertise?
- Do they share your vision for the firm's future?
- How much of an appetite for risk do they have?
- Do they have entrepreneurial flair?
- How confident are you in their abilities?
- Do you respect their work ethic?
- Are you able to communicate well together?
- How complementary are your working styles?

And, perhaps most importantly:

- Can you trust them?

Making the decision to welcome another partner or director into your business should obviously not be taken lightly. This is a choice that will have long term implications, especially if it turns out that you and the new individual do not find it easy to work together.

It's really important not to underestimate the personal side of this decision. You might have found someone who looks perfect for the role on paper, but if you have wildly different management styles and/or ideas for taking the firm forwards, in practice this is unlikely to be a sensible choice.

Developing a partnership agreement or director's service agreement

When you do decide to formally welcome a new partner or director into your law firm, you will need to make sure you have covered all legal bases for doing so.

You will need to draft and execute a partnership agreement or director's service agreement in order to clearly record all terms that have been agreed on. This document will be useful to refer back to in the event of a dispute or if you need to manage a conscious uncoupling.

A *partnership agreement* should include:

Table 14.1

Information	**Details**
The name and address of your business	
The type of business and purpose of the partnership	
The duration of the partnership	This may be for a specific length of time, or it may be until the withdrawal, dissolution or death of a partner.
The investment made by each partner	Contributions may be in the form of cash, property, services or intellectual property. Partners do not have to make equal contributions and contributions do not have to be made at the same time.
What the administrative responsibilities of each partner will be	Include: working hours, skills to contribute, holiday entitlement, sick leave entitlement, etc.
How much authority each partner will have	The voting power held by each partner may be equal, or it may be based on their experience, expertise or their initial investment. This should also include provision on how much each partner can borrow on behalf of the partnership without approval from other partners.
Any restrictions on work that can be done outside the partnership	Some partners may be involved in other businesses.
The division of profit and loss	Unless otherwise specified in writing, general partners will share profit and loss equally, regardless of the initial investment each has made. This should also include a provision for periodic accounting.
Salaries and compensation	Detail what each partner is entitled to receive in terms of salary, bonuses and other compensation. This should also include any expense accounts partners are entitled to.

Information	Details
How company assets would be distributed in the event of the partnership being dissolved	Unless otherwise specified in writing, general partners would be expected to distribute assets equally. Include provision for financial assets as well as premises, customer lists, marketing assets, trade secrets, patents, copyrights, trademarks and the business name.
Reasons for the dissolution of a partnership	This is likely to include the death or incapacitation of a partner, but there may be other reasons specific to your business.
The conditions for the admission of new partners	
A buy/sell clause	This should include the method that will be used to value the business. It could also prohibit a partner from selling their stake in the company to a third party. You may wish to include a 'shoot out', in which each partner sets out a price that they would buy out another partner's interest or sell their own.
How disputes will be settled	This could include arbitration (appointing someone who is given the power to resolve a dispute), mediation (evolving a professional to facilitate a reconciliation) or both.
Provisions for settlement in the case of death or incapacity of a partner	This may be handled through a buy/sell agreement funded by business life insurance.

A *director's service agreement* should include the majority of the above details. However, it will also need to contain additional information:

Table 14.2

Information	Details
The provision of shares	How will these be distributed and administrated between directors?
Voting rights	Should one of the directors be nominated to hold the casting vote to prevent a 'tie' at board meetings?
Fiduciary duties	These are set out in the Companies Act 2006.

Information	Details
Duty of confidentiality	What responsibilities should directors have concerning the confidentiality of company affairs, trade secrets, client lists, databases, etc.?
Restraint of trade	Will there be clauses in place should a director leave or the directorship cease for another reason?

Investing the time to put together clear and watertight agreements will help to ensure that the interests of the firm and any individual partners or directors are protected in the event of disputes, disagreements or unexpected events.

14.4 What risks are involved in growth and expansion?

Any strategy for growth and expansion will come with inherent risks. Whatever direction you choose to move in, you will need to be prepared to make mistakes along the way. And, of course, to learn from them.

Though there is, of course, a great deal to gain from growing and expanding your business, there is also significant potential for loss. You could lose time, money or even damage the existing reputation of your business.

There is no way to completely eliminate risk in business. However, you can seek to reduce it by ensuring that you do your homework as conscientiously as possible.

The more research, preparation and due diligence you do, the more satisfied you will be that you are:

(a) making the *right decision;*
(b) making the decision *at the right time.*

Bringing in expert advisors can also help you to better understand what pitfalls could be ahead and what steps you can put in place in order to mitigate them.

Assuming you have a smart approach and the right support, there's no reason why you wouldn't be able to successfully scale up your business. Constantly being innovative in what is quickly becoming a very disruptive legal market will no doubt pay dividends in the long run.

14.5 Is growth and expansion right for everyone?

Not all law firm owners will want to go down a traditional route of expansion. You may have left your previous firm precisely because you didn't want to be part of a traditional large firm, and if this is the case your aim probably wasn't to end up running one!

Many small law firms are content with their client offering and simply aim to continue to deliver, year after year. There's certainly nothing wrong with this ambition; compound growth isn't the only way forward. Instead, you might want to focus your energies on nurturing a regular supply of clients that will keep your firm going even when economic times are tough. There are certainly some benefits to this option:

- If the law is what you love, you will be able to focus on continuing to offer a high-quality legal service without having to shift your focus to business development.
- You won't have to take on additional responsibilities.
- You'll be able to better stay in control of what your daily work life looks like.
- You may be able to safeguard the time you have to spend with your family.
- You may be better able to protect your capacity for enjoying hobbies, interests and social commitments outside of work.
- You may be able to keep a better reign on the finances of your firm, keep overheads down and, ultimately, increase what actually ends up in your pocket. Bigger doesn't always mean more profitable.

All these reasons are valid and understandable. It's important to assess how you feel about all these factors and, therefore, whether a traditional growth model is going to work for you and your current life situation.

Even if you decide that you don't plan to move forward with a second office or a new area of practice, it's worth keeping in mind that it's never truly possible to stand still when it comes to running a business.

If your aim is simply to maintain your law firm's current position, you will still need to continue to dedicate time to business development work in order to make that happen.

CASE STUDY 14: MANDEEP KAUR VIRDEE

Mandeep Kaur Virdee is a solicitor, a solicitor-advocate and the managing director of KaurMaxwell. KaurMaxwell is an independent and international law firm that champions diversity. They offer a wide range of personal and business legal services including corporate and commercial, dispute resolution and litigation, intellectual property, real estate, private client and employment.

When did you launch your law firm?

I launched my firm in March 2018.

How much knowledge and experience did you have before you started?

In law – I qualified as a solicitor in February 2011 and as a solicitor-advocate shortly after, which means I was seven years qualified before I started KaurMaxwell. I trained and specialised in insolvency and restructuring, in both contentious and non-contentious areas. Over the last few years, I predominantly found myself representing clients in commercial and general litigation.

In business – My parents started their first business when I was 16. Being the eldest – and considering my family's core belief about everyone pulling their weight – I learnt about business very early. From dealing with HR, suppliers or customer issues, this naturally led me to want to know more about our legal position so I could be more useful. I was the first lawyer in the family and always thought I would qualify in order to return back to business . . . though I've never quite found the right moment to leave the law!

In life – I was 32 years old and seven months pregnant with my first born when I began the steps of starting the firm. I can genuinely say that of all the challenges I have ever taken on, this, coupled with being a first-time parent, was the hardest challenge of my life. I had to learn how to be a mum and a boss with immediate effect!

What would you say is the most important lesson you learned in the first few years of your firm?

It's lonely. It's best to prepare yourself for this at the beginning, though it doesn't have to be a bad thing. If you're setting up with someone or others, be clear what your roles are and put a shareholder's agreement/partners agreement in place so there's no confusion or difficult conversations later. You should do this no matter who they are to you, whether they're family or otherwise. You have worked hard for years to qualify and this venture could have catastrophic outcomes if you or your partners get it wrong.

Growth is something any businessperson should have their eye on. Remember that opportunities offer themselves up in different ways. I would strongly advise against giving up equity too quickly. Of course, everyone wants a piece of something they haven't earned. Just don't forget those sleepless nights of worry and let them go in vain!

At various points, I did consider (and even did at one juncture) taking on a non-equity partner in order to provide them with a platform to grow. My personal experience with this is that people can let power and titles get to their head, as though it's a given that they should be a partner, without truly understanding the responsibility it carries. It's fair to say that experience was short-lived!

I would not be dismissive if the right person came along and I do believe that growth is imperative, however the true measures are profit and client satisfaction, along with staying within the lines of the ethos of the law firm. I have seen extremely bright lawyers who make several millions a year for the firm but because of this, they've believed they could push outside of boundaries. That can only be done so far and can very often be the demise of the entire firm.

27 months from inception, KaurMaxwell has grown from me and another fee earner, to me, another partner, practice manager, five fee earners and several introducers. There is a trajectory of growth with various methods to do this: organically or via a merger/ acquisition. I have been advised organically is ultimately the best way forward, but it is slow. Given the current climate, I can't help but be interested in the possible purchase of firms who are failing due to no other reason but cash flow.

Can you tell us how you learned this particular lesson?

I set up on my own and no matter how much people told me they were there to support me – and they did very kindly try – the business was on me. I had been working for someone else who had to close his practice of eight staff in a two-storey building in Soho in a matter of weeks, all while I was pregnant. I went for interviews but none of the options seem to make commercial sense. I decided to make an offer to my employer that I would start my own practice and take my files and some staff.

Everything, from managing the cases from the old firm, to transferring them and making big decisions on the business; it all stopped with me. Once I got over the impact, I just did what my instinct dictated (I didn't have the time to do anything else!). Some things I got wrong but I made decisions that felt right at that time. I had far too many plates spinning to deal with it all at once, so I had to be careful with what I prioritised.

What changes did you make as a result of this?

I realised that I needed to run thoughts, ideas and issues by someone. But I knew my staff were not always the answer for this as they needed to see their leader lead.

Instead, I created an unofficial board. I have great people around me, I just needed to identify them and tap into their experience. From creatives to business owners to people who'd been employers for 30 years, I went to people with the right skill set to bounce my ideas or talk through issues. I confided in my bank manager a lot! It was so helpful to speak to someone completely detached who had excellent commerciality.

It's about being resourceful.

In what way do you think this made you a better law firm owner?

I needed to be an effective boss and owner right away, so I stopped feeling sorry for myself and decided to refocus my energy. I didn't have a huge amount of experience running a firm, but I drafted experience in through family, friends, contacts and clients! Clients have some fantastic insight and were excellent people to sound board from. It made me clearer about decisions and whilst I was alone, it felt like I had an invisible army behind me.

What advice would you give to a new law firm owner about this?

Do not think you know it all. Equally, do not doubt yourself at every juncture. We are lawyers, we can't help but be risk adverse. However, you are now no longer just a lawyer, you have another job and that's a business owner. Be honest about your strengths and weaknesses. Once you're clear on this you can either draft in the skill set you need or borrow time from people you respect.

Finally, the best advice I was given was to imagine you are wearing two different caps: 'working on the business' and 'working for the business'. Create each persona and don't try to do both at the same time. When you're working on the business, you are a business owner and it will be necessary to adopt an aerial view. When you are working for the business you are fee earning and working in a way which you should already know well!

Chapter 15

Exit strategies

There are many reasons why you might be thinking about moving on from your firm. You may have started your business with a big vision and the very best intentions, but that doesn't mean it will always be right for you.

Circumstances change, as do people, and there may come a time when you want to make the decision to step away from your business. The best route for dealing with this is likely to depend on your reasons behind wanting to make an exit, the current position of your business and your own personal circumstances.

If you find yourself in this position, please do take the time to congratulate yourself on all you have achieved. Many people dream of starting their own business, but comparatively few ever take any real steps towards doing so. The courage it took to get your big vision off the ground was no small endeavour, no matter the end result.

Even if you're not yet even nearly at the stage of considering moving on from your business, you may still want to take the time to read about some of the most common ways other business owners seek to do this. Having an awareness of some of the broad options that may be available to you in the future will help you to build a firm that is prepared whatever the future should hold. In other words, starting with a few possible ends in mind will help to make sure you implement policies and procedures that will serve you well in the years ahead.

15.1 When might it be time to move on?

Like almost everything in business, the answer to this question will involve a lot of weighing up of different factors as well as a heavy emphasis on instinct.

You may reach a point of understanding when you realise that running a business isn't the best option for you anymore. Or you may feel that factors beyond your control are forcing your hand on the issue.

It may be the right time to move on from your firm for a wide range of reasons. Some possible reasons for this are:

- it isn't what you expected;
- your personal circumstances have changed;
- you want to pursue other career goals;
- your firm isn't financially viable; or
- you're ready to retire.

15.1.1 It isn't what you expected

You have no doubt realised by now that the realities of running a business are rather different to the idealised image we're often presented with. This is perhaps even more true for legal professionals who will have a very different experience at the head of their own firm than they did when they were employed elsewhere.

The law is already a stressful industry to be in; adding in the worry of finding new clients, paying salaries, complying with regulatory burdens and navigating professional indemnity insurance, it may all become too much.

It takes a very particular type of person to flourish while managing all these competing pressures. You may well realise that this isn't the role for you and, if this is the case, we applaud you for your honesty.

Running a law firm is such a big commitment and is likely to take up a huge chunk of your focus and waking hours. You would need to take a significant amount of enjoyment and professional satisfaction from your firm (as well as a healthy and sustainable profit!) in order to make this sacrifice worthwhile.

If running a firm isn't as rewarding as you expected, or if you're just not enjoying it, it's probably wise to make the decision to move on sooner rather than later.

15.1.2 Your personal circumstances have changed

Personal circumstances can change for all sorts of reasons. Those reasons may be happy ones: perhaps you have a new partner or are expecting a baby. They can also be difficult ones: perhaps you or a family member may be suffering from poor health, you may have had a redundancy in the family or you may be dealing with a divorce or separation.

Whatever the change, you may discover your business is no longer compatible with where you are in life. It might no longer make sense financially to carry on, or you may be finding that you just don't have enough hours in the day to spend enough time with your business *and* your loved ones.

You may well be brilliant at running a business and derive a great deal of enjoyment from doing so. This doesn't mean you can't make the decision to exit your business in order to prioritise other areas of your life.

15.1.3 You want to pursue other career goals

Some law firm owners specifically start their firm in order to boost their job prospects for the future. Perhaps you started out with the intention of boosting your CV and personal profile in order to attract the attention of major industry employers. Equally, you may discover that founding a law firm has opened up new career opportunities for you even without this being your intention.

In these cases, you may choose to distance yourself from your firm in order to accept or pursue an alternative career offer.

Alternatively, you may decide that you're ready for an even bigger career change and plan to leave the law altogether.

15.1.4 Your firm isn't financially viable

Not every new law firm will survive the first few years in business. This is an increasingly competitive industry and you may have to accept that your firm simply isn't profitable enough to survive.

If you reach this point, you're likely to have to make some very difficult decisions about how to move forward.

15.1.5 You're ready to retire

It's probably fair to say that most people don't want to run their law firm forever. Sooner or later, everyone will come to a point where they feel they've done what they need to do in their career and are ready to retire.

Coming to this decision isn't necessarily as straightforward as a business owner as it would be for an employed professional. Once you're sure that the time is right to take a step back, you'll need to think carefully about what will happen to your business when you're no longer there to run it. This is likely to be an easier issue to navigate if you have one or more partners than it would be if you are the sole owner. It might be wise to think about this long ahead of time and have a comprehensive plan in place for when you're ready to activate it.

You might want to consider aiming for a gradual transition into retirement. Running a firm is an important and demanding job: don't underestimate how difficult it might be to suddenly cut out your work routine. Though there's no doubt that running a law firm is hard work – it also offers meaning, structure, mental stimulation and a sense of belonging and purpose. Losing all of that could increase your risk of suffering from loneliness or even depression. Sure, once you retire you will be the master of your own destiny, but in many cases you might no longer be clear about what that destiny might be.

If you think this could be a concern for you, you might want to consider developing a plan that will provide more of a transition period. This could involve gradually cutting the hours you work over a period of a few years. Alternatively, you may choose to leave your position of director or partner of a firm but stay on part time as a consultant.

Whatever you decide is the right way to enter retirement, you will no doubt want to do so with the confidence that you are leaving your firm in good hands.

15.2 What exit strategies could you consider?

In some cases, making the decision to leave your firm can be just as complicated as making the decision to start one.

Depending on how successful your firm is, it's unlikely that you would be prepared to just close the doors and walk away. Rather, you may be interested in selling your firm or merging it with another firm. This would mean that you could walk away with a significant financial boost in return for all the hard work you have put in.

There are so many different ways you could consider moving on from your business. Each option will have a myriad of associated benefits and disadvantages, along with a whole host of legal intricacies to work through.

Below we have touched on some of the most common exit strategies you could consider, though obviously if you do choose to explore any of these options further, a great deal more research will be needed:

- being bought out by other partners;
- management buy-out;
- selling your firm;
- closing your firm.

15.2.1 Being bought out by other partners

If your firm has other partners, the most obvious choice might be to approach those partners and explore whether they might be willing to buy your share in the firm.

This could be a good option whether all partners are equal in the firm, or whether you are a senior partner with other more junior partners.

If you have a partnership agreement in place, you may have chosen to include a clause on partnership buy-outs. This may even have included a 'shoot out' note on how much each partner would be willing to sell their share for.

How you choose to manage a buy-out will depend both on what you are most comfortable with and on what your partners are able to afford. You may choose to take a lump sum in return for your partnership, or you may choose to accept your payments in instalments.

15.2.2 Management buy-out

A management buy-out is when the owner of a company sells all or some of their shares to members of the management team. In some cases, the management team will do this by forming a new company to be an acquisition vehicle. The funds for the purchase are generally a mix of funds from the management team themselves, private equity and bank loans. In these situations, it's fairly common for the previous owner of the company to retain an interest in the company. This interest is usually in the form of a debt, which can be paid off over time.

This could be a good option as an exit strategy if you are the sole owner of a firm but have a management team who would be keen to take over.

The benefits of this kind of sale include:

- the peace of mind that you would be handing your firm over to people you already know and trust;
- you wouldn't need to go through a long process of identifying and approaching potential buyers;
- the sales process may well be quicker as the buyers already know the company well.

This kind of exit could also be really beneficial for the buyers. Being able to take over the company in this way would mean that they could continue to benefit from all the hard work they've invested in the company during their time in management, rather than facing uncertainty or potentially redundancy should the firm be sold to a third party.

If you decide to explore the option of a management buy-out in your company, you would, of course, need to examine the issue from all angles and ensure that both you and your management team have taken legal and financial advice.

15.2.3 Selling your firm

If you are considering selling your firm to a third party, this is certainly not something to rush into. In order to achieve a successful sale, you will need to start preparing your firm for this end a year or two before the planned sale date. This is important as you will want your firm to be in the best possible health in order to get the best possible price for it.

In order to help you focus on the areas where your firm might need some attention prior to approaching potential buyers, we suggest you conduct a SWOT analysis of your firm. This is a strategic planning tool which will enable you to identify strengths, weaknesses, opportunities and threats. Doing this will be very helpful in terms of helping you to highlight:

(a) strengths and opportunities that may attract buyers; and
(b) weaknesses and threats which will need to be addressed.

We also suggest that you get your accountant on board with your plans early on in the process as they will be able to help you prepare financial forecasts, information about goodwill and a full valuation of your firm.

What else will you need to consider?

Tax is an important consideration during this process and we recommend you take professional advice on this as early as possible. This will ensure that you are fully briefed on the tax implications of the sale and that this process is managed as efficiently as possible.

How exactly a sale plays out will depend on the structure of your firm. While sole practitioners, partnerships and limited liability partnerships (LLPs) sell their assets, a limited company can choose to sell their shares in the company (a share sale) and/or its assets (an assets sale).

If your firm is regulated, there will likely be requirements you will need to take into account when selling a firm.

Regulatory requirements from the SRA include the following:

- Any firm that is regulated by the SRA will need to inform the SRA of a change of ownership *before* it occurs.
- If you are selling your practice as a going concern, you must inform all clients of the change in ownership and obtain their consent in advance to transfer their files and any of their money that is being held on account.
- Client confidentiality must be preserved during negotiations for a sale. It is not permitted to share confidential information with third parties without consent. Potential buyers still count as third parties in these circumstances.
- If you will be retiring or taking a break from the practice after the sale of your firm, you will need to provide the SRA with a contact address.

Further involvement

Whether you have any further involvement with your firm after the sale will depend on your preference, along with that of the buyer.

It may seem like a better choice for everyone involved for there to be a completely clean break. This could be a good choice for you if you plan to leave the law entirely or if you are choosing to sell the firm due to it causing more stress than joy.

Alternatively, you and the buyer might want to consider options of you staying on as an occasional consultant. This could be a good option for you if you are selling your firm because it has become too much to handle, perhaps due to other commitments or health reasons.

Whatever your plans on this front, this is something that will need to be discussed thoroughly during the negotiation period.

15.2.4 Closing your firm

There are a number of reasons why you might choose to simply close your firm.

This could be because, for example:

- you haven't been able to find a buyer;
- you don't feel your firm has sufficient value to be sold;
- your firm has been declared bankrupt;
- your firm has been the recipient of disciplinary action;
- your practising certificate has been suspended;
- you haven't been able to secure professional indemnity insurance; or
- serious health problems or a death have required an immediate cessation of business.

Though you could argue that closing your firm might be simpler than seeking a buyer and managing negotiations, it's certainly not an easy option. It would also mean that you would have to walk away from your business empty handed, no matter how much money and time you'd invested into it over the years. For this reason, you probably wouldn't opt for this as an exit strategy unless you had no other choice.

There are a range of issues that need to be dealt with when you close down a firm. However, when you are dealing with these issues it is important to make sure that what you are doing couldn't be construed as continuing to practise. Once you have notified your regulatory body that your firm is closed, you will not be permitted to practise at that firm.

For example, it would be perfectly okay to submit final bills or arrange for any files you have in storage to be transferred. However, it would not be reasonable to apply for a grant of probate or even respond to a query relating to a previous application.

If you do need to engage in correspondence after the closure of your firm (perhaps to chase up unpaid invoices) you will need to make clear that the firm is now closed. If you continue to use any headed paper for any purpose, the headed paper should also make this clear.

Closing a firm after a death

Legal professionals should perhaps know better than most just how important it is to be prepared for even the most unlikely of eventualities. None of us are invincible and it's wise to make sure you have documentation in place that details what should be done with your firm in the event of your death.

This might be a more straightforward procedure to put in place if your firm has other partners or staff members who would be able to step in if necessary. If you are a sole practitioner, you might want to consider appointing another legal professional you trust as an executor in your will or as an attorney in a power of attorney. This would ensure that a trusted professional would be involved with closing down your firm, should that be necessary.

15.3 How to prepare for an exit

Preparing for an exit will include the following:

- telling your staff;
- telling your clients;
- informing organisations;
- getting your firm ready;

and importantly:

- taking care of yourself.

15.3.1 Telling your staff

If you are planning to close, sell or merge your firm, you will need to find a way to sensitively convey this information to your staff.

Ideally, you would be able to share the news with your staff along with information about how this will affect their jobs. However, it is important to balance this with the importance of ensuring that your staff hear of the news from you and not from a third party.

You will need to have covered all eventualities here and may need to consider redundancy pay or payment in lieu of notice as part of the financial arrangements for closure.

15.3.2 Telling your clients

It will also be important to notify your clients of your intentions to exit the business. The tone you will choose for this will no doubt be different depending on the specific exit strategy you have chosen.

If you will be closing your firm altogether, it would be a matter of professional courtesy to ensure you have been able to bring all client matters to an appropriate close. If this isn't possible, you may wish to find an alternative firm for any outstanding matters to be transferred to.

If you are handing your firm over to the other partners or to a new owner entirely, you will need to conduct a handover to ensure all clients have been introduced to the new owners and feel confident that they are still valued and appreciated by the firm.

15.3.3 Organisations to notify

Whether you are selling your firm, closing your firm or your firm is being merged into another, you will need to notify a wide range of organisations and suppliers about your intentions.

This may include:

- your regulatory body;
- your accountant;
- any banks that your business holds accounts with;
- Companies House (assuming you are a limited company or an LLP);
- counsels' chambers;
- any professional or advertising directories your firm is listed in;
- your broadband provider;
- your electricity and/or gas supplier;
- your telephone provider;
- your water supplier;
- HM Courts and Tribunals Service (HMCTS);
- HM Revenue and Customs (HMRC);
- HM Land Registry (HMLR);
- Information Commissioner;
- local authority;
- Probate Registry;
- your professional indemnity insurer;
- Royal Mail and DX; and
- any contractors or freelancers you have worked with in the past.

15.3.4 Getting your firm ready

All firms should have management procedures for closing down written as part of their risk management strategy. This should include processes for managing an orderly closedown and dealing with outstanding issues such as client matters, client money, insurance and other administrative functions.

Run-off insurance cover

If your firm will be ceasing without a successor practice, you will need to have run-off insurance in place for a period of six years. The insurance company that was providing professional indemnity cover on the date that your firm ceased practising is obliged to provide this.

Run-off cover will usually be paid for in one premium that will last for the full six-year period. The cost of the premium will depend on factors including the size of your firm, the type of work it undertakes, its turnover and its claims history. You will usually need to budget around three times the cost of your firm's annual premium.

What if your indemnity insurance policy ran out before your firm closed?

If your professional indemnity insurance policy ran out before your firm closed and you weren't able to take out a new one, your last insurer is obliged to provide you with an extended policy period of an additional 90 days from the end of your previous policy. If you close during this 90-day period, or on the final day of it, your insurer will have to provide you with a run off insurance policy that runs for six years from the start of the extended policy period.

What about run-off cover beyond six years?

Cover beyond the six-year run off period is called 'supplementary run off cover'. This is provided in many cases by the Solicitors Indemnity Fund, although this was due to close to new claims on 30 September 2020. Due to the coronavirus pandemic and its significant impact on the profession, the SRA has decided that the closure of the Solicitors Indemnity Fund should be postponed for one year, until 30 September 2021.

Without further cover, the former principals of firms that closed after 31 August 2000 (or their estate) can be liable for any subsequent claims that are made. The SRA reports that around 11 per cent of claims are made after six years (**www.lawsociety.org.uk/support-services/advice/articles/closure-of-the-sif**), so this is by no means an insignificant risk.

It is generally advised that former law firm owners who are coming to the end of their initial six year run off insurance period contact their insurance providers to see if further cover can be provided. If not, you may wish to contact a specialist insurance broker to find out what other options may be available to you.

The SRA may introduce an alternative to the Solicitors Indemnity Fund at some point, though there is no clarity about this at present.

15.3.5 Taking care of yourself

There are many reasons why you may need to manage an exit from your law firm. Some will be predominantly positive, others will be quite the opposite.

Whatever your situation, it's important to recognise that this is likely to be a difficult time for you emotionally. It will be important to give yourself the mental space to work through your feelings about moving away from your business. This is also likely to be a stressful period with a lot of important decisions to make and regulations to comply with.

We suggest you make sure you have family and friends around to support you, as well as a trusted group of professional advisors.

15.4 How long will it take to complete a managed exit?

There is no definitive framework to use to determine how long it will take for you to manage an exit from your law firm. Some exits will be planned and managed over a period of three to five years, while those with more extreme conditions might need to be completed within a matter of weeks.

Generally speaking, the longer you take to plan and orchestrate an exit, likely the more favourable the conditions will be when you do so. Your plan for exiting your business should aim to capitalise on all your years of hard work. Not only will this hopefully mean that you exit your firm with an attractive profit, it will also ensure that your transition from business owner to former business owner is as smooth as possible.

However, you will not always have the luxury of time, especially if you are being forced by circumstances beyond your control. You can go some way towards minimising the effect of a forced exit by ensuring that you have put policies, procedures and plans in place for all eventualities long before you expect to need them.

CASE STUDY 15: PAUL BENNETT

Paul Bennett is a solicitor and partner of Bennett Briegal LLP. Bennett Briegal is a specialist law practice that focuses on advising lawyers and professionals on matters including the business of law, partnership matters, mergers and acquisitions, business structures, professional regulation and employment. Paul is also a Law Society council member.

When did you launch your law firm?

My first law firm as a sole practitioner launched in 2009, just after the financial crash. It was pre-planned before the crash and I knew it would still work. I sold that firm in 2013 and joined a Top 200 practice as one of 26 partners in an ABS. My aim was always to start, build and sell or to take external investment as I wanted to fast-track my career and use technology to develop a client-focused business, which was rarer in those days.

In March 2019 I launched my second law firm with a colleague, Bennett Briegal LLP, focused on law firms and the professional sector. This time around it is about having a great firm and clients for the next 20–25 years to provide an income with interesting work. Our core clients are solicitors and law firms, but we act for barristers, Chambers, GPs, accountants, independent financial advisers (IFAs) and professionals generally.

How much knowledge and experience did you have before you started?

The lawyer in me says: in what sense? Business knowledge and experience? Legal experience? Knowledge of managing finances, people, marketing? In law, most people get to a position based on a narrow skill set which is usually legal. My career has been built on business experience gathered prior to law which has enabled me to deliver law at a high level because the business aspects are second nature and instinctive rather than additional skills, which they are for many lawyers. My earlier commercial career included flagship projects for Virgin Group, Marks & Spencer, and Orange Mobile Phones. This gave a broad business experience which 99.9 per cent of solicitors simply do not have.

By 2009 I had spent almost five years as a paralegal prior to being a trainee and had just over three years' PQE, so I had nine years of legal experience and business and management experience going back to the mid-1990s. I had run non-law businesses, I was a DJ and nightclub promotor and also had an experience in both the manufacturing and service sectors in commercial roles.

What would you say is the most important lesson you learned while running your firm?

You have to stretch yourself and others. We all have to keep learning and self-development is key. As a smaller, niche firm, clients expect excellence and depth of knowledge and that's a given for solicitors who specialise. However, the client care, marketing, PR and the process of managing the team will all stretch you and offer evolving challenges to you as a business owner and manager.

I learnt early on that, unlike in other businesses, you have to stretch those elements in a smaller law firm to be effective. In larger firms you can hide, and I have seen lots of solicitors who are great at the law but who do not have leadership, marketing or financial skills so simply could not be effective in a role without developing themselves. However, those skills are capable of being learnt. Remember, at one stage none of us could drive or ride a bike, but we learnt when we were ready to do so and committed to it.

Can you tell us how you learned this particular lesson?

When it was all going so well in late 2010 and early 2011, I took my foot off the gas thinking I had cracked the leadership of a law firm lark. In doing this I realised my team and clients needed me to push myself a little further as the performance of others dropped off.

Everyone I have worked with since, including those I helped recruit in the Top 200 firm, had a skill or knowledge or expertise which I lacked – whether in a support role or as an equity partner. This ensured I was stretched and had confidence in them. Those recruited had to have that hunger to self-develop further because they want to be the best.

What changes did you make as a result of this moving forward?

I have adopted a constant evolution mentality. I have a hunger for knowledge and excellence which is mirrored by my clients and my business partner. We know our field, we develop each other, and self-development is key for smaller law firms.

In what way do you think this made you a better law firm owner?

It has ensured we are super profitable; clients have fun working with us, we enjoy it. It is a cultural thing: we seek to work with those who share our values.

Instead of focusing on turnover, growth and career opportunities for staff, I quickly learnt to focus on happy clients and profits. These two things are intrinsically linked. Happy clients will pay a premium for service and legal excellence, but unless you have a self-development ethos you will not have happy staff, happy clients or profits to reflect your hard work. This is, in my view, a critical but often-overlooked part of a successful law firm business.

Staff will be loyal if they are involved in great work and are fairly paid. The quality of the work and clients is key for holding onto good staff.

What advice would you give to a new law firm owner about this?

Come out of your comfort zone and aim to be the best you can be for your clients and your business; this is the right approach. If marketing is your weakness, develop that skill. If motivating others scares you, work on confidence and supervision. Stretch yourself, it is the least your clients and your business deserve if you decide to leap into self-employment in this sector.

Focus on happy clients and good profit margins on each and every job – the rest will then take care of itself.

Chapter 16

COVID-19 – the ultimate disaster recovery test

The last third of this book was written during the COVID-19 lockdown in 2020. The idea of publishing it with no more than a passing reference to events that have rocked not just the legal industry but the world as a whole seemed implausible.

The COVID-19 pandemic has created a very difficult period worldwide. Hundreds of thousands of people have lost their lives, healthcare professionals and key workers have made huge sacrifices, and large numbers of people have been plunged into unstable financial situations.

This, of course, is a book about starting and running a law firm. Though there are no doubt more serious and more tragic implications of the pandemic and the subsequent lockdown, our remit is to examine how they have impacted law firms, law firm owners and the legal industry in general. What are the business implications of this current global reality? And how might things evolve and change as we emerge at the other side?

At the time of writing (June 2020) we are still in the relatively early days of the pandemic. Though we can be certain the effects of COVID-19 will be felt for many years to come, it's difficult to know exactly how these effects will manifest.

The new reality that we are facing goes far beyond the question of running a business. It concerns our health and wellbeing, our families, our finances and our perspective in every sense. Even if you feel that you and your firm have been well-placed to continue as usual during this time – or perhaps even to thrive – it's impossible to be sure that this will last. Yes, there are plenty of factors you can control within your own business, but how the wider economy responds will be very much out of your hands.

16.1 The ultimate test for your disaster recovery plan

At various points in this book we've talked about just how important it is to make sure you've planned for all eventualities as a business owner. Planning for crisis management in advance can make all sorts of business hiccups easier to deal with as and when they happen.

You may have disaster recovery plans in place for things like staff illness, technology break-downs or sudden incapacity. Of course, we suspect very few law firm owners had the foresight to plan how they would manage a worldwide pandemic.

16.1.1 How important are disaster recovery plans?

Disaster recovery and crisis management plans are absolutely vital when it comes to building a strong and sustainable business. Though these aren't particularly enjoyable subjects to think about, investing regular time to establish policies and keep them up to date can reap dividends in the future.

Many of the law firm owners we have spoken to about their experiences of running a firm during lockdown have spoken of how fortunate they felt to have had robust disaster recovery policies in place long in advance. This meant that these professionals had a head-start on crisis management and were able to move forward within lockdown regulations with a much smaller impact on their business.

16.1.2 What aspects of disaster recovery plans have been most helpful?

When you put a disaster recovery plan together you are, in large part, working on the basis of educated guesswork. Though in many cases you can take advice from other law firm owners on their experiences, in others you will need to try to walk through different scenarios in your mind to try to identify potential pitfalls.

Once again, it is unlikely that law firm owners had a specific crisis plan in place for managing a pandemic. However, they may well have had procedures in place for dealing with being shut out of their office temporarily or for dealing with a sudden downturn in work.

Some of the disaster recovery plans that are likely to have been most beneficial during this period include plans for:

- effective remote working;
- being able to access all documents digitally;
- identifying key personnel (perhaps with a view to furloughing non-essential staff);
- communicating effectively with your client-base;
- nominating who is able to make key decisions, and who needs to approve them;
- supporting staff in working from home.

16.2 The initial impact for the profession

During the early stages of the COVID-19 pandemic, legal professionals of all levels were under a great deal of pressure. Law firm owners and their employees all suddenly found themselves having to juggle working from home, childcare responsibilities, sharing a home workspace with other members of their household, having to participate in virtual client meetings or court hearings, and missing the social and collegiate atmosphere of their usual workplaces.

There are a range of ways that we can examine the initial impact for the profession:

- the quick shift to working from home;
- access to governmental support programmes;
- pay cuts and redundancies;
- short-term changes in the courts;
- other innovations in the industry.

We will examine each of these, and then discuss how firms have fared.

16.2.1 The quick shift to working from home

When lockdown was announced there was certainly a sense of panic among all business owners. A crucial element of lockdown was that no one should be travelling to and from a place of work except where this was 'absolutely necessary and could not be done from home.'

Generally speaking, almost everything we do in legal services can be done from home. There are some obvious exceptions for barristers, litigators and in cases where documents need to be signed and witnessed in person. However, in theory it should not have been too difficult for legal professionals to make the switch to working from home. Indeed, many sole practitioners and members of remote teams already do this full-time.

This is an area where firms who already had a fantastic grasp on technology are likely to have initially fared better.

A team who were already used to . . .

- storing and accessing documents digitally;
- communicating with clients and each other using video messaging services;
- working from home either using a company laptop or remote log in access to their office PC

. . . are likely to have been able to make the shift far more easily than teams who did not already have these skills. Indeed, in the weeks leading up to the government's lockdown announcement we are aware of many firms who had already had a trial-run of these systems and processes, which meant they were able to address any resulting issues ahead of time.

Firms also needed to navigate the process of ensuring that all staff members had the right tools and equipment to allow them to carry out their roles, not to mention a space at home where they could do this.

For many firms this involved:

- thinking ahead to send staff home with technological equipment such as PCs, scanners and monitors ahead of time;
- buying additional equipment and having it delivered directly to staff members;
- giving each staff member an allowance to purchase vital home working equipment such as desks or chairs;
- purchasing and introducing new software packages;
- having to navigate the process of providing remote technological assistance to staff members who are used to having this on site;
- redistributing responsibilities that would previously have been carried out by furloughed staff members;
- introducing new policies to manage flexible hours for staff members who were now having to work with no available childcare.

Managing the emotional impact

Many law firms likely found that it was easier to address the practicalities of the shift to working from home than it was to support their staff members through the process emotionally. There is, of course, no one-size-fits-all approach to helping employees through a stressful situation. Though many staff will no doubt have enjoyed the convenience of working from home, others will have found it very difficult to have a sudden change to their usual routine.

With all the complications involved in this period, it's no wonder that HR departments and professionals that provide specialist employment services have been incredibly busy. For many firms, the advice provided by these specialists has been vital in ensuring that they are supporting their employees in the most effective ways possible. The value of this kind of specialist advice can never be underestimated.

With this in mind, many law firm owners learned how important it is to add in plenty of flexibility to disaster recovery plans in order to accommodate their staff members and keep morale high.

Did all law firms shift to home working?

Not all firms felt they were able to make this change. This is generally true for law firms who don't already have a digital infrastructure in place and are still very reliant on a paper filing system.

Those law firms who did keep operating from their offices during the lockdown period had to make some other changes to make this possible.

Many had to rearrange desks and other furniture in order to abide by social distancing guidelines. It was also necessary for many to reduce the number of personnel in the office. This problem was generally addressed by requiring staff to work on rotation, and/or by furloughing some staff.

How have these changes impacted on productivity?

Potential loss of productivity has always been a key reason cited by companies who don't want their employees to be able to work from home. This is a hotly contested claim, and would likely be enthusiastically argued against by those law firm owners who have actively chosen to work remotely. Indeed, many of the law firm owners we've spoken to about this during lockdown have been very quick to tell us that their productivity has increased exponentially.

It will be interesting to see whether firms who have been able to switch seamlessly to remote home working have experienced any tangible effects to their productivity. Though it's likely that there was an initial adjustment period while staff familiarised themselves with new systems and processes (particularly if new technologies and software were being introduced), has this translated to any noticeable impact on the bottom line?

It may well be that firms have found it easier to determine which staff, particularly fee-earners, are meeting key performance indicators (KPIs). It is much harder to hide a lack of productivity behind 'soft skills' when working remotely.

Many firms have also enjoyed a boost of productivity in switching from face-to-face client meetings to virtual ones. This is due to a complete removal of travel time for legal professionals, as well as the fact that clients don't need to be met at the door or provided with tea or coffee during a virtual meeting. This particular development is likely to be one that many firms choose to continue in the future, especially now that so many more of their clients will be more familiar with virtual meetings and open to this option.

Despite these initial positive signs, we do need to be wary of how sustainable these new working practices might be over time. Yes, many firms have experienced a productivity boost during these first few months, but would this continue over time?

Questions that need to be considered here include:

- Are managers having to spend more time supporting less autonomous team members?
- Will morale fall over time without the usual office camaraderie?
- Is the training and supervision of more junior staff less effective when carried out remotely?
- Will innovation suffer without people having physical colleagues to bounce ideas off?

- Will there be an increase in mental health diagnoses for staff members who have had to balance working from home with increased family pressures, such as a lack of childcare?

All things considered, we suspect switching to remote working may have had a lesser impact on a firm's overall productivity than those who stayed in their offices but had to use the government's furlough scheme to cut down personnel numbers.

It's currently too early to have access to any specific data on this from the legal industry, though we have seen some firms make big decisions on this front. For example, Slater and Gordon has publicised its decision to close its London headquarters in a bid to embrace remote working (**www.lawgazette.co.uk/practice/slater-and-gordon-to-close-london-office-as-remote-working-becomes-norm/5104404.article**). Many big companies in other industries have also made a commitment to offer more options for remote working in the future. Facebook, Twitter and Shopify are some of the big-name technology companies leading the charge with this (**www.forbes.com/sites/jackkelly/2020/05/24/the-work-from-home-revolution-is-quickly-gaining-momentum/#7675026d1848**).

16.2.2 What governmental support has been available?

The government has set out a range of support packages and mechanisms to help business owners and self-employed individuals to get through this period.

The support packages that may have been available for law firm owners and sole practitioners include:

- **Coronavirus Job Retention Scheme**, whereby business owners have been able to furlough employees while the government pays 80 per cent of their wages in addition to any employee-paid national insurance (NI) and pension contributions. (Though these proportions have changed over the lifetime of the scheme.)
- **Deferral of VAT payments**, whereby business owners could choose to defer any VAT payments due between 20 March and 30 June 2020.
- **Deferral of Self Assessment payments on account**, whereby anyone due to make a second self-assessment payment on account by 31 July 2020 could choose to defer this to the 31 January 2021.
- **Coronavirus Small Business Grant Fund**, whereby small business owners who pay little or no business rates were entitles to a one-off grant of £10,000.
- **Coronavirus Local Authority Discretionary Grants Fund**, whereby small or micro businesses who were not eligible for other support could apply to their local authority for a one-off grant.

- **Self-employment Income Support Scheme (SEISS)**, whereby self-employed individuals earning up to £50,000 per year could claim a grant for up to 80 per cent of their average monthly income.
- **Coronavirus Business Interruption Loan Scheme**, whereby small and medium business owners can apply for loans for up to £5 million. 80 per cent of this was guaranteed by the government, and it also paid interest and any fees on the loan for the first 12 months.
- **Coronavirus Future Fund,** whereby innovative businesses facing difficulties due to the outbreak could apply for convertible loans of between £125,000 and £5 million.
- **Coronavirus Bounce Back Loan scheme**, whereby small to medium businesses could borrow from £2,000 up to 25 per cent of their turnover (maximum £50,000). The government guaranteed 100 per cent of the loan and there were no fees or interest to pay for 12 months.
- **Coronavirus Large Business Interruption Loan Scheme**, whereby medium- and large-sized business could access loans of up to £200 million, with the government guaranteeing 80 per cent of the finance to the lender.
- **COVID-19 Corporate Financing Facility**, whereby the Bank of England will buy short-term debt from large companies who have been affected by a short-term funding squeeze.

Though these schemes have certainly been very helpful for businesses during the initial period, it's important to note that reliance on such schemes shouldn't necessarily be part of any disaster recovery plan you put together for any future events of these sort. It's impossible to know whether these sorts of schemes would be available in the future, either during another coronavirus pandemic or another economic event of this scale.

It's also important to note that many law firm owners have found themselves exempt from all the support on offer. This might be because they are paid via dividends, or because they are self-employed and earn over £50,000 (which was the cut-off point for accessing government support under the SEISS).

16.2.3 Pay cuts and redundancies

No business can survive a period of change or disaster without remaining profitable. For some firms this may have involved some quick thinking and innovation to bring in new services or reach out to new groups with existing ones. For others, it will sadly have involved having to significantly cut costs through pay cuts or redundancies.

A lot of firms have had to make some very tough decisions about how they will move forward. Others have still to make these decisions.

Many firms have already had to implement pay cuts. As early as April 2020 there were reports of partners at magic circle firms having to take pay cuts, or perhaps even having to give up their pay completely for the foreseeable future (**www.thetimes.co.uk/article/magic-runs-out-at-city-law-firms-as-partners-set-to-suffer-pay-cuts-b8x22rksr**).

16.2.4 Short-term changes in the courts

Unprecedented times are a huge motivator for change. An excellent example of this is the changes seen in the courts system.

Though many courts have remained open during COVID-19 and we have heard stories of crowded criminal court rooms with little to no social distancing adherence, other courts have taken a rather different stance. In March 2020, the Lord Chief Justice announced that civil and family courts were to take place via video link.

The Court of Protection was the first in England and Wales to conduct a hearing entirely online due to the pandemic (**www.familylawweek.co.uk/site.aspx?i=ed210438**). The first hearing was no small feat as it involved 11 witnesses and three expert testimonies, all of which were conducted over Skype for Business.

Equally, on 24 March 2020, *Fowler* v. *Commissioners for Her Majesty's Revenue and Customs* [2020] UKSC 22 was the first UK Supreme Court case to be conducted entirely by Cisco WebEx video conferencing.

In this way, the pandemic can be said to have pushed forward the use of technology in the judiciary by at least five years. It has certainly saved a great deal of public money which otherwise would likely have been spent on consultation papers concerning the right type of technology to be used in these situations. Necessity meant these steps had to be taken without extended consultation. Thus far, the system does not seem to have hit any major issues.

As for the criminal courts, initially all jury trials were suspended. However, some jury trials were able to resume in May in courts where it was felt those in attendance would be able to sufficiently socially distance.

16.2.5 Other innovations in the industry

Periods of difficulty are often times where we see a great level of innovation. When there are more constraints in place, individuals and groups of people often have to think more creatively about how to get around them. There have been some suggestions that this may be the case with the coronavirus pandemic.

One way in which legal professionals have certainly had to think outside of the box is in terms of how to manage the growing demand for wills and lasting powers of attorney (LPA) documents. Both these documents need to be officially signed and witnessed in order to be valid, but social distancing regulations obviously made this difficult. There have been many examples of documents being witnessed on car bonnets or through office windows.

Some firms have really taken their technology use to a new level. Some have been able to adopt the remote signing of documents over video messaging software, while many have seamlessly managed to move client meetings onto these platforms.

16.2.6 How firms have fared

We've stressed at various points during this book that law firms are no different than any other business. You may be offering a very specialist service, but you will still need to abide by tried and tested general business principles in order to sustain profits, manage overheads and come out as profitable enterprises.

The legal industry has no doubt been in a far better position to weather this particular storm than other industries. It has been reasonably straightforward for many of us to transition to working remotely and meeting clients via video messaging software. Unlike other businesses such as restaurants, bars and non-essential shops, we have not been forced to stop trading.

Of course, though many law firms have managed to sustain themselves reasonably well thus far, others have not been as lucky:

- Firms that were slow to adopt remote or digital working practices have had to invest quickly in order to catch up.
- Many firms have had to furlough staff or reduce working hours.
- Many partners have had to agree to pay cuts or salary freezes.
- Many firms have had to quickly reduce overheads.
- Many firms have had to put recruitment plans on hold.

Research conducted by the Law Society suggests that in a survey of nearly 8,000 small firms in March and April 2020, one in five said they were already feeling an impact on cash flow and fee income; 63 per cent of sole practitioners and 71 per cent of firms with four partners or fewer said that these pressures could put them out of business by autumn (**www.lawgazette.co.uk/news/many-high-street-law-firms-face-collapse-research-suggests/5104096.article**).

A Bar Council survey from April 2020 found that 53 per cent of self-employed barristers would not survive six months under current conditions without some sort of financial aid, while 74 per cent would not survive the year. The criminal bar was the hardest hit: 31 per cent said they would not last three months without financial aid, 69 per cent would not last six months and 88 per cent would not last a year (**www.lawgazette.co.uk/news/81-of-chambers-will-fold-within-a-year-bar-council-survey-finds/5103761.article**).

Does firm size matter?

The question of firm size and whether bigger or smaller practices are better placed to deal with such an unexpected business interruption is an interesting one. It might seem obvious that bigger firms with bigger clients would be stronger and more able to withstand turbulent times, and perhaps they'll end up even bigger thanks to buying out smaller firms who haven't been able to survive.

Equally, you might be more supportive of the idea that smaller firms are more flexible and therefore more likely to be able to innovate themselves through this period. Larger firms may need to drastically cut costs by issuing redundancies, which is likely to result in the splintering of larger firms and many of the staff who have been dropped choosing to open their own firms.

Smaller firms are often simpler to run. If you're the director of a small firm, you are probably generally aware of what's in the bank, what invoices are outstanding and what overheads and expenses are coming up. This is likely to make it much easier to make key changes as a result of economic circumstances, without the constraints a big firm may find themselves up against.

However, big firms that cover multiple areas of practice often do well in these periods as those departments that have been more affected can be propped up by those who either haven't been affected or potentially have become more profitable. A big firm may also be better placed to divert fee-earners to areas of the firm where demand has increased rather than simply continuing to pay staff despite there not really being enough for them to do.

With all things considered, there seem to be both advantages and disadvantages to being a larger or smaller firm. We suspect that firm size will have less to do with the ongoing success of a firm during this period than factors including how effectively the firm is able to manage its finances.

Ultimately, those businesses who know their numbers well are likely to fare better in the medium and long term than those who don't.

Does area of practice matter?

The area of practice a firm deals in has certainly had a big impact during the early stages of the pandemic. We suspect this is likely to continue over the rest of the pandemic and the recession that will follow it.

Some areas of the law are more recession-proof than others. Those practices that deal with inevitable necessities such as end-of-life planning and probate are likely to see less of an impact than those that deal with more aspirational areas of the law such as property purchases.

It's also important to consider how much of an impact world events could potentially have on your firm. During the lockdown period, conveyancing firms were affected very badly due to government rules that property sales were not able to continue as normal. Alternatively, many firms who offer will writing, powers of attorney and probate services found themselves extremely busy due to more people wanting to ensure that their family's future was secure and, tragically, significantly more people dying than normal.

There have been some further effects of lockdown on the popularity of legal services:

- More than a dozen cities in China reported a surge in demand for divorces post-lockdown (**www.ft.com/content/11990ff0-c8f5-4f60-9b0a-be06324a4ddb**). Many commentators have predicted a similar outcome in the UK and across Europe, though in the early stages of lockdown in the UK demand for divorce lawyers seems to have dropped (**www.telegraph.co.uk/family/relationships/contrary-popular-belief-divorce-actually-lockdown-and**).
- It's expected that firms that deal with insolvency may experience high demand due to issues concerning business loan defaults and the forfeiture of leases relating to commercial property becoming commonplace.
- Commercial lawyers may find themselves inundated with enquiries regarding policy wordings and whether COVID-19 is a valid reason for a business interruption insurance policy to pay out. (At the time of writing, in July 2020, the Financial Conduct Authority (FCA) is taking a test case regarding this to the High Court. The full judgment, from 15 September 2020, can be read at **www.bailii.org/ew/cases/EWHC/Comm/2020/2448.html**.) The construction of force majeure clauses may also provide plenty of work for commercial lawyers.

16.3 What are the predictions for medium- and long-term impact on the profession?

It's understandable to want to try to predict what might happen in the industry on a medium- and long-term basis. This feels particularly important after a period of social and economic uncertainty, as nobody really knows what to expect from the coming months and years. Will we soon be able to drop straight back into normal business trading? Or will the impact of the COVID-19 pandemic be felt for many financial years to come?

You may be particularly keen to make these sorts of predictions in regards to what you can expect from your business. It's impossible to truly know whether this is a good time to seek to expand or even to start a new business, but you may find some clues by looking back at how businesses have fared in the wake of previous economically difficult periods.

Though we haven't seen anything like the COVID-19 pandemic in our lifetimes, we are all no doubt familiar with the impact of the 2008 global financial crisis. This resulted in a period of recession which is officially recorded as lasting for 18 months, from December 2007 to June 2009 (**www.law.com/americanlawyer/2020/03/13/the-coronavirus-this-recession-and-how-law-firms-need-to-plan-now-to-protect-their-business**). During this recession, demand for law firms dropped, especially for those working within the areas of property and conveyancing. This was a direct result of the drop in house prices – a reported 15.9 per cent in 2008 according to a Nationwide survey of house prices.

16.3.1 What could we expect from the coming recession?

The Organisation for Economic Co-operation and Development (OECD) released predictions for the coming economic outlook in June 2020. They forecasted an 11.5 per cent drop in gross domestic product (GDP) in the UK assuming a second major outbreak is avoided, and a 14 per cent drop assuming there is a second outbreak (**www.oecd.org/economic-outlook**). They believe we are facing the worst economic recession in over a century. This has been supported by further figures from the Office of National Statistics showing that the UK economy shrank by 20.4 per cent in April 2020, which is the largest monthly contraction on record.

Though we can be reasonably certain that we have entered a recession, there's no real way of knowing how long it will last or how best for legal business to protect against it.

In times of economic difficulty, business owners will need to pay closer attention to their finances than ever before. A crucial aspect of this will be developing cash flow models so that you can compare and contrast the possible effects of your business decision-making. This may involve having to invest in financial software that offers this kind of modelling capability, but you'll likely find that this is invaluable at a time like this when there are so many unknowns.

16.3.2 Will more legal professionals become self-employed?

This period has certainly enabled professionals to see their career from a whole new perspective. For some, the period of intense introspection demanded by the pandemic is likely to have enabled them to find greater clarity on what they want from their life.

Many would-be law firm owners have been put off in the past by the cost of what they have considered to be necessary overheads such as the rent for an office space. Now that so many more of us are familiar with remote working – as well as the process of conducting meetings over video messaging software – many of these concerns may have been completely allayed.

There's also the question of job security. Many legal professionals will be facing the possibility of redundancy or massively reduced job prospects. They may therefore be considering other opportunities.

These factors are very likely to have led to more legal professionals making the decision to start their own firm, whether in terms of a more traditional firm or deciding to become a sole practitioner or freelance solicitor.

After a time of much uncertainty, it's not hard to see why many professionals may want to take significant steps towards having greater control over their working lives.

There's an argument to say that the period after economic difficulty is the best time to start something new and dynamic. These types of events involve business casualties: firms who are nimble and quick to adapt will invariably be able to pick up clients from those firms who have not been able to sustain themselves.

16.3.3 Will remote working become the norm?

Early reports seem to indicate that the majority of legal professionals are embracing the fact of working from home and have actually found themselves to be more productive. It's unsurprising, then, that many firms that do have offices are now looking to reduce their physical space.

We believe that in the future, the home office will be more popular than ever, both for sole practitioners and for teams of remote employees. Large office spaces, if they are retained at all, will likely be used less as many employees will visit only a few days a week or for occasional meetings. Of course, offices that do continue to function will not be able to do so completely as normal. Many will need to be redesigned with social distancing in mind. This could result in firms needing larger spaces to accommodate fewer employees.

A sustained growth in home working could have a really positive impact on the environment, especially in large cities like London where we might expect use of the public transport system to be commensurately reduced and for roads to be far less congested. It may also significantly benefit our wellbeing and work/life balance, as remote working is likely to cut commuting times and increase the availability of flexible hours.

16.4 The new normal

The 2020 coronavirus pandemic has introduced radical changes on both a professional and a personal level. Millions of people have had to adapt to remote working more-or-less overnight. Video messaging services have become the norm, while daily commuting and business travel has come to a very abrupt stop.

It is clear that whatever the new normal is, it will be significantly different to life before the pandemic. We believe this period may well have turbo-charged the legal industry ecosystem for clients, legal professionals and the judiciary.

Clients might now expect faster solutions to their problems, perhaps assisted by the combination of minimal human touch and maximum technology, all at a reduced cost. Legal professionals will have to change the way they offer their services in order to incorporate digital and virtual means.

The judiciary and court services will need to secure greater investment in technology to ensure that cases can be heard virtually across the whole court service, and not just in certain courts. This will ensure that the whole system of administration of justice is totally modernised and fit for purpose. The concept of online courts that has been talked about since Lord Justice Briggs's 2016 Final Report on the Civil Courts Structural Review, may now be accelerated.

Those who are hoping that technological changes across the industry will be temporary are likely to be disappointed. Rather, we expect a Darwinian *survival of the fittest* scenario, where those firms that survive and thrive will be those who are willing to adapt and embrace the pace of change.

CASE STUDY 16: JANE CASSELL

Jane Cassell is a solicitor and the founder of JC Independent Wills and Probate Ltd. JC Independent Wills and Probate is an unregulated legal firm that specialises in wills, lasting powers of attorney (LPAs), probate and contentious probate.

When did you launch your law firm?

When I realised that I'd only get more than evenings and weekends with my husband when we both retire, unless I was to set up on my own and enjoy a more flexible lifestyle than a traditional law firm can offer an employee. This was in 2010.

How much knowledge and experience did you have before you started?

Not enough to do it perfectly on day one! Specialising in a particular area of law (wills and probate in my case) does not teach you about running a business and all the many and varied tasks behind the scenes.

I had been qualified as a solicitor for nine years when I set up my will writing business. I'm approaching 20 years qualified now and there's always something more to learn.

What would you say is the most important lesson you learned in the first few years of your firm?

If you have a compelling personal reason for specialising in a particular area of law: share it. For some considerable time, I was simply a woman who went on and on about wills and taking action and moaning about lawyers' fees sometimes being unfair. Then I had a chance encounter which resulted in me deciding to reveal a very personal story about why I run my legal practice the way I do, and why I'm so passionate about wills.

This was a game changer and allowed people to understand where all that energy about wills comes from. Perhaps I should have spoken about my personal experience before I did. It's built up an incredible amount of trust, as clients now understand what shaped me and therefore my law firm.

Can you tell us how you learned this particular lesson?

My personal background is that I was a little girl who received nothing from her mum's estate. My mum had remarried and that marriage cancelled her previous will that included provision for me.

When I encountered the man who took all the financial assets decades later, while running my own law firm, the experience had a profound impact on me. I knew I needed to share the story to explain why I was so passionate about helping my clients to avoid situations like this.

When I shared this very personal experience, the response I received helped me understand how necessary it is for people to understand me as a lawyer. This helps them reach out and discuss their very private concerns. Getting a will in place can be an emotional and significant life event for many – it is a kind of expression of love – and the level of care and attention required for this needs an individual bespoke service.

What changes did you make as a result of this?

I now share my experience through the Telegraph newspaper, the Law Society blog and LinkedIn. I hope that people who were previously uncertain about getting on with their will are nudged into action.

In what way do you think this made you a better law firm owner?

I've found that people now open up more freely to me. It was surprising at first the number of people who approached me to explain they had a similar experience in their family.

I also do my best to raise awareness about fixed fees. My personal background means I have a heightened sensitivity about lawyers charging for time spent rather than results achieved.

When people can relate to lawyers and see that some of us truly are in the profession to serve, then trust increases.

What advice would you give to a new law firm owner about this?

Always remember that people deal with people. I know it's a cliché, but it's so true. Lawyers are far more specialised than they used to be. Even when I qualified as a solicitor back in 2001, there were still general practitioners. Most people will work on the basis that expertise is assumed.

People want to be heard. They want their particular requirements to be met. Some people need to chat, some need a snappy service and some want something in between.

Please take personal responsibility for legal fees never being a surprise to your clients. And do your best to give more value than your client can reasonably expect! Giving more is rarely a wasted effort.

How has the coronavirus pandemic impacted your firm so far?

It's early days. At the time of writing we're a couple of months into lockdown and apparently some shops will start opening next month.

My area of law is relatively unaffected, though sadly there are more deaths and therefore more probate work than normal. Some people just need to chat through what's required, and others need to hand everything over and ask us to handle it all.

What was the biggest issue you had to overcome in the initial stages of lockdown, and how did you overcome it?

Within a week of shifting my office to my home I was struck down with COVID-19. I was completely out of action for almost two weeks and it took several weeks after that to fully recover. I am grateful to be a survivor and feel blessed that someone who understood far more than me made me promise to respect the recovery. That promise allowed me to be gentle with myself.

I accepted that afternoon naps were an essential element of building strength, and I've now progressed back to running the sort of distances that were part of my life pre-COVID-19.

How do you see the ongoing coronavirus pandemic changing the future of your business, whether positively or negatively?

A couple of years back I struggled to accept that it was okay to meet with clients by video. Of course, we're now all embracing the technology and this is developing more and more the longer lockdown goes on.

I've always enjoyed going to my office to work and coming home to enjoy family time. I try to have clear boundaries about when I work, even if I'm working from home. I think when I can return to my office in future months, I will likely continue to work from home regularly.

Afterword

What will success look like for you?

Over the course of this book we have touched on the many different ways there are to run a law firm. Some of you will be setting out with ambitious plans for establishing an industry-shaking firm. Others will be dreaming of a quiet home workspace with few distractions. Many will be hoping to become a well-known and respected part of their communities, while others will be planning to work remotely from wherever they can plug in their laptop.

The reality here is that what you consider the perfect law firm set-up is as individual as you are.

It's important to carefully consider the law firm you're building and think about how well it fits with your vision for your ideal work life. If you want to have the flexibility to travel frequently, you probably won't want to build a firm that's reliant on seeing clients face-to-face in a physical office. If you're a social person who loves to be surrounded by a friendly team, you probably don't want to set up as a freelance solicitor working from home.

Many of us have been brought up on the belief that professional success is determined by the number on your bank statements, the size of your office and the number of people employed under you. Though there is certainly nothing wrong with striving for success under these criteria . . . ask yourself whether this is really what you want.

Just as there are countless different ways to set up a law firm, there are also countless different ways to measure how successful those law firms are. The trick here is to reassess and adapt your understanding of success in order to accommodate the future and the firm you are setting out to build.

It's important not to get swept away in the idea of always needing to work towards being bigger, better or more profitable in order to be a success. Rather, we invite you to measure your success in terms of how happy you are with your working life and how well your firm aligns with your own personal visions and goals.

When we measure using these terms, a sole practitioner at their kitchen table could be considered just as successful as the director of an international multi-practice firm, if not more so. And why shouldn't they? If you are able to build a firm that works for you, your clients, your lifestyle and your financial requirements, then this is most certainly something to celebrate.

Ultimately, you will need to develop your own personal criteria for success and focus on building a law practice that is right for you, not anyone else.

We wish you the very best of luck.

Appendix

Sample cash flow forecast

	Jan	Feb	Mar	Apr	May	Jun	Jul	Aug	Sep	Oct	Nov	Dec	Total
INFLOWS													
Sales													
Capital													
TOTAL RECEIPTS													
OUTFLOWS													
Salary													
National insurance													
Professional indemnity insurance													
Practising certificate													
Rent													
Rates													

	Jan	Feb	Mar	Apr	May	Jun	Jul	Aug	Sep	Oct	Nov	Dec	Total
Water													
Electricity													
Gas													
IT software													
Website													
Marketing													
Advertising													
Seminars/Networking events/CPD													
Online subscription to legal journals													
Online library subscription service													
Accounting fees													
Telephone													
Travelling													
Postage													
Bank charges													
SRA – payment for authorisation													
TOTAL PAYMENTS													
NET CASH FLOW													

Index